SPECIALISTS AND GENERALISTS

SPECIALISTS

AND

GENERALISTS

*A comparative study of the professional
civil servant at home and abroad*

EDITED BY F. F. RIDLEY
*Professor of Political Theory and Institutions
University of Liverpool*

London
GEORGE ALLEN AND UNWIN LTD
RUSKIN HOUSE · MUSEUM STREET

PRINTED IN GREAT BRITAIN
in 11 *on* 12 *pt Times type*
BY SIMSON SHAND LTD
LONDON, HERTFORD AND HARLOW

CONTENTS

INTRODUCTION

Several factual studies have been published of Civil Service structures in other countries, but very little has been done on the organization and functions of what in Britain are called the 'professional' classes or even on the wider question of the relationship between 'specialists' and 'generalists'. The present authors were asked to make an independent survey of the role of the 'specialist' abroad by the Institution of Professional Civil Servants. This followed the appointment by the Government of the Committee on the Structure, Recruitment and Management, including Training, of the Home Civil Service, under Lord Fulton. The Fulton Committee was asked to recommend any changes which it thought necessary to ensure that the service is properly equipped for its role in the modern State.

The Institution represents the professional, scientific and technical classes and many other specialist classes in the Civil Service, the Atomic Energy Authority and various other public bodies. Membership covers a great diversity of professions and skills. In its own evidence to the Fulton Committee, it has argued that the present structure, organization and management of the Civil Service are no longer appropriate to modern needs. In the view of the Institution, the structure of the Civil Service is based on concepts which were valid in the nineteenth century, when the prevailing belief was in liberalism, private enterprise and local self-government, but are no longer valid today. At the time of the Northcote-Trevelyan Report of 1854, the concept of civil service administration was largely that of a night-watchman. The outcome of the report was a service in which management and administration at the highest levels were almost exclusively the monopoly of the Administrative Class. The Civil Service has since developed in a largely unplanned way to accommodate the changing functions of government but the role of the professional has remained largely subordinate to that of the administrator; he is regarded primarily as an adviser when it comes to responsibility for policy determination. The need to provide careers sufficiently attractive to recruit able people is fully accepted so far as administrative and executive staff are concerned, but the career expectations of the professional have been kept lower.

In very general terms, this is the broad thesis of the Institution's evidence.

It felt that an independent survey of the role and the career expectation of the professional *vis-à-vis* the administrator in other countries might well prove useful to the Fulton Committee and five of the present authors were asked to undertake a study. France, Germany, Sweden, Australia and the United States were selected because they seemed representative of different traditions. The authors are all University teachers concerned with public administration. The sixth contribution, written subsequently, is by the Deputy General Secretary of the Institution. It would not have served any useful purpose merely to have recorded the facts about the grading structure of the civil service in these countries. What was required was information about the position of the professional within the general structure of the service and, in turn, to see this within the framework of the administrative machine as a whole. His position had also to be seen in terms of the functions of the civil service of his country. If there is to be full understanding of the reasons why professionals in other countries play such a different role from those in Britain, still wider factors would have to be considered. The time limit, dictated by the need to submit this symposium to the Fulton Committee while its views are still in a formative stage, has prevented this from being done uniformly by all contributors. What emerges is that reform should not be considered too narrowly. Much of the factual material in this survey will not be found elsewhere and there is a certain amount of originality in interpretation and comment. The work seems worth doing for its immediate purpose and one may hope that it has a wider and longer-term interest for practitioners and academics alike.

The Civil Services studied here are very different. The contributors show that their differences must be seen against their wider institutional, social and historical background. Underlying such organizational differences, however, there are differences of principle. One may be tempted to dismiss these as mere rationalizations but that would be to miss a good deal. There are different theories about civil service organization and few claim to be as narrowly culture-bound as one country. Attention could be drawn to many points of interest and to a number of common strands. One major lesson seems to emerge. Even a superficial reading will show that nowhere does one find anything like a theory justifying the separation, either of persons or of functions, into generalists and specialists, administrators and advisers. For various reasons, Britain has developed a Civil Service structure which makes it very much the odd man out. While reform can only take place in the context of our constitutional order and must take into account many other factors, we can learn from other countries that alternative principles of organization work and that, unless we claim that Britain does uniquely well in the modern world, they work at least as effectively. Though each has its own problems, they largely avoid some of the problems facing our Civil Service at the moment.

First point. None of the countries have anything like our Administrative Class, generalists in functions and generalists in background. Recruitment to the higher Civil Service on the basis of an entirely non-vocational education is rare. It is true that in most continental European countries there are administrators who are not specialists-professionals in our sense and who, in the European context, can be described as all-purpose administrators. In each case, however, they have legal training directed to their work (administration in administrative law countries has a higher legal content than in Britain). They are no exception to the finding that higher civil servants are generally recruited for qualifications and/or experience related in some way to their duties. The countries differ only in whether they define these requirements broadly or narrowly. Some recruit into specific posts, evaluating candidates' education, skills or experience in terms of the job specification; others recruit into broad classes for which relevant educational qualifications are prescribed. Most foreign civil servants would therefore be surprised at our preoccupation with the rival merits of generalists and specialists. All of them can be regarded as specialists of one kind or another, their knowledge and training related to the kind of work they do. The notion that a man who has done well at Cherokee is *ipso facto* likely to make a good civil servant is not found elsewhere.

Second point. Even where the higher Civil Service contains generalists-jurists as well as specialists-professionals, this reflects no theory about the organization of government work. There is no structural separation of specialist or advisory work from general administration (policy-making/management). Indeed, it is most unusual for any distinction to be drawn between the nature of the work involved in policy-making and in other more technical functions. One rarely finds abroad the parallel hierarchies of administrators and specialists common to British Government departments. If the work of a section requires specialized knowledge, then it is likely to be put in charge of a professional official with the appropriate training and experience. He will take responsibility for whatever policy questions arise. Ministries are usually organized on the assumption that it is impossible to distinguish technical and advisory functions from general administration: they are not structured to separate advisory staff or advisory functions. Indeed, there is difficulty abroad in understanding the importance of advisory posts in the British scheme of things. It is generally assumed of men in senior positions that their specialized knowledge will not merely contribute to good administration but that it will also enable them to give the best advice to their political superiors.

Third point. Senior posts may be restricted to specialists (how-ever defined), especially where job specification is used, or they may be open to all higher civil servants. The likelihood in the latter case is that a man with relevant qualifications will be appointed. It is hard to find examples of the opposite: of positions either formally reserved for generalists or restricted to them in practice. In most cases specialists tend, if anything, to do better career-wise than generalists. In America a man trained in the sciences and the professions based on the sciences finds it easy to move up into higher administrative posts. A large proportion of senior officials have qualifications in engineering, the sciences, business and public administration, medicine and law. The federal service is one of specialized officials doing either specialist jobs or general administrative work in offices in which their particular knowledge is considered essential. In Sweden, where jurists occupy many of the policy posts, profes-sionals in turn fill many of those in the top management of public services. In France the professionals hold a large share of the directorial posts in those branches of the administration for which their training has prepared them. The Australian system is one in which professionals are dominant; it is heavily weighted to give preference to the officer who can demonstrate com-petence in his particular job. Specialists generally enjoy parity of esteem; in some cases their prestige is actually higher than that of the generalists. As a rule career opportunities are as good, if not better, and salary scales are often advantageous.

GREAT BRITAIN

1. INTRODUCTION

This paper deals with the respective roles and status of 'generalists' and 'professionals' in the British Civil Service. By 'generalists' is meant the administrative and executive classes in the home Civil Service, i.e. those who have had a good non-vocational education; by 'professionals', those recruited to posts for which a professional, scientific, technical or other specialist qualification is essential, e.g. corporate membership of a recognized professional institution, honours degree in science, economics or statistics, an appropriate technical qualification, etc. The professionals include architects, engineers, surveyors, scientists, doctors, lawyers, economists, statisticians, psychologists, and many other professions and disciplines.

This paper has a modest purpose, no more than to give background to those which follow on the roles of these two groups in the civil services of five other countries. It describes the organizational pattern of the home Civil Service and deals in some detail with the qualifications and work of some of the professionals, a subject largely neglected in most of the published material about public administration. A comparison is made of the 'career values' of the generalists with two main groups of professionals. It is not practicable to refer in detail to all the professional grades as there are literally hundreds of them employed in the service but a selection has been made of groups which are sufficiently representative to enable general conclusions to be drawn.

Comparison with the structure of the civil services of other countries should add a great deal of interest to questions now being asked about the future structure of the British Civil Service. For example, does the present class structure of the British Civil Service enable it to cope efficiently with its modern role in a complex technological society? Is the present demarcation between policy making and administration on the one hand (the generalists' role), and the giving of professional advice on the other (the professionals' role), the most efficient way of administering the affairs of the country? What sort of education, qualifications and aptitudes should a civil servant possess to perform his functions in contemporary government? These important issues are currently being debated, and while this paper does not attempt to answer them in detail, it provides the factual information on which conclusions can be drawn and comparisons made with other countries.

Those with only a casual acquaintance with the Civil Service are surprised to find how diverse is its role today and how many civil servants are engaged on non-traditional tasks. A reflection of this is the relative numbers of the generalist and professional classes. The figures are:

CIVIL SERVICE GRADES 1966/7[1]

Administrative	3,500
Executive	74,300
Professional, scientific, technical	86,900

The organization of the British Civil Service is based on the separation of both persons and functions into generalists and specialists. To the generalist is assigned responsibility for advising Ministers, the formulation of administrative policy, control of the Governmental machine and, of great importance, financial control. The role of the professional is to carry out the work of the various specialist branches of the service, under the ultimate financial and administrative control of the generalist, and to advise the generalist on policy matters. Basically this structure has its origins in the deeply rooted British practice of selecting Ministers, not on the grounds of their expert knowledge of the department of which they take charge, but because they are men judged to be capable of coming to balanced decisions on the evidence submitted to them by experts. The same principle has been extended to the administrative and executive sphere of the Civil Service. The generalist case is that by the nature of his education, and training in the service, he can bring to bear on the work of the department the same type of consideration that the Minister would himself bring, and act accordingly.

Those who enter the administrative class direct from outside the service primarily have good honours degrees in subjects that are unlikely to have any direct connection with their work. The breakdown according to disciplines of an intake of 77

[1] *Source:* The Financial Secretary's Memorandum on Estimates.

assistant principals in 1966, as published in the Civil Service Commission's report for that year, shows history students taking the largest number of places, 34, followed by modern languages, 13, English, 10, classics, 10, and science and mathematics, 10. Under the present system the top fliers from the direct-entry intake are destined to become the permanent secretaries of the future. Of the current 36 posts at permanent secretary level, 33 are filled by members of the administrative class. The administrator receives an extensive training mainly of an in-service kind and, when fully trained, is expected to be able to administer practically anything in the Civil Service and to advise his Minister on almost any subject. That is the basic purpose of his training. The executive class, which supports the administrative class, consists mainly of staff without university degrees but recruited at two GCE 'A' levels. They carry out Civil Service work at the lower and middle management level and below major policy decision making. In parallel with these two classes are the professionals. These include doctors, lawyers, architects, surveyors, engineers, scientists, research officers, planners, accountants, economists, statisticians, etc., and their supporting technically qualified staff.

As the functions of government have changed markedly in recent years the Civil Service now tends to use the term 'managerial responsibility' for functions previously described as 'administrative' or 'executive'. To some extent this blurs what is really a sharp distinction in roles. In highly technical branches of the service the professional is, undoubtedly, in managerial command, though under the ultimate control of the generalist. Inevitably there is a substantial managerial content in professional work. Moreover, some very senior professional officers—the Chief Scientific Advisers—have influence on the formulation of policy. But it should be explained that, although departments differ in size, function and complexity, there are certain features in common. An administrative permanent secretary is at the head and he has one or more deputy secretaries, according to the size of the department, and a varying number of under-secretaries and assistant secretaries. There is usually a principal finance officer and a principal establishments and organization officer. All these are members of the administrative class. In the larger Ministries there is a chief scientist or scientific adviser with a small staff in addition to any research and development, production or inspectorial staff the department may also employ. These senior advisers put the 'professional' point of view when policy is being decided. Nevertheless, and allowing for this influence on policy, it is certainly the case that the British Civil Service is structured on the basis of a demarcation between those who administer and those who advise.

A central issue is whether the responsibilities of the professionals should be extended so that they take full administrative and executive control of the work on which they are engaged. An example will illustrate the point. Local authorities submit to the Ministry of Housing and Local Government requests for permission to vary planning arrangements. The request for the variation of an approved plan comes first to the generalists. They, in turn, refer it to the planning officers, the research and estate officers for a professional opinion. Having examined the proposed variation, the professional staff sign a report saying 'Our recommendation is that this variation should be permitted' or 'Our recommendation is that this variation should not be permitted'. The request then goes back to the generalist, be he executive, administrative principal, or administrative assistant secretary, who makes a decision in the light of the recommendation and says 'Yes, it will be allowed' or 'No, it will not be allowed'. The generalist's case is that in taking the decision he brings to bear on it the same kind of consideration as would his Minister were he personally dealing with it, and that this is a function for which the professional is not equipped because of his narrower specialist background and training.

Many professionals adapt to the system and accept the overall control of generalists. Indeed, there are quite a number who would contend that specialization and division of function as between administration and the giving of professional advice is the most convenient way of running the Civil Service, and certainly one most compatible with the British temperament. Professional colleagues holding a contrary view, and conscious of friction in their relationship with the generalists, criticize the conformists for embracing subordination as lemmings do the sea. Officialdom is aware of the problem, but is a little apt to adopt an ostrich-like attitude towards it. They hope when they look up it will have gone away. A fruitful field for research would be to find out what happens to newly appointed professionals when they have to fit themselves into the organizational control of the generalists after several years' experience outside. Do they become more creative and more effective because of the generalist support which the organization provides? Or is it that the system of ultimate generalist control dominates rather than assists them? Professionals accept that a carefully planned organizational network is essential for any undertaking of size. But to think of the central issue as being whether or not there should be an organizational network supporting the professionals would be to miss the real point. The issue is whether the class structure of the Civil Service, with its system of control by generalists and its limitation of professional responsibility, is a necessary way of organizing the Civil Service and one which leads to efficient decision making. To emphasize: the vertical class structure of the British Civil Service is based on this theory of two separate roles—the generalists, who 'specialize in the awareness of ministerial responsibility'[1] and the professionals, about whom C. H. Sisson comments, 'The senior administrative officials have to learn to extract from the specialist flowers around them the honey their Minister needs, explaining as they do so that the Minister does not live on honey.'[2]

2. THE DUTIES OF THE ADMINISTRATIVE AND EXECUTIVE CLASSES

Much has been published and is readily available about the work of the administrative and executive classes, so brief summaries will serve here.

The administrative class function is cogently stated, as one would expect, in the published evidence to the Fulton Committee of the First Division Association. The FDA represents all administrative grades, including Permanent Secretaries, having over 90 per cent of the class in its membership. It said:

'The need for and function of the Administrative Class derive from the Ministerial and Parliamentary system of government. Under this system all executive power is vested in Ministers. They are few in number and hold office for only a comparatively short time. They rarely come in as specialists in any aspect of the work of their Department and in this

---

[1] C. H. Sisson, *The Spirit of British Administration*, p. 13.
[2] Ibid., p. 16.

B

respect they reflect the generally accepted principle in this country that non-specialists should take the major policy decisions on behalf of the community as a whole. In these circumstances the volume of work demands that a Minister should be supported by a body of staff which can bring to bear on the work of the Department the same type of considerations that the Minister would himself bring and act for him under his general direction in matters either of a minor policy or quasi-judicial nature.

'The essential function of this group of staff is to bring together the disparate issues involved in taking major decisions of policy, to advise on what these decisions should be and subsequently to put them into effect. The Administrative Class is uniquely able to perform this function because of its broad background, intellectual capacity and experience of operating in government. Administrators become conversant with the special subjects with which individual departments are concerned; collectively they know about the whole range of Governmental and Parliamentary affairs; they know how to cope with the complexities of the Government machine; finally they are politically aware in the sense of regarding politics as the art of the possible.

'These are the traditional functions of the Administrative Class but the continued extension of direct Government influence and control has meant that the managerial skills of the Class are increasingly required in running projects and programmes, work more akin to that performed in industry. We believe this trend will continue in the future.'[1]

A similar brief statement will serve for the Executive Class. The Society of Civil Servants represents the general executive class having 92 per cent of the class in its membership. It described their duties to the Fulton Committee as follows:

'A full description of all the duties of the Executive Class would not be practicable within the range of this memorandum, but the chief categories can be summarized briefly. They comprise the placing of Government contracts for a vast range of equipment and supplies, for research and development, and for building and civil engineering works; the con-

[1] Evidence presented by the Association of First Division Civil Servants to the Fulton Committee on the Civil Service, paragraphs 3 and 5.

trol and issue of stores and the organization of transport; the work of Government accounting and the internal auditing functions of Government Departments; and a wide range of case work arising from the interpretation and application of law and regulations. The development of the Welfare State and the creation of large local office organizations have involved the Executive Class in a vital role in social administration and have placed it in direct contact with the general public. In the Departments concerned with trade and industry and with the oversight of nationalized industries, members of the Executive Class have become increasingly involved with the economic and industrial life of the country. With the widening of Government responsibilities, it is the Executive Class which has provided the link between Whitehall and the community.'[1]

It will be convenient to reproduce here the current salary scales and grading structure of the administrative and executive classes as references are made to the various grade levels in the following sections. It is not practicable to list the grade structure at the senior adviser levels, for they are on individually assessed rates. For comparison purposes they will be listed separately.

ADMINISTRATIVE CLASS (National scales)

£ a year

Joint Permanent Secretary to the Treasury	9,200
Permanent Secretary	8,600
Deputy Secretary	6,300
Under-Secretary	5,250
Assistant Secretary	3,500–4,500
Principal	2,250–3,107
Assistant Principal	926–1,574

EXECUTIVE CLASS (National scales)

£ a year

Head of Major Executive Establishment	up to 5,250
Principal Executive Officer	4,000
Senior Chief Executive Officer	3,156–3,500
Chief Executive Officer	2,571–2,999
Senior Executive Officer	1,977–2,411
Higher Executive Officer	1,574–1,874
Executive Officer	568 (age 18)– 970 (age 25)– 1,457

[1] Society of Civil Servants' evidence to the Fulton Committee, paragraph 3.

3. THREE 'TRADITIONAL' DEPARTMENTS

Before examining the structure of those departments which are predominantly scientific or technical in character, it may be of interest to look at three traditional departments, and note the extent to which professionals have been introduced into them at the highest levels, and their role and status.

The Cabinet Office which operates under the direction of the Prime Minister is at the apex of the Civil Service. It has a secretariat of permanent officials which 'has grown into an instrument of great importance in the co-ordination of policy at the highest level'.[1]

The functions of the Cabinet were described by the Haldane Committee in 1918 as:

1. the final determination of the policy to be submitted to Parliament;
2. the supreme control of the National Executive, in accordance with the policy agreed by Parliament;
3. the continuous co-ordination and delimitation of the authority of the several Departments of State.

These functions have not changed materially but certainly has the content and significance of many of the problems with which it has to deal. For information on the staffing position in the Civil Service the British Imperial Calendar is always a very informative publication. The 1967 Imperial Calendar records that the Secretary of the Cabinet is Sir Burke St John Trend, KCB, CVO. Sir Burke was educated at Whitgift and Merton College, Oxford, where he obtained a First Class Honours Degree in Literature (Hum.). He is an Honorary Fellow of Merton College. He joined the Home Civil Service administrative class in 1936 and was at the Ministry of Education for one year, and then transferred to H.M. Treasury and became Assistant Private Secretary to the Chancellor of the Exchequer. He has had a distinguished Civil Service career, his subsequent appointments being: 1945 to 1949 Principal Private Secretary to the Chancellor of the Exchequer; 1949 to 1955 Under-Secretary, H.M. Treasury; 1955 to 1956 at the Office of the Lord Privy Seal; 1956 to 1959 Deputy Secretary of the Cabinet; 1959 to 1960 Third Secretary, H.M. Treasury; 1960 to 1962 Second Secretary, H.M. Treasury; 1963 he became Secretary of the

[1] COI Reference Pamphlet 40, *The Central Government of Britain.*

Cabinet. Sir Burke holds one of the three highest posts in the Civil Service administrative hierarchy, the other two being held by the Joint Permanent Secretaries at the Treasury. Associated with Sir Burke is the Government's Chief Scientific Adviser, Sir Solly Zuckerman, KCB, FRS. Sir Solly is classed as a temporary civil servant. Until recently the Economic Adviser to the Cabinet was Professor T. Balogh, a post he held since October 1964. Professor Balogh was educated at the universities of Budapest, Berlin and Harvard. He is a Fellow of Balliol. His economic publications, his published papers and the expert positions he has held are too well known to need recording here.

The Central Statistical Office is an integral part of the Cabinet Office. Its role is to act as a central advisory, consultative and co-ordinating office for Government statistical services. Its newly appointed director is Professor Claus Moser of the London School of Economics. He is the son of a Berlin banker who left Germany in 1936. Professor Moser's statistical studies have covered various aspects of British life ranging from crime to nutrition. In 1961 he became the statistical adviser to Lord Robbins' investigation into higher education. Largely as a result of Moser and his team, British education statistics are probably among the best in the world.

Cabinet members are bound by their Privy Council oath, and civil servants by the Official Secrets Act, not to disclose information about the proceedings of the Cabinet. Also forbidden is the publication of Cabinet and other State papers. While therefore it may be of interest to speculate on the respective influence and roles of the professionals and generalists at this high level, it probably would serve no useful purpose. Whether it was Sir Solly who single-handed was responsible for the demise of the British aircraft carrier, is shaping the defence policy for the next ten years, and who will have the major influence in determining the division of future scientific effort between military and civilian requirements, must be left to journalistic speculation as must the influence Professor Balogh had on Government economic policy. It is at levels below this that one is able to see more clearly the separatist system at work and assess its relevance to contemporary problems of government. What is clear, however, from this brief description of the Cabinet Office, is that the scientist, the economist and the statistician occupy advisory positions in the hierarchy.

These are the salaries and gradings at the higher levels in the Cabinet Office:

Cabinet Office

Secretary of the Cabinet	£9,200
Deputy Secretaries (3)	6,300
Under-Secretaries (4)	5,250
Assistant Secretaries (5)	3,500–4,500
Chief Scientific Adviser	8,600
Adviser on Economic Affairs	7,100
Chief Scientific Officers (2)	5,000–5,250
Senior Principal Scientific Officer	3,500–4,000

Central Statistical Office

Director	£6,300
Deputy Director	5,250
Assistant Director	5,250
Chief Statisticians (6)	3,500–4,500

Second in the Civil Service pecking order is the Treasury. Under Article 6 of the Civil Service Order in Council the Treasury is empowered to make regulations or give instructions for controlling the conduct of Her Majesty's Home Civil Service. Subject to compliance with Treasury regulations and instructions, the responsibility for the proper administration of a department rests with the head of that department. Departments may make rules or regulations and give instructions for controlling the conduct of their establishments and providing for the conditions of service of their staff, but these rules, regulations or instructions must not be inconsistent with any regulation or instruction given by the Treasury under the Order in Council. Departments must refer to the Treasury before they make rules or regulations or give instructions which deal with any point of particular importance or general principle not clearly covered by Treasury instructions.

Public finance was the Treasury's original concern, but nowadays it is involved in a great deal more than that. Although there is an indeterminate area between its functions and those of the department of Economic Affairs, the closer concern of Government with economic planning means that the Treasury's horizon has been extended to the national economy as a whole. One of the most important Treasury functions is to present the civil estimates for all departments to the House of Commons. Departments must submit their departmental estimates to the Treasury, which weighs the advantages of the proposals against the monetary and economic cost, having regard to current Government policy, and decides the relative merits of expenditure proposed by different departments. It lays down general rules of financial and accounting procedure and exercises a general supervision over all departmental expenditure. The Treasury also keeps a very close control over such matters as rates of pay and the aggregate size of the staff in all Government departments. Armed with these powers, the Treasury obviously is able to exercise a very considerable influence in the overall policies and running of Civil Service affairs. It is, therefore, of particular interest to see the extent to which professionals have been brought in at the higher levels. The Treasury's organizational tree as at October 1966 is:

H.M. TREASURY ORGANIZATION CHART

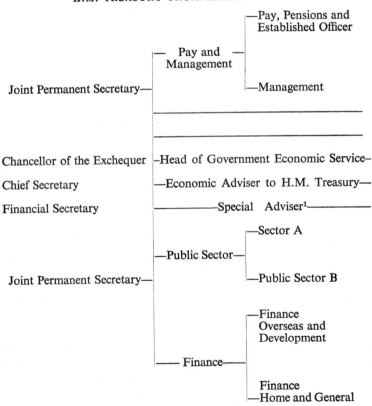

[1] Special Adviser to the Chancellor of the Exchequer on the social and economic aspects of taxation policy.

Sir Laurence Helsby, GCB, KBE, and Sir William Armstrong, KCB, MVO, as joint Permanent Secretaries, share with Sir Burke Trend, Secretary of the Cabinet Office, the three highest Civil Service posts at joint Permanent Secretary level. Sir Laurence was educated at Sedbergh and Keble College, Oxford, and is an Honorary Fellow, Keble College, Oxford. He became a lecturer in Economics at the University College of the South-West, 1930 to 1931, and then as lecturer in Economics, Durham Colleges, University of Durham, 1931 to 1945. In 1946 he became Assistant Secretary, H.M. Treasury, and in 1947 Principal Private Secretary to the Prime Minister. From 1950 to 1954 he was Deputy Secretary at the Ministry of Food; in 1954 the First Civil Service Commissioner and in 1959 until 1962 Permanent Secretary to the Ministry of Labour. He has been joint Permanent Secretary to the Treasury and Head of the Home Civil Service since 1963.

Sir William was educated at Bec Grammar School and Exeter College, Oxford. He is an Honorary Fellow of Exeter College, Oxford. His civil service career has been: 1938 Assistant Principal, Board of Education; 1940 Assistant Private Secretary to the President of the Board of Education; 1943 to 1946 Private Secretary to the Secretary of the War Cabinet; 1949 to 1953 Principal Private Secretary to successive Chancellors of the Exchequer; 1953 to 1957 Under-Secretary, Overseas Finance Division, H.M. Treasury; 1957 to 1958 Under-Secretary, Home Finance Division; 1958 to 1962 Third Secretary and Treasury Officer of Accounts. Since October 1962, he has been joint Permanent Secretary to the Treasury. The two Second Secretaries are responsible, respectively, for pay and management and finance. There are six Third Secretaries and supporting administrative and executive staff. All are permanent administrative civil servants.

Professor A. K. Cairncross, CMG, is Head of the Government Economic Service, Mr M. V. Posner is Economic Adviser to the Treasury, and Mr K. E. Berrill is the Special Adviser to the Chancellor of the Exchequer on public sector problems and the long-term growth of public expenditure. Professor Cairncross has been Head of the Government Economic Service since 1964. He was Professor of Applied Economics at the University of Glasgow from 1951 to 1961. His public and civil service career includes: Director of Programmes, Ministry of Aircraft Production 1945; Adviser to the Board of Trade; Director of the Economic Development Institute, Washington; Economic Adviser to the Organization for European Economic Co-operation, etc., etc. Mr Posner was formerly Director of Economics in the Ministry of Power on leave from Pembroke College, Cambridge. Mr Berrill is a Fellow of King's College, Cambridge.

Although there is a close relationship between the work of the economists and the formulation of policy, and indeed on recruitment economists have to be capable of participating in policy matters, nevertheless the organizational tree shows that the basic Civil Service pattern still holds; the generalists have overall responsibility for the organization and the specialists' role is that of advisers.

Inland Revenue, the third traditional department selected, is of particular interest because the characteristic feature of its organization is the complete separation of administrative policy from its execution. It too is subject to changing conditions, for taxation is no longer simply a means of raising money for Government expenditure, but is now an important instrument of Government economic policy. The Inland Revenue administers the laws relating to income tax and surtax, corporation tax, capital gains tax, estate duty and stamp duty. It is also responsible for the valuation of real property for such purposes as compensation for compulsory purchase, local rates in England and Wales and estate duty; tithe redemption annuities; and compensation for war damage to land, buildings and chattels. It has a total staff of approximately 60,000. The actual execution of work is devolved on branches, such as the Estate Duty Office, Solicitor's Office, Tithe Redemption Office, Chief Inspector of Taxes Office, and Office of Chief Valuer. Administrative control is vested in the Board of Inland Revenue which consists of a Chairman, two Deputy Chairmen and five other Commissioners, all full-time civil servants and senior members of the administrative class. The Board advises Ministers on questions of taxation policy, conducts necessary Finance Bill business, decides questions of principle raised by the public, representative bodies and branches, and controls and co-ordinates the various branches. The Chairman is equivalent to a Permanent Secretary (£8,600) the two Deputy Chairmen to Deputy Secretaries (£6,300), and the five other Commissioners to Under-Secretaries of other departments (£5,250). The Board's Secretariat consists of three parts: the Stamps and Taxes Division which deals with the general administration of Inland Revenue taxes, the Establishments Division which deals with general organization and efficiency, and a Statistics and Intelligence Division staffed by professional statisticians. These former two divisions are staffed by members of the administrative class, the only place in Inland Revenue in which they are employed. It is from their number that appointments to the Board are normally made.

The Chief Inspector of Taxes (£6,300) is the professional head of his branch. He controls a staff of over 40,000, a figure well in excess of many departments with Permanent Secretaries at their head. The Civil Service structure, with its division into classes, means that no matter how efficient a Chief Inspector of Taxes may be he cannot be eligible for any higher posts within the service. His job is the organization and management of his branch and to advise the Board on all matters relating to income tax, profits tax, corporation tax and all capital gains tax. He is not a member of the Board but reports to it. There are two Deputy Chief Inspectors (£5,000) who deal, respectively, with the technical and establishments work. In the Head Office section of the Chief Inspector's Branch are thirty Senior Principal Inspectors (£4,430) studying a narrow field of taxation work in depth and advising the Board, through the DCI and CI, on policy, and the districts on individual cases.

The strict separation of policy from execution is based on a reorganization of the Secretary's Office carried out by Sir Warren Fisher in 1918. He said:

'Control and co-ordination [of the branches] depend on the secretariat which, with a different viewpoint, has to direct, supervise and criticize the main lines of their varied activities, and, in the process of linking them together and relating them to Ministers and to Parliament, to provide the type of perspective which continuous absorption in specialized work cannot be expected normally to produce. . . . The numbers [of the secretariat] can be small and the exclusion from its scope of any work not strictly conforming to the tests laid down must be rigidly enforced.'

Sir Alexander Johnston, present Chairman of the Board, firmly supports this separation. He says:

'For example, the Chief Inspector of Taxes, the head of the branch which deals with income tax, is responsible for a total staff of 37,000 working in some 700 tax offices. If he were a member of the Board and responsible for income tax policy as well as for the execution of the Acts, he would necessarily spend a great part of his time on the annual Budget and Finance Bill, that is to say, on policy matter; he would not in fact have the time to exercise full executive control of his branch. That part of his functions would have to be left largely to his deputies and his responsibility for carrying out the policies he had helped to frame would thus be largely nominal.'[1]

The Association of Inspectors of Taxes does not consider satisfactory the separation between the administrators and the specialists. In its evidence to the Fulton Committee it stated:

'20. Moreover, when able men are at a premium we suggest that the double tier system is uneconomical in time and numbers of staff. The safeguards of processing day-to-day problems through two chains of comparable intellectual ability are outweighed by the sheer waste of time and effort involved. Also, the theory of the highly intelligent but technically uncommitted administrator making decisions on the basis of the technical advice supplied by the Inspectorate on the one hand and the Solicitor of Inland Revenue on the other is impossible to maintain, since the administrator is forced by the extremely technical nature of the work to acquire technical knowledge and become an expert himself. The situation then becomes one in which the dominant partner—and expert by evolution but without the first-hand practical experiencing of implementing tax legislation or dealing with the tax-paying public—is covering the same ground as men professionally trained for and practically experienced in the work. In this situation the Association cannot but doubt the soundness of the present Head Office organization which rigidly separates, on a caste basis, the

[1] Sir Alexander Johnston, *The Inland Revenue*, pp. 23 and 24.

Administrators who make policy and advise Ministers from the Specialists who advise the Administrators.

'In making this analysis it should be clearly understood that we are not criticizing the calibre of the Secretariat but the system—the limitation of training and experience on both sides and the severance of function.'

4. THE WORK OF 'PROFESSIONAL' DEPARTMENTS

As practically every profession and skill is represented in the Civil Service the work of professionals cannot readily be summarized. For example, in the engineering profession alone the modern Civil Service includes representatives of every branch; mechanical, electrical, civil, electronic, nuclear, heating, ventilating and air conditioning, public health, marine, aeronautical and automobile. It may help first to give a brief account of the work of some of the departments in which professionals are employed so as to illustrate why the service employs professionals in such diversity and number.

The Ministry of Defence is responsible for defence policy and control and administration of the three Fighting Services. It has a comparatively small Central Secretariat and three Service Departments, the Army Department, the Navy Department and the Air Force Department. The Secretary of State for Defence is supported by a Minister of Defence for Administration who is responsible for personnel and logistics matters affecting all three Services and a Minister of Defence for Equipment who is responsible for matters concerning all three Services in research, development and production and in procurement and sales. There is a Parliamentary Under-Secretary of State in charge of each of the three Service Departments. The estimated total expenditure on research and development alone for 1967/8 is estimated at £260 million,[1] and this is of course only a small part of the total expenditure. In some respects the Ministry of Defence resembles a huge industrial company. It employs a very large number of professional staff and is a purchaser and user of some of the most expensive capital equipment in the country. It is concerned with the management of the Fighting Services, the procurement of weapons and military equipment and all aspects of defence research and weapons development.

[1] Statement on Defence Estimates, 1967 (Command 3203).

The Ministry of Public Building and Works is the largest building organization in the country and possibly in Europe. It meets the construction needs including the operational work of the Armed Services; and provides accommodation and services for all civil departments at home and abroad. It constructs and equips research establishments; builds prisons; maintains the royal palaces and parks, Houses of Parliament and a number of museums and art galleries. It designs, purchases and maintains furniture and equipment. Examples of its work are the new Post Office Tower in London, new Embassy Offices in Washington, new military hospital in Hong Kong, and a high-temperature laboratory for the National Engineering Laboratory at East Kilbride. It is the liaison point for the Government with the construction industries and the building materials industries and has some responsibility for building, research and development work. The Building Research Station is attached to this Ministry. It disseminates the results of research and encourages industries to make full use of them. About £250 million per year is spent on capital projects, £130 million of it on regionally controlled projects and another £40 million on overseas schemes.

The Ministry of Technology is science and technology's largest single central organization certainly in Europe and very possibly in the world. It is responsible for stimulating a major national effort to advance technology and new processes in British industry. It does scientific research, disseminates results and furthers the practical application of scientific research. It is the sponsor department for technical and electrical engineering industries, machine tools, electronics, computers and telecommunications. It has a number of research establishments and aids with grants many autonomous research associations. From the recently defunct Ministry of Aviation it acquired vast responsibility for research, development and procurement relating to aircraft, guided weapons and electronic equipment for both military and civil purposes. Over 8,000 staff are employed at its headquarters and regional offices and a further 28,000 in its research and development establishments and inspectorates, many of whom are professional, scientific or technical. It has an annual gross expenditure of about £750 million.

The Ministry of Agriculture, Fisheries and Food administers Government policy for agriculture, horticulture and fishing in England and Wales. It pays out large sums in deficiency payments schemes and allocates various grants and subsidies designed to improve the efficiency of these industries. It operates a large, expert and free scientific advisory service. The control and eradication of animal and plant diseases is its concern, as is the operational control of certain diseases in animals. It is concerned with legislation about food, slaughter-houses, quality and cleanliness of milk, and issues arising from the supply and manufacture of food, its consumption, composition, preservation and nutritional qualities.

The Board of Trade has a general responsibility in respect of the country's commerce, industry and overseas trade. It is also responsible for general distribution of industry policy and for the shipping and ship-building industries. It promotes exports and compiles statistics of industry. Recently it acquired from the Ministry of Aviation certain civil aviation functions including civil airports policy, a national air traffic control organization, air safety and accident investigation, international regulations of civil aviation and negotiation of traffic rights, functions in relation to the air corporations and air transport licensing.

The Ministry of Transport has powers and duties relating to inland transport. It is the highway authority for trunk roads and motorways in England, allocates funds for road expenditure and has many powers and duties relating to road traffic and safety. It has responsibility for general policy in connection with the development of British ports and for the operation of ports in the event of war.

Ministry of Power is charged with the effective and co-ordinated development of fuel and power supplies in Great Britain and promoting economy and efficiency in their distribution and consumption. It has certain functions in relation to the iron and steel industries and is specifically responsible for the use of atomic energy as a source of industrial power and for the safety of nuclear installations other than those operated by the UKAEA. It co-ordinates fuel research, safety and health of workers in or about coalmines and quarries, etc., and it conducts research on these matters.

The Department of Education and Science is responsible for the development of primary, secondary and other education, including the supply, training and superannuation of teachers, the building of new schools and other institutions, a school health service, education of handicapped children and provision of school meals and milk. It has specialist branches 'available to provide professional advice for health, building, statistics, law and information'.[1]

The architects in the Ministry of Education and Science examine and advise on the suitability of designs submitted for approval by local authorities and voluntary bodies. Modern English school design developed and executed by them has won world-wide acclaim. They undertake development work on projects and on particular aspects of design and construction. This involves them in design and the supervising and erection on site of buildings which are part of a local education authority's normal programme. The work is done after a thorough investigation of the educational needs of the school; it includes the development of building techniques, particularly of industrialized methods, cost planning and the design of furniture and fittings. There is a building productivity group which is concerned with dimensional co-ordination, industrial building systems and other aspects of greater productivity. Multiprofession teams are engaged on this work. The department is also responsible for a vast field of civil science which it discharges through research councils—the Medical Research Council, Agricultural Research Council, Natural Environment Research Council, Social Science Research Council and the Science Research Council. It is also responsible for museums and galleries.

The Ministry of Housing and Local Government exercises a general responsibility for local government in England. It also has wide powers in regard to housing, town and country planning, administers the housing statutes and the national housing programme. On the town and country planning side responsibility includes confirmation of the acquisition and disposal of land by local authorities; payment of grants in certain cases of acquisition, clearing and compensation; designation of new towns and other development corporations.

The Ministry of Health administers the National Health Service in England and Wales and has overall responsibility for the welfare services of local authorities. It also has functions concerning food hygiene and welfare foods, and is concerned with the medical and surgical treatment of war pensioners. To give one example of the work of its professionals, they advise

[1] COI Reference Pamphlet 40, *The Central Government of Britain.*

on the provision of adequate accommodation for the Health
Service and the implementation of a consistent approach to the
planning of a ten-year capital building programme costing £800
million for hospitals and £200 million for construction by local
authorities.

5. RECRUITMENT STANDARDS AND CLASS STRUCTURE OF THE PROFESSIONALS

The Works Group

One of the larger groups of professionals is the 'Works Group'.
It is not a single class in the way the administrative and executive
classes are organized but a complex of separate groups, each of
which has broadly comparable or related standards. Its nucleus
is called the Works Group of Professional Classes. The five
largest professions in this group are mechanical and electrical
engineers (1,100), civil engineers (950), architects (600), lands
officers (600) and quantity surveyors (550). There are also about
250 estate surveyors, 200 maintenance surveyors, a score of
public health engineers and a dozen structural engineers. Half
the group is employed in the Ministry of Public Building and
Works. The other principal employers are the Ministries of
Agriculture, Fisheries and Food, Defence, Housing and Local
Government, Transport, and the Scottish Departments. The
Works Group of Professional Classes is only part of a complex
of professions linked with each other for pay and other conditions of service. Allied to it are several departmental classes,
i.e. a class recruited to work in one department only. They include the valuers in the Inland Revenue (2,100) and several
classes of engineers in the Post Office (2,000), the Ministry of
Technology (ex-Aviation) (900), the Ministry of Defence (Army)
(700) and the Ministry of Defence (Navy) (200). Other classes
with over 100 members are the Signals Officers in the Board of
Trade (ex-Aviation), the Industrial Chemists in the Ministry of
Defence, and the Housing and Planning Inspectors in the
Ministry of Housing and Local Government. Some of these
allied classes have the same pay and structure whilst others
differ from the Works Group of Professional Classes to varying extents. In Civil Service jargon these other groups are
called 'departmental variants' or 'related classes' of the Works
Group. The distinction is largely one of recruitment arrangements, though, for some, salary differentials are also important.

The Works Group complex, including the variants and related classes, totals over 11,000. Its members may be designing, planning, erecting, and maintaining building and engineering works and equipment, managing a large engineering or other production unit such as a Royal Ordnance Factory, acting as consultants for other bodies, supervising production contracts with private industry, carrying out inspectorial duties, or doing research and development work in close association with scientists in all the research and development establishments. The professional estate surveyors, land officers, or land commissioners are responsible for the purchase, sale, lease and management of both urban and rural real property. Other professionals carry out investigations into accidents on railways and to shipping. The survey, construction, equipment and crew standards of ships also comes within the scope of the professionals in this complex. The architects, civil engineers, maintenance, quantity and estate surveyors are mainly in the Ministry of Public Building and Works; lands officers and land agents in the Defence departments, Ministry of Agriculture, Fisheries and Food, and the Department of Agriculture and Fisheries for Scotland; mechanical and electrical engineers in the Defence departments, Ministry of Public Building and Works, Board of Trade, and Ministry of Transport; road engineers in Ministry of Transport; planning officers and housing and planning inspectors in the Ministry of Housing and Local Government; valuers in Inland Revenue, and marine surveyors in Board of Trade.

There is a common grading structure, irrespective of profession, for those in the Works Group of Professional Classes proper. It consists of a basic grade to which staff are normally recruited, a main grade which is numerically the largest, a senior grade, a superintending grade and a number of directing grades. Some of the variants and related clases have the same structure. Others, particularly those engaged on inspectorial duties, have the same structure excepting there is no grade below the main grade. The Board of Trade marine surveyors, the Royal Corps of Naval Constructors and the Royal Naval Engineering Service and several others have a different grading structure. The grades and numbers of the Works Group and, with some exceptions, the variants and related classes, and their current salary scales, are:

C

		£ a year
		(Works group proper)
Top posts	24	5,000–7,200*
Directing grades	254	4,500 and 4,825*
Superintending grades	624	3,500–4,000*
Senior grade	2,138	2,639–3,105
Main grade	4,647	1,894–2,510
Basic grade	3,729	1,242 (age 25)–1,894
	11,416	

* Individually assessed within this range.

Recruitment to the Works Group is normally by open competition between the ages of 25 and 34 through the Civil Service Commission. There are opportunities for class-to-class promotion from the technical and drawing office classes. The minimum qualifications required for the basic grade of the Works Group are given below, those for the variants and related classes being broadly comparable. These qualifications must be supported by evidence of professional ability and several years' appropriate professional experience in private or outside practice or in the service of a local authority.

Architect: Must be a registered Architect.

Maintenance Surveyor: Must be a registered Architect, or must have achieved corporate membership of the Royal Institution of Chartered Surveyors (Building Section).

Civil Engineer: Must have achieved corporate membership of the Institution of Civil Engineers.

Public Health Engineer: Must have achieved corporate membership of the Institution of Civil Engineers, having qualified in the subject 'Hydraulics', or must have achieved corporate membership of the Institution of Municipal Engineers.

Structural Engineer: Must have achieved corporate membership of the Institution of Civil Engineers, or corporate membership of the Institution of Structural Engineers.

Quantity Surveyor: Must have achieved corporate membership of the Royal Institution of Chartered Surveyors (Quantities Section).

Estate Surveyor and Lands Officer:	Must have achieved corporate membership of the Royal Institution of Chartered Surveyors, or of the Chartered Auctioneers and Estate Agents Institution or of the Land Agents Society, or must hold a degree in Estate Management (BA Cantab. or BSc London), provided corporate membership is achieved within the period of probation. (There are special requirements in some departments.)
Mechanical and Electrical Engineer:	Must have achieved corporate membership of the Institution of Civil Engineers, or of the Institution of Mechanical Engineers, or of the Institution of Electrical Engineers.

Candidates are also recruited if they have passed Parts I and II of the examination of the appropriate professional institution, or have passed the examinations for corporate membership, provided corporate membership is achieved during the probationary period which is normally two years. Exceptionally, alternative evidence of high professional attainment may be accepted.

The Technical Classes

Associated with the Works Group of Professional Classes and its complex of professions is the Technical Works Engineering and Allied Classes. This is a group of classes between the industrial staff who are engaged on production and maintenance, and the fully qualified professionals whose work has been described above. Their concern in this work is executive—interpreting current technical practice, arranging and supervising its execution, and inspecting the results. The technical staff are complementary to the drawing office staff which are referred to later, and they translate the drawings into actual production and operation. Their work tends to divide itself into three broad divisions: detailed technical planning and progressing, which is mainly a desk job though very close contact with the factory or the site must be maintained. Secondly, jobs concerned with direct labour production in factories, dockyards, airfields, on sites, etc.; and a third group dealing with inspection work in outside industry engaged on Government contracts. These functions are exercised in connection with practically every kind of mechanical, electrical, and other manufactured material and equipment, ranging from aircraft, ships, mobile or stationary land power units, to precision measuring instruments and minor accessories. The technical classes are also concerned with apprentice training and the management of labour. The two largest sections of this group are engaged on mechanical and electrical engineering and building construction work. The group is, however, very diverse and the staff are employed on a whole range of technical duties.

Recruitment is normally on a temporary basis in the first instance and opportunities are provided for establishment by means of open competition through the Civil Service Commission. Candidates must be at least age 25 but there is no upper age limit. They have to prove an adequate standard of technical education, and for the technical grade III this is an Ordinary National Certificate, or equivalent technical qualification. In addition the candidate is required to have five years' apprenticeship or its equivalent and, after apprenticeship, three years' workshop or other relevant practical experience. Direct recruitment to technical grade II is exceptional, but where it does take place weight is given for the possession of Higher National Certificate or equivalent standard of technical education. The grading structure of the technical classes, their numbers and the current salary scales are:

		£ a year
Above Technical A	46†	
Technical grade A	439	1,951–2,277
Technical grade B	799	1,842–2,096
Technical I	4,407	1,490–1,842
Technical II	7,784	1,283–1,490
Technical III	7,855	1,076 (age 26)–1,283
Technical IV*	265	854 (age 25)–1,149
	21,595	

† Individually assessed.
* An obsolescent grade.

The Draughtsmen Classes
Complementary to the Works Group of Professional Classes

and the Works Technical and Allied Classes is the Architectural and Engineering Draughtsmen Classes. The work of this group falls into three broad categories: architectural, civil engineering, and mechanical and electrical engineering. They prepare engineering or architectural drawings and plans needed for production purposes or for building operations—thus assisting in the designing of engineering, civil engineering, and architectural projects. The majority are employed in the Ministry of Public Building and Works, though there are considerable numbers in other departments and, in particular, mechanical and engineering draughtsmen are used extensively by the Defence departments.

The grades and numbers of the Architectural and Engineering Draughtsmen Classes and their current salary scales are:

		£ a year
Chief Draughtsman	176	1,904–2,277
Senior Draughtsman	1,022	1,527–1,879
Leading Draughtsman	2,470	1,263–1,480
Draughtsman	4,694	1,030 (age 25)–1,263
	8,362	

Recruitment is done departmentally either in a temporary capacity initially, with opportunities to become established, or direct to an established post. Before a temporary draughtsman can become established he must compete through the Civil Service Commission limited competition. Subject to sufficient of the limited competition candidates reaching the qualifying standard, at least 50 per cent of the vacancies may be reserved for them.

The Scientific Civil Service

Although there is a wide diversity of disciplines and skills in the Scientific Civil Service, the scientists are organized, with some exceptions, on a uniform class and grading structure. There are three separate classes: the scientific officer, experimental officer and scientific assistant classes, and within each class there is a series of grades. In total, about 15,000 scientific staff are employed in the Scientific Civil Service. A few departments operate separate departmental classes for scientific work which is special to them, such as the advisory staff in the National Agricultural Advisory Service and research officers with veterinary qualifications in the Ministry of Agriculture, Fisheries and Food, but this is very much the exception. Permanent recruitment is by continuous open competition through the Civil Service Commission, but many scientists prefer to come in, initially, as temporaries and decide later whether or not they wish to apply for a permanent post. A number of Research Fellowships are offered throughout the Scientific Civil Service for scientists of outstanding calibre; they are attached for a period of three years to the Government scientific establishment which is doing the kind of work they wish to pursue. As an individual scientist will bring to his work his own personal qualities and experience, a system known as flexible complementing operates in the scientific officer class up to, and including, the principal scientific officer grade. This means that a scientist does not have to wait until a vacancy arises in the grade above before he is promoted, promotion taking place when the individual is judged on merit to be ready for it. There are also 'special merit' promotions above the principal scientific officer grade, which enables individual researchers to be promoted on merit without having to take on any managerial responsibilities. The Treasury has recently extended this scheme of special merit promotions to engineers on Works Group gradings who work in research and development establishments. There is also flexible complementing between the two lowest grades in the experimental officer class.

The scientific officer class, which is the senior of the three, is recruited mainly from candidates with first or second class honours degrees or diplomas in technology, or higher qualifications. The normal age limit on entry is under 32 years of age. It has the main responsibility for scientific advice, research, design and development in the Civil Service. The experimental officer class may be graduates or have higher technical qualifications, such as HNC, or enter direct from school with GCE 'A' level. Recruitment normally takes place between ages 18 and 31. The experimental officers act as support for the scientific officers. They carry out a large proportion of the experimental work and manage groups of junior staff. Normally they do not initiate research, except on the authority of scientific officers. The scientific assistant class is normally recruited between the ages of 16 and 17. They must have a minimum of one year's laboratory experience and at least four GCE 'O' level passes before they can compete through the Civil Service Commission for established posts. They assist the more highly qualified staff by undertaking the care and preparation of apparatus and materials, by observing and recording any experiments and tests, by making related calculations and maintaining records. With few exceptions, every Government scientific establishment has members of all three classes on its staff and the typical working unit consists of teams of all three scientific classes.

To give some examples of the work, scientists in Ministry of Agriculture, Fisheries and Food do research on food standards and on the peaceful uses of nuclear energy in agriculture and food processing, the control and the disposal of radio-active waste from nuclear installations, plant pathology, animal health, research into the classification, growth, structure and uses of plants, fisheries research, pest infestation, etc. Ministry of Technology conducts a wide range of research and development work, much of which has important industrial and civil applications, e.g. aeronautics, astronautics, gas-turbine technology, radar, telecommunications and navigational aids. The Royal Aircraft Establishment, Farnborough, is the largest research establishment in the country. The Ministry of Technology is also responsible for many laboratories which were formerly under the control of the Department of Scientific and Industrial Research, such as the National Physical Laboratory, Forest Products Research Laboratory, Hydraulics Research Laboratory, Government Chemist's Laboratory, National Engineering Laboratory, National Lending Library for Science and Technology and the Warren Springs Laboratory. Scientists in the Navy, Army, and Air Force departments also do wide-ranging research which may be fundamental in character and involving the provision of scientific knowledge in fields largely of interest to the Fighting Services, or applied research and development work. The Meteorological Office is responsible for advances in the science of meteorology as well as for the provision of weather forecasts and other meteorological services. The Post Office Research Station researches into communications problems.

The scientific officer class is composed of the following grades:

	Total	Current pay £ a year
Posts above chief scientific officer	21	5,525–9,500*
Chief scientific officer	69	5,250 and 5,000
Deputy chief scientific officer	158	4,175–4,625
Senior principal scientific officer	557	3,500–4,000
Principal scientific officer	1,572	2,250–3,107
Senior scientific officer	1,167	1,744–2,155
Scientific officer	573	926–1,574
	4,117	

* The top posts are graded individually in this range.

The experimental officer class is composed of the following grades:

		Current pay £ a year
Chief experimental officer	228	2,571–2,999
Senior experimental officer	1,549	1,977–2,411
Experimental officer	4,008	1,365–1,734
Assistant experimental officer	1,694	568–1,243
	7,479	

The scientific assistant class is composed of the following grades:

		Current pay £ a year
Senior scientific assistant	1,127	1,031–1,359
Scientific assistant	4,589	396 (at 16)– 776 (at 25)– 985
	5,716	

Professional Accountants

There are numerous other distinct groups of professionals, e.g. accountants, doctors, lawyers, statisticians, etc. Although the total Government expenditure for 1965/6 was £8,456 million, only 333 professional accountants were employed by the Civil Service in that year. There was none in the Home Office, Ministry of Health, Ministry of Housing and Local Government, Department of Economic Affairs, Ministry of Technology, Ministry of Overseas Development, and in the now defunct Ministry of Land and Natural Resources. The Treasury, with its wide sphere of accountability and responsibility for giving advice, employed only one accountant. The explanation is that the basic accounting work for the Civil Service is done by the executive class, with the administrative class contributing the higher direction and policy element. The professional accountants are employed primarily on work being done on Government contracts outside the service in the industrial sphere. Consequently professional accountants are employed mainly by those departments whose work involves them in commercial accounting or who are concerned with the financial operations of commercial organizations. The main employing departments are Ministry of Defence, Board of Trade, Inland Revenue and the Post Office. The accountants give advice on the financial viability of contractors, comment on firms' published accounts; supply reports on contractors' overheads, on the figures of capital employed; and the costs of production, which are required for negotiation of profit rates; and average earning rates and actual costs incurred against specific contracting. In the Board of Trade they have to examine and prepare evidence on the financial aspects of monopolies, mergers, and restrictive trade practices, and advise on the financial and accounting aspects and implications of legislation such as the Companies Act and the Industrial Development Act. The structure of the professional accountant class provides for five grades; their numbers and current salaries being:

		£ a year
Director	6	3,500–4,265 and 4,500
Assistant Director	21	3,081–3,650
Chief Accountant	81	2,335–2,925
Senior Accountant	195	1,682–2,319
Accountant	30	1,194–1,682
	333	

Recruitment is by open competition between the ages of 25 and 40 through the Civil Service Commission. Membership of one of the following bodies is essential: Institute of Chartered Accountants in England and Wales, Institute of Chartered Accountants in Scotland, Institute of Chartered Accountants in Ireland, Association of Certified and Corporate Accountants. Also an essential requirement is professional experience, including experience in a professional office.

Other classes

With the exception of the professional accountants, the classes referred to in the previous paragraphs are all in large groups. There are many important smaller groups, including the doctors, lawyers, economists, statisticians, but it is not practicable to deal with all. The economists and statisticians do, however, occupy a significantly different position from most of the other professionals and this difference is worth noting. It is that the Treasury recognizes a close relationship between the work of certain of the economists and statisticians and the formulation of policy. Candidates for these two classes must be judged capable of participating in policy matters and be able to exercise administrative judgment, in addition to their own professional techniques. Presumably it is for this special reason that both the general service class of economists and also that of statisticians have grades and salary scales which correspond with the administrative class up to Assistant Secretary level but not beyond. At the higher levels salaries and gradings are *ad hoc*. There are about 100 economists, of which twenty or so are permanent civil servants, and about 250 posts for statisticians, of which fifty-two were unfilled at the end of April 1967. But this does not account for all the economists and statisticians in the service. They are also recruited to the research officer class and the scientific classes. When recruited to these classes, they are graded and paid on the scales of their appropriate class which are different from those of the administrative class.

6. THE SEPARATION OF PROFESSIONAL AND GENERALIST FUNCTIONS

The class structure of the service is responsible for considerable rigidity and inflexibility. Merging of functions is a rarity and transfer to another class, whether or not it involves promotion, usually means an elaborate process of selection and re-certification. It is quite exceptional for an officer in one class to transfer for a short period to a job regarded as appropriate to another class. More importantly, from the point of view of the professional, transfer to the generalist classes means giving up his professional activities. There is little prospect of acquiring administrative skills and techniques while serving as a professional, because of the separation of generalist and professional functions and, effectively, the professional is confronted with the choice of abandoning early in his career the profession for which he has been trained, or reconciling himself to a lifetime career within the confines of his profession.

The system works on the following lines: the objectives of departments are assigned by the Government or, equally likely, emerge from the department's 'own philosophy'. Plans are made for the achievement of these objectives—the formulation of policy stage, and then these plans are put into effect—the execution of policy. The generalist analyses and co-ordinates the ideas and proposals, relates them to the political and economic conditions and expresses the decisions in a form which he considers can be assimilated and carried out by the departmental machine.

Apart from the highest levels where the generalists are in final control, the extent to which generalists are used for departmental activities depends on how far the activity involves such things as:

(*a*) co-operation between a number of functional units within the department;

(*b*) resolution of conflicting objectives or priorities;

(*c*) interpretation of the public's needs;

(*d*) liaison with other departments, public bodies and organized interest such as trade unions;

(*e*) international and strategic interests;

(*f*) the necessity for sophisticated financial control;

(*g*) important Parliamentary and legislative complications; and

(*h*) important economic effects.

One or more of these factors are involved in a considerable part of any department's activities, even those of a department whose work is predominantly engineering or technical. This explains, for example, why the generalists play an important part in the work of a Ministry such as Ministry of Public Building and Works, which is predominantly a vast building organization.

It may be of interest to describe briefly how some of the departments are organized to accommodate both the generalist and the professional functions. The Ministry of Health, Ministry of Housing and Local Government and the Scottish departments have certain common features. Each has a number of activities outside the professional sphere, and, with the exception of the large number of doctors employed in Ministry of Health, each employs a relatively small number of professionals of various disciplines who examine and advise on constructional and ancillary projects being carried out by outside bodies. The professionals influence such projects at the formulation and design stage, the policy decisions being both made and executed from headquarters rather than regional or local offices. In all three departments the professionals are organized separately from the generalists and are required normally to act in an advisory, consultative, or research capacity. This is a fairly general system of organization known as 'separate hierarchies'.

Reference has been made to Ministry of Public Building and Works. It is of interest in this context because it is so predominantly a professionally based department, though there are, of course, others such as Ministry of Technology and Ministry of Defence. The Government decided in 1963 to merge the former Ministry of Works and the large works services organizations of the then Air Ministry, Admiralty, and War Department into a single Ministry—the Ministry of Public Building and Works. It is a vast building organization at home and overseas and the professional staff obviously play an important role. Since it was brought into being it has suffered from a malaise in the relationships between the professionals and the generalists. Two reorganizations have taken place since the merger, each designed to regulate the relationships between professionals and generalists and to strengthen the executive chain of command in the Controller-General's organization, i.e. on the professional side. Under the most recent reorganization the Controller-General, who has responsibility for the activities of about 12,000 professional and technical staff and their supporting staff, will be the top professional, with a production side and a research and development side organized separately from each other under his control. On the opposite page is an organizational chart of the new set-up.

There is little to cavil at in the new organization on the professional side, but the question still remains as to the relationship between the professionals and the generalists. There is a duality in the organization; at all levels the generalists are involved in the formulation and execution of policy. A principal feature of the headquarters organization is a number of distinct works directorates and secretariat branches, the heads of which

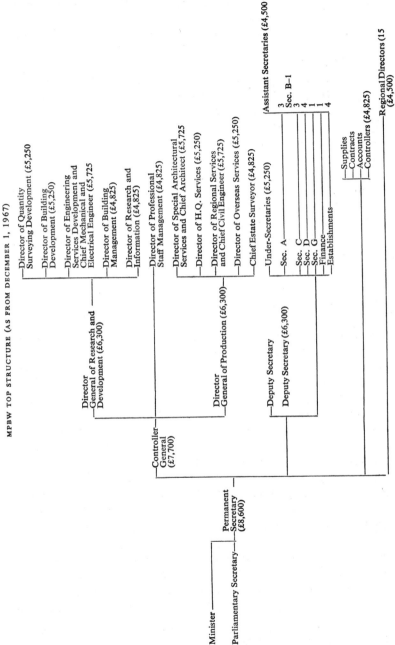

MPBW TOP STRUCTURE (AS FROM DECEMBER 1, 1967)

Minister

Parliamentary Secretary

Permanent Secretary (£8,600)

Controller-General (£7,700)

Director General of Research and Development (£6,300)
- Director of Quantity Surveying Development (£5,250)
- Director of Building Development (£5,250)
- Director of Engineering Services Development and Chief Mechanical and Electrical Engineer (£5,725)
- Director of Building Management (£4,825)
- Director of Research and Information (£4,825)
- Director of Professional Staff Management (£4,825)

Director General of Production (£6,300)
- Director of Special Architectural Services and Chief Architect (£5,725)
- Director of H.Q. Services (£5,250)
- Director of Regional Services and Chief Civil Engineer (£5,725)
- Director of Overseas Services (£5,250)
- Chief Estate Surveyor (£4,825)

Deputy Secretary (£6,300)

Deputy Secretary
Under-Secretaries (£5,250)
- Sec. A
- Sec. C
- Sec. D
- Sec. G
- Finance
- Establishments

Assistant Secretaries (£4,500)
- 3
- Sec. B–1
- 3
- 4
- 1
- 4

- Supplies
- Contracts
- Accounts
Controllers (£4,825)

Regional Directors (15) (£4,500)

are, respectively, professionals and generalists. The responsibilities of each are clearly defined to avoid doubt as to where responsibility for any duty or decision lies. Each Director-General works in partnership with an administrative deputy secretary, and the directors with the appropriate under-secretary. It is a system known in the service as 'parallel hierarchies'; one used where the work is considered so complex that it requires both professional and administrative contributions. The official reason given for the adoption of parallel hierarchies is the need to establish a close relationship between professionals and generalists while, at the same time, retaining clear definitions of responsibility considered essential for the control of large executive programmes of work. The administrator's role includes ascertaining the requirements of clients and deciding what should be met, where, and at what cost; a role which is recognized as being practicable only if there is constant collaboration with professional officers. The system has its peculiarities and its official justification. The justification is that, unlike professional people in private practice, the clients of the Ministry's professionals are other Government departments and there is a task of reconciliation to be performed which is a function of the generalist. The client department will want its resources to be used in accordance with its own policy and the Ministry of Public Building and Works will have its own programme for the scale and development of financial and other resources, taking account of the demands of all its clients. It is the generalists' function to bring these conflicting demands into harmony so that the Ministry's professionals 'are given a reasonable degree of protection against conflicting requirements'.[1] One of its peculiarities is that the system inevitably means interposing an intermediary between the professional and his client, which is something quite contrary to the relationship outside the Civil Service between, say, an architect or a consultant engineer and his client. Space does not permit of an analysis of the special problems which this system throws up, nor of the special precautions that have to be taken to ensure that each plays his allotted role in the department's business. For the purpose of this essay it is sufficient to describe the organizational pattern so that comparisons can be made with the organizations of other countries. The

[1] Report of the Official Working Party on the Role of Professional Engineers in the Civil Service, January 1966.

system is inevitable if one accepts the doctrine that only general-ists can reconcile conflicting demands and interpret ministerial policy. The central question again is whether there are really two men's jobs to be done, or if both functions could, and should, be concentrated under the control of one person. The regional structure of the Ministry is quite different, the Regional Directors being either administrative or professional officers selected solely on the basis of merit.

The Department of Education and Science has introduced an organizational arrangement which avoids some of the diffi-culties inherent in the system of parallel hierarchies in which latter there is strict separation of roles. In this Ministry the pro-fessionals work together with administrators and executives under the joint direction of an assistant secretary and a chief architect. There is no rigid definition of functions and the normal pattern is that the senior professionals participate on equal terms in the formulation of policy and its execution. A similar organization is to be found in a limited area of Ministry of Transport. It is in the Headquarters Highways Organization of that Ministry. A 'Heaton Committee' was appointed to in-vestigate whether engineers in the Ministry of Transport were too much engaged in checking and examining the work of local authorities. It found this not to be so. It did find, however, a malaise in the relationship between engineers and their adminis-trative colleagues. The morale of the engineers was under-mined by the feeling that they were kept in the background and that the most important decisions were taken by administrators. It was considered that this had an adverse effect on morale and recruitment. In consequence the Heaton Committee recom-mended a 'joint hierarchy' headed by a Deputy Secretary and a professional Director of Highways Engineering reporting jointly to the Permanent Secretary. Three years later in 1965 a professional was put in charge of this organization with joint heads below in certain groups at Under-Secretary level. In parallel with this the committee recommended greater delega-tion of engineering, administrative and financial matters to Divisional Road Engineers 'in order to clear the channels of communication with the Ministry, eliminate delays and generate a fuller sense of responsibility where work is generated'. In implementing the Heaton Committee recommendations that greater financial delegation be made to the Divisional Road

MINISTRY OF TRANSPORT HEADQUARTERS ORGANIZATION

Deputy Secretary

Under-Secretary (Railways) — Asst. Secs. (Railways A and B Divisions)
    Ch. Insp. Officer (Railway Inspectorate)

Under-Secretary (Channel Tunnel)

Under-Secretary (Nationalized Transport) — Asst. Secs. (Nationalized Transport A and B Divisions)

Under-Secretary (Road Transport) — Asst. Secs. (Road Transport [Goods and Passenger] Divisions)

Under-Secretary (Ports and Shipping Operations) — Asst. Secs. (Ports and Shipping Planning Divisions)
    Director (Sea Transport Division)

CHIEF SCIENTIFIC ADVISER

Under-Secretary (General and international transport, and statistics) — Chief Statistician (Statistics Division)
    Asst. Sec. (General Division)
(Reports to both Deputy Secretaries according to nature of the work) — Asst. Secs. (2) (Regional Development Division)
    Asst. Sec. (International Transport Division)

ECONOMIC ADVISER

Under-Secretary (Road Safety and Vehicle Regulation) — Asst. Secs. (Road Safety [Traffic and General] Divisions)
    Asst. Secs. (Vehicle Regulation and Driving and Motor Licences Divisions)

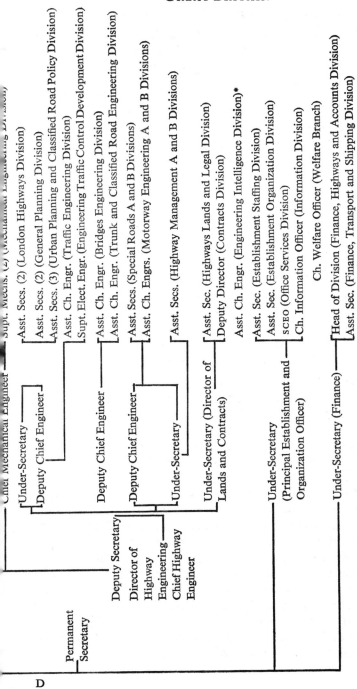

HONORARY ADVISER TO THE MINISTER ON ROAD TRAFFIC

* Reports direct to the Chief Highway Engineer working in liaison with all highway divisions.

Engineers an annual allocation of funds was approved enabling them to authorize contractual action on schemes by local authorities up to £100,000. This ceiling was later raised to £250,000. This method of organization is known as 'joint hierarchies'; an arrangement whereby professionals and administrators jointly run the same units. It is intended to cope with the situation in which engineering and administrative aspects are so closely associated together that if one brain could provide the expertise for both aspects, one man should be responsible for both. A detailed analysis of the changes made appeared in an article by D. E. Regan in *Public Administration* (Volume 44). The article concluded:

> 'Although much depends on the nature and volume of work, one may very tentatively conclude that the modified joint unit head structure is the most satisfactory integrated organization. Joint professional and non-professional heads at division and branch level are especially valuable but perhaps there should normally be a single person in charge at group level. In fact the Ministry's second reorganization has tended to be on these lines . . . in general, however, professional civil servants must play a greater role in policy and administration than they have usually in the past.'

The professionals in Ministry of Transport are critical of the reorganization in that it does not go far enough. They see it as a reorganization enforced on the generalists because of the increasing technical complexity of the work. Their criticism is that it has integrated administrators and professionals on the basis of the rigid class structure of the present-day Civil Service with its separation of roles, and that it has failed to deal with the central problem whether there are really two different roles requiring two differently educated and trained people to carry them out. They feel that the qualities of political awareness, ability to control the Civil Service machine, and ability to assess competing demands, are not the sole prerogative of the generalists and, at least in the area of their own professional work, they ought themselves to be allowed to exercise these judgments.

As the chart on pages 48 and 49 shows, the joint hierarchy is confined to the Directorate of Highway Engineering, the remaining divisions being organized on the conventional Civil Service basis with the generalists in control.

7. COMPARATIVE CAREER VALUES

There are several official sources from which one is able to calculate in a rough and ready way the average career prospects of a civil servant of proved ability in any given class. The following analysis of the relative career prospects of the generalists and two of the professional classes is derived from the following two sources:

1. Civil Service Commission booklets which are designed mainly as recruitment literature. They are entitled *Administrative Group of Appointments 1966, Engineers in the Government Service 1965* and *The Scientific Civil Service 1965*, and
2. *Civil Service Manpower 1966*, compiled by the Statistics Division of H.M. Treasury.

In calculating the total amount earned in a normal career in any given class, assumptions have to be made about the average age of promotion from one grade to another within the class. In the following calculations based on the Civil Service Commission booklets the 'normal age' at which the booklet states that promotion can be expected has been taken. For the calculations based on the *Civil Service Manpower 1966* statistics the median age of those promoted to each of the grades has been used as published in that publication. The results from these two sources differ but point to similar conclusions. Calculations based on either source show that the professional has a materially worse career value than the generalist.

Taking the Civil Service Commission booklets first and calculating on current salary scales the following careers are reached:

DIRECT ENTRANTS (23–60 years in each case)

	Assumptions	Total £
Administrative	Entry at 23, Principal at 28, Assistant Secretary at 39	130,931
Works Group	Entry at 23, Main Grade at 31, Senior Grade at 40	94,580
Scientific Officer	Entry at 23, Senior Scientific Officer at 28, Principal Scientific Officer at 36	95,845

The calculations based on the statistics in *Civil Service Manpower 1966* show that the career expectations in the professional fields as stated in the Civil Service Commission booklets are

over-optimistic. The manpower statistics give the median ages
of those who are actually promoted and, of course, take no
account of those who are *not* promoted. One would expect
career value calculations made on this basis to reflect a much
better picture than an analysis based on the average expectation of every member serving in the class. In fact they do not do
so, as the following shows:

DIRECT ENTRANTS (23–60 years in each case)

	Assumptions	Total
		£
Administrative	Entry at 23, Principal at 29, Assistant Secretary at 42	124,970
Works Group	Entry at 23, Main Grade at 43, Senior at 46	84,654
Scientific Officer	Entry at 23, Senior Scientific Officer at 30, Principal Scientific Officer at 38	92,324

As the median age for those actually promoted has been used
above, no account has been taken of those who do not get
promoted above various levels and, therefore, do not attain
what is normally described as a 'typical' career.

Comparing the various stages in the careers of professionals
and generalists in the three classes listed above, and again
basing the calculations on the careers which emerge from the
Civil Service Manpower 1966 statistics, it is possible to see the
rapid way in which the administrative class draws away from
the professionals:

Age	Administration	Works Group	Scientific Officer
		£ per annum	
23	926	1,035	926
30	2,340	1,569	1,744
35	2,817	1,848	2,155
40	3,107	1,894	2,534
45	4,000	2,196	3,015
50	4,500	3,105	3,107
55	4,500	3,105	3,107
60	4,500	3,105	3,107

So far the comparisons have been made on the basis of those
who *are* promoted. Obviously the balance in favour of the
generalists would rapidly be redressed if substantially more
professionals were promoted at the ages given relative to the
generalists. The age distribution in the grades of each of the
classes must therefore also be taken into consideration, as
these will reveal the opportunities of promotion from one grade

to another and will take account of those who are unlikely to receive further promotion. Tables have been prepared and are reproduced (p. 55). These show the age distribution of the Administrative, Scientific Officer, and Works Group Classes and also the 'pyramid' of the grades within each class. To look at the 'pyramid' of the grades first it will be seen that the percentage of the three classes reaching the 'upper echelons' is as follows:

		Per cent of class
Administrative	Assistant Secretary and above	46·6
Works Group	Superintending Grades and above	8·7
Scientific Officer	Senior Principal Scientific Officer and above	23·6
	or	
Administrative	Under Secretary and above	15·34
Works Group	Directing and above	2·87
Scientific Officer	Deputy Chief Scientific Officer and above	7·24

This clearly illustrates that a far greater percentage of the Administrative Class reaches the highest grades in the Civil Service than does the Scientific Officer Class. It demonstrates even more strongly the relatively poor career prospects of those recruited into the Works Group. As a further illustration of the poor career prospects of the Works Group 50·8 per cent of the class is in the main grade (salary £1,894–£2,510) and a further 18·5 per cent of the class in the basic grade—that is, nearly 70 per cent of the class is in the two lower grades. The disparity can be expressed in a table showing the percentage of the classes in the lower grades:

		Per cent of class
Administrative	Principal and Assistant Principal grades	43·2
Works Group	Senior Grade and below	91·1
Scientific Officer	Principal Scientific Officer and below	76·3

The age distribution shows that approximately one-third of the basic grade of the Works Group is 55 years or over and approximately one-third of the main grade is 55 years and over. The comparison of equivalent salary grades shows:

	Per cent of grade			
	55 years and over	45–54 years	35–44 years	23–34 years
Administrative Principal	12·1	36·7	36·4	14·8
Principal Scientific Officer	18·8	36·6	43·8	under 1
Senior Grade	44·2	40·6	14·7	under 1

The figures and conclusions drawn above leave room for error, but the comparisons have a common source and the final career values all leave out of account those who are not promoted to the normal career expectation grade. Nevertheless, they clearly indicate that at all levels the scientific officer and works group professional classes have career earnings well below the generalists.

8. CONCLUSION

There are obviously variations on the three forms of organization of professionals and generalists which have been described, but, in substance, they all come down to these three broad classifications:

1. Separate hierarchies—in which policy is determined by the generalists and the job of the professionals is to execute it;
2. Parallel hierarchies—in which each class has its own separate hierarchy parallel one to the other, co-ordination being achieved by frequent liaison; and
3. Joint hierarchies—the system in which the professional and administrative aspects are so closely integrated that administrators and professionals must, of necessity, work together in the same division or unit of organization.

The basic assumption of all three is that there are two different roles which cannot be combined. There are some posts on both the generalist and the professional sides, the content of which is clearly managerial. There are other posts, almost exclusively on the generalists' side, which are concerned with control in a more general sense. These posts are concerned with the development of governmental policy, negotiation in particular fields, the political implications of the department's objectives and of its day-to-day working. The higher one goes on this side of the service, the closer are the links with the Minister. These posts are reserved almost exclusively for the generalists because they have to apply the same kind of consideration to their work as would their Minister. They have to be 'politically aware'. The basic assumption is that the professionals cannot do this kind of work. Half of the entrants to the administrative class are promoted from the executive class, but it is mainly the graduate direct entrant who fills the top jobs. These, as has been shown,

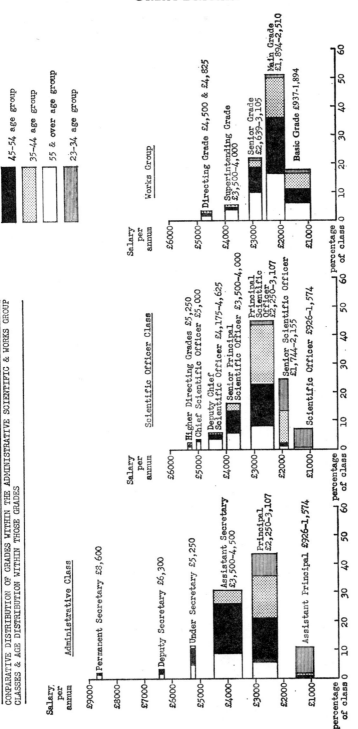

COMPARATIVE DISTRIBUTION OF GRADES WITHIN THE ADMINISTRATIVE SCIENTIFIC & WORKS GROUP CLASSES & AGE DISTRIBUTION WITHIN THOSE GRADES

45-54 age group
35-44 age group
55 & over age group
23-34 age group

Salary, per annum

Administrative Class

£9000
£8000
£7000
£6000
£5000
£4000
£3000
£2000
£1000

Permanent Secretary £8,600
Deputy Secretary £6,300
Under Secretary £5,250
Assistant Secretary £3,500-4,500
Principal £2,250-3,107
Assistant Principal £926-1,574

percentage of class   0 10 20 30 40 50 60

Salary per annum

Scientific Officer Class

£6000
£5000
£4000
£3000
£2000
£1000

Higher Directing Grades £5,250
Chief Scientific Officer £5,000
Deputy Chief Scientific Officer £4,175-4,625
Senior Principal Scientific Officer £3,500-4,000
Principal Scientific Officer £2,250-3,107
Senior Scientific Officer £1,744-2,155
Scientific Officer £926-1,574

percentage of class   0 10 20 30 40 50 60

Salary per annum

Works Group

£6000
£5000
£4000
£3000
£2000
£1000

Directing Grade £4,500 & £4,825
Superintending Grade £3,500-4,000
Senior Grade £2,639-3,105
Main Grade £1,894-2,510
Basic Grade £937-1,894

percentage of class   0 10 20 30 40 50 60

Derived from Civil Service Manpower 1966

come mainly from Oxbridge and most are arts graduates in spite of the Civil Service Commission's best endeavours to broaden its field of recruitment. Reserving the administrative and most of the managerial work for the generalist classes means that professionals who wish to remain as professionals are unable, in their formative years, to gain broad administrative experience. If they have a real potential for management and administration, it will probably never emerge because of lack of opportunity. Admittedly, they have a choice. They can abandon their professional careers immediately after qualifying and compete for administrative posts through the Civil Service administrative class competitions; or, alternatively, after a few years practising their profession in the Civil Service they can apply for for class-to-class promotion to the administrative class. Either choice means abandoning their professional career. The service is so structured that one must be a member of the administrative class to participate in administration in the general sense described above. The assumption is that only a career in administration can give one the necessary background knowledge, training and skills to enable one to run the Civil Service machine, be politically aware and advise the Minister. The changing functions of the Civil Service demands that at least some of those engaged in administration should be professionally qualified in the subjects they are administering. The home Civil Service is not so rich in managerial talent that it can afford to neglect the potential ability on the professional side. Clearly the higher Civil Service must be opened up to all the talents. It is right that thought should be given at the present time to what kind of Civil Service the country needs today, and what changes, however fundamental, should be made to its structure. What follows in this book on the structure of the civil services of other countries should prove very useful in this context.

AUSTRALIA

1. INTRODUCTION

Like most modern governments, the Australian Commonwealth (that is, the federal) Government is now a big employer of some scattered and some concentrated groups of variegated but predominantly white-collar workers. Its overall employment is now over 300,000, as a result of increases which had already begun to show before the Second World War, but which have been more important during and since then. Federation began with the century. The first functions of the Commonwealth Government were limited by an international situation in which it could rely on the u.k. to provide its defence and much of its foreign policy. Its functions also seemed to be limited by an apparently restrictive constitutional allocation of powers and finance between the federal and the states' authorities, outside of certain judicial rather than administrative processes and activities. Hence the Postmaster General's Department and the Customs were very much the dominant original Commonwealth employers. That has not been unimportant for the whole tradition and development of the Commonwealth public service. However, a degree of change from that starting point occurred rapidly and the radical alteration of that first simple and desirable state of affairs has been statistically very impressive. The gross total of Commonwealth employment has increased from 25,000 in 1903 to 70,000 before the war, 250,000 by the 1950s and so to the present figure. As a part of the whole Australian population it has increased from ½ per cent to 1 per cent before the war to 3 per cent today while the population itself has increased rapidly enough, although only at half that rate.

As elsewhere, again, the whole of Commonwealth employment does not fall within the public service proper, that is fully within the terms of the Commonwealth Public Service Acts (a neat definition of a public or civil servant not available in the u.k.). Apart from the armed services (about one-sixth of the whole) the Commonwealth, like all other Westernized governments, whatever their ideological position, operates many business enterprises: banks and airlines, for example. It operates still more non-business enterprises falling outside the public service proper. However, the control of the public service and of other ranges of Commonwealth employment is not without some elements of distinctiveness.

The distinction lies in the role of the Commonwealth Public Service Board. The bulk of Commonwealth civilian public employment (apart from some very few organizations, like the Australian National Airlines Commission, for example, whose control of their own employment is much like that of any ordinary public company) is within the influence of the board at least as far as overall wage policy and co-ordination. Further, the Commonwealth public service itself is in fact two-thirds, an unusually high proportion of the whole of federal employment compared with some other national governments, and compared with some of the Australian States, like Victoria. The management of that public service falls fully under the aegis of the board. It is not, then, exactly comparable with the U.S. Civil Service Commission or Budget Bureau or with the U.K. Treasury or Civil Service Commission. The limitation of its position, other than political support, lies only with another institution: arbitration and its application to the service.

If much of the experience and position of Commonwealth employment is highly comparable with that of other Western States some of it is peculiar enough. The special position of the board, of which more will be said later, is the most important aspect of this. As between the British Civil Service and the Australian public services a second aspect of difference is the respective positions of professional officers.

2. THE CONDITIONS AND THE STATUS OF THE PROFESSIONAL

It may be useful from time to time in looking at the Australian situation to think of professionals according to their qualifications and their conditions of recruitment as professionals; their classification in the service; the sorts of people they are; or the jobs they do, the careers they have and the careers they may expect to have. For the most part it is useful to look at professionals as people who come into the service and then are paid and classified because of certain qualifications which enable them to do particular work; they may later in their careers go on to do other things. Thus, the criterion for a professional public servant used by the Commonwealth public service in Australia (e.g. for classification in the Third Division) is, 'acceptance for membership by an association of professional officers'.[1] The main interest in comparing the positon of such professionals in different public services is twofold: a matter of the salaries and conditions they do get; and a matter of their status particularly as it concerns their relation to the top administrative jobs. In both respects the Australian public services offer a sharp contrast with the U.K. Civil Service. The contrast covers both the Commonwealth and the State public services, but this discussion will be mainly concerned with the Commonwealth as offering the fairer comparison.

The contrast is often vivid.[2] For example, the failure of the IPCS in 1960 to gain salary increases for the Works Group of engineers, etc., in U.K. was followed very quickly in June 1961 by quite startling awards granted by the arbitration machinery to engineers in Australia.[3] Similarly, in a paper in 1962[4] the Chief Inspector of the Public Service Board of Victoria accepted as a necessary doctrine for the Australian public services that 'for specialists, it is necessary for the salary pattern to offer a reasonable guarantee of progression through to a much higher salary level than might be expected on the same "guaranteed" basis by an administrator'. He went on to explain that, 'Beyond a relatively low level, the administrator must, to progress to higher salary levels, gain promotion in competition. Probably this is because all specialists are required to have professional qualifications, and must, therefore, be offered a career inducement to acquire them. . . . Further, while specialist qualifications are usually easily measurable up to a fairly advanced level of work, administrative qualifications are not.' Mr Gardner's words indicate a good deal of the Australian situation. His was the doctrine accepted in the Engineers' Awards, as the 1961/2 decisions were called. So the full measure was applied despite

[1] Commonwealth Public Service Board. Information on the Commonwealth Public Service prepared for the Arbitration Court: Margins Appeal Case, 1955, p. 8.
[2] V. Subramanian, *41 Public Administration*, London, 1963, p. 357.
[3] Commonwealth Arbitration Reports, 19, 1961, and 29, 1962.
[4] A. J. A. Gardner, *Specialists and the Administrative Career*, Royal Institute of Public Administration, Canberra, 1962, p. 21.

any difficult implications it had for the relations between people in engineering and in administrative positions.

The awards actually represented two decisions by the Commonwealth Conciliation and Arbitration Commission in 1961/2. The first was in the case between the Association of Professional Engineers and others *v.* various employers' organizations scheduled on lists A (mainly private) and B (including various State public service boards).[1] The second was between the APE together with the Professional Officers' Association (the POA, the Commonwealth public service staff association for the bulk of professional officers) and the Association of Architects, Engineers, Surveyors and Draughtsmen (AAESD) *v.* the Commonwealth Public Service Board and others.[2] The awards covered 'all employed as professional engineers' (under current legislation, whether members of the APE, etc., or not) so that the very definition of 'professional engineer' was important. Professional engineering duties were taken to mean 'duties carried out by a person in any particular employment the adequate discharge *of any portion* [italics, B. B. S.] of which duties requires qualifications of the employee as (or at least equal to those of) a Graduate Member of the Institute of Engineers, Australia'. A professional engineer meant an 'adult male qualified for those duties'. A qualified engineer meant someone who had done a four or five years' recognized course; an experienced engineer meant anyone qualified for Associate Membership of the Institute.

The minimum scale for a qualified engineer was to be £1,400[3] for a non-graduate; for an experienced engineer the minimum was £2,200, if he were an Associate Member over 25, a graduate with four years' experience or a non-graduate with five years' experience. For the Commonwealth public service the award meant basic or minimal scales for an engineer Grade 1 of £1,298–£2,098, and for a graduate from a four to five years' course of £1,438—1 by 140—1 by 160—2 by 180—£2,098 (i.e. one incremental advantage).

That would cover any employee being an 'adult male who possesses professional engineering qualifications and is em-

---

[1] Commonwealth Arbitration Reports, 97, 1961, Pt. II, p. 345 ff. Wright and Gallagher, J. J., and Portus, Commr.

[2] Wright and Gallagher, J. J., and Galvin, Public Service Arbitrator.

[3] Figures are quoted as £1 Australian=16s sterling or $2 Australian. Most figures used here relate to the period before decimalization, 1965/6.

ployed temporarily or permanently in the Public Service as defined by the Public Service Arbitration Acts'. The definition thus included the Commonwealth public service proper plus certain other Commonwealth organizations. As we have seen, that sort of extension is usual.

While the generosity of the scales was notable, perhaps, and their application to both public and private employment was a result of amended procedures, the method and care of the definitions were typical; the application to State authorities new; and the implications important throughout public and professional employment. Thus by the end of 1964 the following scales applied, subject to variation since by any increases in the basic wage. Examples:

(i) VICTORIAN PUBLIC SERVICE
Agricultural scientist: four-year degree course minimum: £1,685

(ii) COMMONWEALTH PUBLIC SERVICE

a. Grades	Meteorologist, etc. £	Architect £	Experimental officer £
1	1,458–2,347	1,579–2,370	1,458–2,347
2	2,450–2,765	2,500–2,824	2,450–2,765
3	2,869–3,175	2,954–3,337	2,888–3,254
4	3,296–3,540	3,470–3,722	3,376–3,620
5	3,672–3,937	3,860–4,134	—

	Engineer £		Scientific Officer £
1	1,515–2,347	base grade	1,672–2,172
2	2,502–2,817	research sc.	2,445–3,105
3	2,971–3,337	senior r. sc.	3,235–3,755
4	3,489–3,733	principal r. sc.	3,885–4,485
5	3,885–4,149	senior principal r. sc.	4,690–4,840

(plus positions up to £6,465)

b. *The graduate minimum:* £
1,515 (£1,685 for an architect)
1,660 for a four- or five-year course
2,347 for an Associate Member of the
Institute of Engineering

c. *Female scales were £200 less*

The minimum qualification for the scientific officer scale is a first or second class honours degree.

Scales had continued to improve after 1961, mainly due to automatic increases and to increases in the basic wage, applied even at that level. The position of engineers was still very favourable as compared with other scales, but all have improved, on the engineers' backs as it were, and research scientists stand still higher. There are slight variations in the scales so that (to anticipate) particular definitions remain very important in the Commonwealth public service's treatment of professionals: an example is the starting point for architects, even allowing for the length of the architects' minimum course. There are certain common points, like the graduate's starting rates, which recognize the difference between the common Australian pass courses of three years and the longer honours course. Very high top salaries are available, e.g. to engineers; but the good starting points and quick movement are more significant. The Royal Australian Chemical Society survey, for December 1964, showed a male median salary for its members as £2,900; 90 per cent earned over £2,080 and 3 per cent over £6,000. A member in the Commonwealth would be likely to do as least as well as this average. For example, any honours chemistry graduate would already have been earning well over £2,000 after five years' service, that is (university courses in Australia often starting at under 18 years) when he was 26 or 27, at that time.

Gardner's thesis perceived that the public service has to offer a different sort of career provision to professional recruits, whatever the hope of the professional to move into top administrative positions. One motive for such a move was blunted by the Engineers' Awards. However, if it exists the hope is much more likely to be realized in Australian than in U.K. conditions. That is, precisely, the second major point. More will be said about this, but six of eleven Commonwealth professional or technical departments still have professional permanent heads. The Postmaster General's Department and Works are always headed by engineers and National Development by a scientist; Health statutorily has to be headed by a doctor. Elsewhere, both in Commonwealth and in State departments, where there is an administrative head (like the Queensland Department of Education with an under-secretary) the professional head (e.g. the Director-General in that case) has at least equal and usually better status, pay and ministerial access. For example, in South Australia four professional departments have administrative heads, but the professional chiefs earn twice as much.[1] Both by opportunity and by status the professional is well treated. That is the tradition.

[1] V. Subramaniam, op. cit., p. 361.

The combination of better professional conditions and better status has meant that in the Commonwealth and in the State public services the professionals have always provided the bulk of the top paid positions: e.g. in the Commonwealth 1956.[1]

Above £2,000	
Professional officers	53·2 per cent
Clerical officers with qualifications	17·5 per cent
Other clerical officers	29·3 per cent

3. CLASSIFICATION AND THE PUBLIC SERVICE BOARD

The points of difference indicate that conditions and status of professionals in the Australian public services are a part of a peculiar system and of a different set of social experiences and attitudes. The position is not isolated or accidental. In the first place, as has been said, the organization and control of the Commonwealth public service is, unlike the position in the U.K., enshrined in legislation and regulations thereunder, particularly the Commonwealth Public Service Acts. The service falls into three groups: permanent; temporary; and (about 25 per cent of the whole) exempt, the bulk in the 4th Division, and over half in one department, the Postmaster General's, and most of the rest in two others, Works and Repatriation. Of the four Divisions, the 1st consists, essentially, of the heads of departments; the 4th of minor technical and sub-clerical grades, like printing staff, linesmen, clerical assistants and stores and transport workers. The 2nd and 3rd Divisions therefore include the majority of permanent officers on administrative, clerical and professional work. The 2nd Division itself is quite small, about 5 per cent of the whole; the 3rd Division is therefore in some way the most important and interesting. Both the 2nd and 3rd Divisions are highly miscellaneous. It has been generally argued that, save for the 1st and 4th Divisions, the divisional structure itself is without significance. For example, Scarrow says, 'Apart, then, from separating the 4th Division from the rest of the Service, the present divisional classification [sic] serves little practical use.'[2] However, we shall see that, since 1964, the Public Service Board has been attempting to make the concept

[1] Commonwealth Public Service. Sample Survey, 1956.
[2] H. Scarrow, *The Higher Public Service of the Commonwealth of Australia*, Duke, 1957, p. 24.

of a 2nd Division more meaningful. In any case, it could be argued that the combination of top professionals and others in the same Division was not, in fact, without point.

Professionally qualified officers can then be found in all three of the top divisions. In particular, in the 3rd Division, where over 17 per cent are professionals, the classification of a position as such has a very real importance. Indeed, classification is the dominant feature of personnel (or establishments) work in the Commonwealth public service. What the service means by classification has been well defined as follows:[1]

(a) Division of work into specific classes;

(b) Delineation of classes in terms of all factors which are decisive in fixing the allocation of positions to a particular class, e.g. qualifications required, responsibilities exercised, staff supervision, etc;

(c) Maintenance of equitable internal relationships within and between classes;

(d) Maintenance of proper relativity with external and community rates of pay;

(e) Prescription of procedures and rules for determining the rates of pay applicable to the various classes and for determining the allocation of positions to the appropriate class.

That sort of position (or job, or task) classification would make inconceivable in the Australian system such an inclusive rank class as the u. k. clerical or executive or administrative.

The system of classification is operated by the Public Service Board whose statutory and, effectively, major work it is. The Board has many other functions, as in recruitment, under s. 17 (O and M work) and in training. Nevertheless, classification predominates and, further, is peculiar to the Board, while other personnel work is not: for example, even in recruitment it is not concerned with the employees it has exempted from the Act, and it has also delegated to the Postmaster General's Department many of the examinations for the recruitment of that department's permanent staff. While, with the exception of one department, it initiated training in the public service, most other departments now do much of the work. In conjunction with its other functions about pay and conditions, classification is, as one

[1] B. White, *The Commonwealth Service: Multiple Checks and Balances*, Canberra, 1959, p. 3.

writer says, 'the most contentious area of the Board's work'.[1] The existence and role of the Board make a major difference. The Board is a body of three commissioners appointed by Governor-in-Council for five years, with one appointed as chairman. It is directly responsible to Parliament, and its members can be dismissed only by Governor-in-Council in a message received from both Houses. The chairman and commissioners have very high status in the service. They are normally re-appointed until retiring age. The chairman is usually referred to and looked on as head of the service. All three will have held high office in the service before appointment. Of the eight since World War II two were former permanent heads of departments, four were former senior members of the Board's own staff and the present chairman was formerly Treasurer of the ILO. They have always been appointed from Commonwealth employment itself. The Board's staff is about 600. They are employed in the Canberra headquarters or in regional offices each under a public service inspector in the State capitals and in Canberra.

The Board is, of course, responsible to the Cabinet. The relations between the Board and the Government of the day inevitably vary with conditions and policy. For example, the conditions governing recruitment pre-war and post-war have, as in other countries, varied widely. One Government may allow the Board, within these conditions, a fairly free hand. Another may issue specific instructions, for example about the size of the service. In any case, the Board can only operate within the limits of its resources of budget, time and support which the Government provides. In this, whatever its formal position, it is no different from any other Governmental structure. Over and above those limitations the formal rules created by the Act itself somewhat confuse the authority of the Board. The Board's regulations, for example for changing classification structures, have to be approved. To be more precise; a recommendation to create or abolish a post is subject to Ministerial approval; but reclassifications, since 1951, are things for the Board itself. The choice between these two methods is not unimportant in technical effect on the individual officer, the amount of work involved or suitability for general reorganization.

Again, the Board is responsible for classification under s. 29; the permanent head of a department is responsible for organizing

[1] G. E. Caiden in *Australian Politics : A Reader*, ed. H. Mayer, 1967, p. 480.

E

his department's work under s. 25. Accordingly, the actual initiation of a review of the classification of a position is not necessarily done by the Board; a department may initiate it and so may the individual officer or the public service union of which he is a member. Nevertheless, subject to arbitration, the Board's is the effective decision.

In coming to its decisions the Board draws on three types of material. The first is its interpretations of principles about the two basic grades; the base grade clerk and, separately, the base grade professional officer. These principles have to do with problems of recruitment and with the concept of a base grade itself. The important thing is that the principles are differently stated for each base grade, professional or clerical. To quote an authoritative source again,[1] the principle is 'the fixation of an appropriate salary range, in the case of a professional officer, to provide a career for the normal qualified man and, in the case of a base grade clerk, to bring him to the maximum of his range at the predominant marrying age for the Australian community'.

The consequence is a very different treatment: professional scales are given above. The base grade clerical scale was £870—5 by 61—£1,175: a short scale to fulfil the rule about marriage age; thereafter, for the clerical officer, there were no fewer than twenty scales in the 3rd Division, each short and, with the three bottom scales, overlapping. The 1965/6 report of the Board indicated a change to eleven scales, a structure already established for the taxation field. The scales get shorter as they go up. Thus progression for the non-professional comes more and more to depend on promotion from one scale to the next at fairly frequent intervals. The distinction is very much in line with Gardner's explanation.

The second sort of material used by the Board relates mainly to the special problems of the clerical scales. The third is more relevant by far to professional positions, namely, the types of comparability to be taken into account. The Board has its own highly specialized machinery about classification, especially the classification bureau and the industrial and arbitration section. In addition departments have classification committees, with Board chairmen, departmental representatives and union representatives, to conduct reviews and to make recommendations to the Board. The committees, with the joint council and promotion

[1] G. E. Caiden, op. cit., p. 4.

appeals committees, were part of the changes introduced in 1945 by the Chifley Labor regime. But professionals have gained far more from arbitration than from these committees. We shall see later how arbitration was introduced into the service. In any case, the way in which the decisions of the Arbitrator are brought into effect is relatively complicated. His determinations do not as such vary the classification (i.e. the salary range) of a particular office. What a determination does is to change the salary of an officer in relation to the duties which are the subject of the arbitration; hence the personal classification of the officer is varied. What then happens is that, generally speaking, the Board will then go on to vary the classification of the office; hence the effect of the determination tends to be extended to all other officers who are doing work which the Board regards as comparable with that of the officer and the duties which were the subject of the arbitration determination.[1] The working out by the Board of these internal relativities is most important in the effect of arbitration.

That has of late all tended to benefit the professionals. Many of the other principles, methods and materials available to the Board have worked in the same way. The Board, for example, also has reference to external comparisons; special qualifications; changes in the work of specific classified positions; relativities to other positions previously classified at the same levels, and relativities affecting the flow of officers to and from positions, a matter of special importance since the Engineers' Awards; and material on the highest function of a classified position, and not merely its major or preponderant duties.

According to the Board, in its 1965/6 report, the Engineers' Award disturbed long-established relativities. That was obviously true, to the advantage immediately, at least, of groups like the engineers. However, the Board goes further. The Commission, in making the award, laid down that even groups doing work like engineers' would have to make specific claims 'for salary increases dependent upon proper proof of work value'. Accordingly the Board admits that there has been increasing emphasis on the establishment of specific salary structures and pay levels for individual groups, as we have seen with the variations in some of the scales and as against the attempt by the Board in the 1950s to go in the opposite direction. The change was already clear by

[1] Commonwealth Public Service Board, op. cit., pp. 20–1.

1963: that is, the Board now gives greater stress to the specific 'work value' of the particular group and less to traditional internal relativities. The Board itself may have wished to go another way. The fact is that the 1961 and 1962 Engineers' Awards and the Commission's dictum have led to a situation in which what matters is the specific: the distinctive group and the particular work value. That is a situation which must suit professional groups perfectly well, at least as far as their conditions as professionals are concerned.

4. RECRUITMENT AND OTHER CONDITIONS

The classification system has indubitably worked in the interests of the specially or professionally qualified person. Recruitment has also treated the professionally qualified in a quite distinct fashion.[1] Recruitment to the 1st Division, governed by s. 54 (and, potentially, by s. 47), is in practice a matter of promotion from the 2nd Division. Similarly, the 2nd Division is mainly recruited by promotion from the 3rd, under s. 50, though there could be some direct outside appointment under s. 47, and that does, in fact, sometimes occur. But the bulk of recruitment is direct to the 3rd Division, both for clerical and for professional appointments.

There are two important facts, however. One is the difference between clerical and professional recruitment. The other is one of the most peculiar features of the Australian system. Normal professional recruitment is managed by the perfectly effective use of what was originally intended as an exceptional provision in the Act: s. 47, as it now is. As to the first point: leaving aside temporary (ss. 82–82b), exempt (s. 8a), and 4th Division (ss. 34, 39, etc.) recruitment, clerical and administrative recruitment is normally to the base grade clerical position by examination under s. 34. There is a specifically limited amount of graduate recruitment (s. 36a). There is also ex-service recruitment (s. 84). Now special, it was at one time virtually exclusive, particularly in the 1920s, and to a lesser extent after the Second World War. Most professionals, though, are recruited either as cadets or under s. 47.[2] To take recruitment figures for a fair post-war year, 1957:

[1] Report of the Committee of Inquiry into Public Service Recruitment, Canberra, 1958: esp. pp. 85–90, para. 28, and app. 5.
[2] Public Service Board, *Annual Report*, 1964–5, p. 22.

total 3rd Division recruitment (excluding 4th Division promotion) was 1,677 of which there were:

811 by examinations,
299 by reg. 153 (ex-servicemen),
16 by s. 36a (graduates),
415 by s. 47 (mainly professionals).

For the six months ending June 30, 1958:

(a) clerical and administrative appointments to 3rd Division (excluding 4th Division promotion) were 1,138, of which: only 15 under s. 47,
(b) professional groups: 110, of which: 96 under s. 47
(c) (in addition, 10 of the 12 'technical' appointments were under s. 47) Cadetships: 136, of which: 70 from Leaving Examinations, 66 under s. 47.
(d) Total s. 47 appointments: 192, of which: 74 had Leaving Examination (mainly appointed to cadetships), 111 had tertiary qualifications, of which: arts degree 5, economics degree 1, science, etc., degree 51, professional diplomas, etc. 54.
(e) Total appointments with science, etc., degrees and professional diplomas: 133 of which: 105 under s. 47.

1964/5 cadetships: in force 645 at June 30, 1965, and selected 242 (1964/5), of which all were professional.

Thus professionals are appointed either as cadets or as already qualified men; they are predominantly appointed either to cadetships or under s. 47; and s. 47 is predominantly used only for such professional appointments. There are, it may be said, two distinct systems, therefore; and the system used for professionals is an unintended one. Because that method, though now normally used, means the management of what was originally meant as an exceptional provision it looks clumsy. It actually required a certificate by the Board that no officer already in the service was capable of filling the position. It works well enough, however.

No right of appeal (despite the width and efficacy of those rights in the public service generally) exists against any such appointment.

It looks clumsy to have the Board's certificate and to have to have copies of its recommendations going before Parliament. However, what actually happens is public advertisement for the vacant job and, usually, competitive interview by the employing department. Cadets are recruited either after their School Leaving Certificate or its equivalent, taking certain subjects into account, or in a few cases after university entrance. A cadet does his university or other tertiary training on salary with his tuition fees paid, working in the department during his vacation. There is little tradition in Australia of study in vacations, so that it is likely that non-cadet university students would also be working through their vacations.

Cadetships now cover a very wide range. They began before the Second World War in the Postmaster General's Department, for cadet engineers. By 1939 four other types were available. They now cover twenty professional specializations. Significantly, the application of cadetships to diplomatic and personnel positions proved, especially in the second case, unsuccessful. The cadetship system has indeed so far proved itself a success for professionals and a failure otherwise. It is a highly Australian system in a number of ways: its vocational attitude to tertiary education; its acceptance of the bonding arrangements which go with it; and its use of university vacations wholly for paid employment.

Professionals are also rather peculiarly placed in relation to promotion appeals and to public service unions. As we have seen, most of their appointments lie outside the appeals system. All promotions in the service are gazetted provisionally and within twenty-one days other officers may appeal on the grounds of superior efficiency or equal efficiency combined with seniority (a ground which the Boyer recruitment report wished to see go). The committees which hear the appeals have a constitution similar to the classification committees; but in the case of the bulk of appeals in professional promotions the committee reports would, as a result of the salary level involved, have to go to the Board itself. The system as a whole is effective, much used and important: something like 30 per cent of promotions are appealed against and something like 17 per cent of appeals are successful. Seniority rather than superior efficiency (the proportion is 4:1) is the usual basis of the successful appeal. But all this works differently for the professional officer.

Again, their union position is somewhat special. Public service unions have to be registered, but there never has been any legal restriction on the setting up of such unions or associations in Australia. Nevertheless, they were, though only by local standards, a little slow in appearing, probably because of the importance of patronage in Australian public services in the last century, when advancement depended on support from Ministers or Members, and partly because of white-collar apathy. Since then, however, their strength has been most impressive. Perhaps the outstanding case is in Victoria. Since the 1946 legislation, which was materially negotiated by the Victorian Public Service Association, the Victorian Public Service Board has had a staff representative in an entrenched position. By now there are over seventy registered associations in the Commonwealth Public Service field. The unions are of two main types: purely public service, like the Professional Officers or the Amalgamated Postal Workers; and those with outside and often mainly outside members like the AEU. Most of the public service unions themselves are organized into the High Council of Commonwealth Public Service Organizations, which is a very influential body though not a registered one. While that covers the 3rd Division pretty completely, some of the important 4th Division associations are affiliated to the Trades Halls, i.e. to the State trade union structures, where they have their own political pull. The High Council, on the other hand, has been of great importance not only within the public service directly but as a major part of the new Federal Council of Salaried and Professional Associations, which has tackled the whole problem of organizing professionals together and affecting their salary levels: this in its turn has had an effect in the public service, particularly in relation to professionals. The High Council is also recognized in the constitution of the public service Joint Council (reg. 72b), which has a Board chairman, six departmental and seven association representatives. While not lodging claims on its own behalf it nevertheless arranges for claims to be lodged with the Abritrator in the name of individual organizations. Thus the High Council is well placed overall. The Postal Workers and the AEU are outside it; the professionals are well placed within it, and through it and in other ways with the Federal Council.

5. THE PRE-WAR SITUATION

Clearly the Australian is a public service system not without faults or oddities; unlike the U.K.; and certainly one in which professionals have been and are dominant. As Scarrow says, 'The whole system of personnel administration is heavily weighted to give preference to the officer who can demonstrate competence for a particular job.'[1] His words are a little ungenerous in tone, for his preference is for something different, but they state the essence of the matter. It is not an accident; nor is it disliked or hidden or misunderstood; on the whole, attempts to move away from it, like s. 36a recruitment, or the Boyer report, or the current 2nd Division policy of the Board, have had limited success. To understand the system, its results and its persistence, one needs to know a little of the Australian situation and the present circumstances.

In the first place there were many factors in the Australian nineteenth-century experience conducing to two characteristics: a neglect, or alternatively a suspicion, of the amateur, of the generally educated, and of administration itself. On the other hand, there was necessarily a notion of public service work as divided not on Trevelyan-Northcote lines between higher and routine but between professional and clerical. In particular the colonial services had themselves to engage in much technical work elsewhere left to private industry and speculation.[2] These two characteristics have always expressed themselves in Australian legislation. For one thing the legislation has been intended to protect the rights of the base grade recruited clerk. Hence the apparently and intentionally restrictive language of s. 47 of the Commonwealth Act, like ss. 34 and 35 of the NSW Act or s. 18(3) (iv) of the Queensland Act. The fact that s. 47 has come to be the basic method for professional recruitment may indicate a difference between the two strands of the Australian tradition. It also shows that it can in fact be accommodated, where others cannot. It is quite distinct from the administrative-clerical or the administrative-professional dichotomies.

Secondly, the earlier divisional or classification systems of Australian public service systems always recognized two sorts of public servants: professionals and clericals. The Victorian Public

[1] H. Scarrow, op. cit., p. 134.
[2] A. G. L. Shaw, *Economic Development of Australia*, 1955, ch. i; B. Fitzpatrick, *The Australian People*, pp. 59–61, etc.

Service Act 1862 distinguished the Professional and the Ordinary Divisions. All Australian public services at one time or another recognized a separate professional division, however egalitarian the systems were in other ways. The Commonwealth public service at any rate began with a separate Professional Division. The 1883 amendment to the Victorian Legislation, which introduced a separate division for permanent heads, was the first example of any distinction for others than professionals. It was, therefore, bitterly attacked. The reply of the premier, James Service, was a sort of apology. 'The status of the permanent head was not above that of the chief professional officers in that department, some of whom were in receipt of higher salaries . . . the professional man stood alone.' The distinction of professionals was acceptable. Any other was not.

Two things are evident. One is that the basic Commonwealth public service legislation, at least in 1902, enshrined that tradition. Entry, for example, was either according to an education sufficient for clerical occupations or according to a certificate of professional competence. The second thing is that great changes in this century, particularly in education and in Governmental functions and scale, have produced challenges to the system. Adaptations have been made, during the Second World War, for example, and again in recent years. But the peculiar combination of an apparent clerical egalitarianism with specific recognition for professional competence, and that alone, still remains the essential key to the service.[1]

The Australian services have also had a close attachment to what elsewhere is better understood as job rather than rank classification, but in Australia is more usually called position rather than personal classification. It originated in Australia in the New South Wales Public Service Board's first report, 1896, and was applied to the Commonwealth service by D. C. McLachlan, its first Commissioner, in 1904.[2] Unfortunately for the earlier years of the service, this very tight principle of evaluation had to be fitted into a system of classification in broad salary bands, itself derived from the Victorian and hence from the colonial service.

The first Commonwealth service had four divisions—Administrative (permanent heads and others), Professional, Clerical

---

[1] S. Encel, 32 *Public Administration*, London, 1954, p. 217.
[2] Commonwealth Public Service Classification Report, CPP, 1904.

and General. The salary classes in the major divisions were few and wide. Subsequently McLachlan introduced sub-classes—subdivisions as they were called—and attempted to control promotion between them in a highly discretionary way. There were five classes in the clerical division, each with several subdivisions which were, in effect, simply incremental stages subject to this discretionary control: the top four classes each had five, and the lowest nine, stages. With the professional division there were also five classes, the top with six, the bottom with eight and the other three with five stages. The superiority of the professional survived the structure. Except for the bottom classes, where the professional had, in effect, one incremental advantage, the professional classes were in each case well above the clerical. The maximum for the comparable clerical class was below the minimum for the professional.

Changes were introduced into the Commonwealth service in two ways. One was the operation of the arbitration system.[1] Arbitration was introduced into the service not at federation (when public service staff associations had been severely disorganized by the federal take-over of parts of their memberships) but by the 1911 Arbitration (Public Service) Act. That brought the service within the ambit of the Court set up for industry as a whole. Arbitration, like protection and restrictive immigration, had been one of the settled policies for the new Australian nation established in its first decade. One effect of the Act was on public service unions. It led to a great increase in union strength, size, number and activity. McLachlan and the Ministers had already recognized them. More than a dozen unions gave evidence before the 1909 Royal Commission on the Postal Services: the dominance of the public service by the postal services has to be remembered; if a little less so today than once, they have always constituted something like one half of the service, more once, less now. But it was the 1911 Act, granting access to the normal arbitration system and restricting benefits to association members which gave the real spurt to the associations.

The Court's interpretation of McLachlan's own principle of work value, it has been pointed out,[2] had two important effects. One was that the simple lines of McLachlan's broad-banded

---

[1] E. E. Crichton, *Arbitration in the Commonwealth Public Service*, Canberra, 1964, ch. iii.

[2] *The Evolution of Classification Practices and Patterns in Australia*, p. 6.

classification system were severely distorted, especially in favour of any group, however small, which could demonstrate some concrete example of increased work value. That certainly did not work against the interests of the more specialized professional groups. Nor did it work against the interests of the associations, to whose members the Labour Government's legislation had restricted the direct benefits of awards. The second effect was a growth of emphasis on 'minute job evaluation' which is, indeed, still a part of the Commonwealth Public Service. Between 1911 and 1920 the Court made thirty-six primary and thirty-nine variation awards.

The importance of arbitration in public service history and practice cannot, indeed, be over-estimated. It was the 1911 Act which, as far as McLachlan was concerned, destroyed his original system: in his 1918 Royal Commission report he described arbitration as wasteful, inefficient, destructive of the unity of classification and leading to indiscipline. The Hughes Ministry could not face the implementation of his radical recommendation to return the sole authority over salaries to the Commissioner. Instead it legislated for a separate Public Service Arbitrator, a provision once again affected by more recent legislation. It was the threat by the Bruce-Page Government in 1929 to abolish public service arbitration which helped to lead to its downfall, with the commonwealth public service associations directly campaigning against the Government in the general election. Arbitration is then dear to the unions. It is so in more senses than one for making claims in this way can be expensive. Appeals from the Arbitrator can be taken (since 1952) to the Commonwealth Court of Conciliation and Arbitration (now the Conciliation and Arbitration Commission). Arbitration is now that much longer and more costly still.

The second great change was not so much McLachlan's own Royal Commission report as the way in which it was implemented. The importance of the report was that McLachlan himself never gave up his earlier belief in few classes, wide bands and discretionary increments of promotion. However, he had changed his mind about one point: he was now in favour of combining the clerical and professional divisions into one, and here he was going against the clear tradition of the State services, which always had and still do have separate divisions for permanent heads, general staff, clericals and professionals. McLachlan had been annoyed by what he called the 'caste' quality of professionals' treatment. Arbitration by an outside institution (McLachlan's main enemy, as he saw it) had certainly not diminished it. Most of what he wanted was only very partly followed, or not followed at all. The Hughes Government could not face implementation. Arbitration continued, though by a separate Public Service Arbitrator. Classification was to remain the function of the new Public Service Board. The new Board's first classification regulations, 104–6, provided for an enormous possible number of scales: the actual number of 1930 was, in fact, 140, and still 108 in 1940, in the 3rd Division alone. But the striking thing is that the apparent combination of professionals and clericals in the Divisions was, as we have seen, much more apparent than real as far as the 3rd was concerned, and not at all to the disadvantage of professionals as far as the 2nd was concerned.

In some ways the balance of emphasis in the service from the beginning, at the start of the century, up to the Second World War, seemed to lie more heavily on the principles of equality (as they happened to be interpreted in Australian politics) than on special professional recruitment. But, firstly, special professional treatment was sufficiently notable early enough to annoy McLachlan. In 1917 the Commonwealth Arbitration Court in an award to the Professional Division 'deliberately raised professional salaries well above clerical salaries in each case and characterized the institution of the same salary class as "not fair nor wise"'.[1] Yet s. 31 (the predecessor of s. 47) was still used as a genuinely exceptional provision. Less than 1 per cent of the whole service was in the Administrative (i.e. permanent heads) or Professional Divisions, though the increasing majority of professional employment rapidly moved into the upper parts of the service: only 8 per cent of all professional employment ranked as in the higher classes in 1907, but 56·8 per cent by 1912. Perhaps the main point was not that professionals were not well treated as yet, but simply that there was not yet much employment of them, certainly as compared with later standards.

Secondly, from 1915 to 1934 the operation of ex-service preference meant that for the most part recruitment was regarded as a benefit to be exercised pretty exclusively for ex-servicemen.

[1] Royal Institute of Public Administration, ACT Group, *The Significance of Recruitment Practices for Higher Administration in the Commonwealth Public Service*, 1957, p. 6.

There was, in effect, no other clerical recruitment over this whole period. That was a blow against normal clerical and against administrative sectors. It was not against professionals, who constituted the main part of the exception. Indeed, it tended to strengthen their dominance at the top. Thus, while little or nothing was being done about the clerical cadres of the service, certain important steps were taken to deal with the needs of professional recruitment. The 1922 Act replaced the original s. 31 with the present s. 47. In the inter-war years that had already become a regular basis for recruitment. It was under that provision that the service got its engineers, architects, draughtsmen and biochemists (then the main professional groups) and the medical and veterinary officers and analysts (the other significant groups). Of course, the sheer weight and variety of professional recruitment did not develop between the wars: in 1938/9, for example, 26 officers were recruited for 10 types of post, as compared with 318 for 27 in 1955/6.

The inter-war years saw great steps forward in Australian secondary and university education. At least one new department, the Commonwealth Department of Health, emerged to create new demands for professional recruitment. Against that sort of background three particular changes may be noted. The first was the institution in 1925 of part-time free places for university education for serving officers. There was a new service policy of co-operating with the universities, though the policy still included a healthy respect for the professional, enshrining a notion of 'the importance in specialized and higher professional and administrative positions' of graduates. About eighteen places were then to be given each year. The scheme has not been statistically a great success. It was important for certain individuals, not mainly, as it happened, in strictly professional positions.

Significantly, it was the cadetship scheme which was much the greater success, and that was restricted to professionals. In the 1930s its main role was to recruit cadet engineers for the Postmaster General's Department. Cadetships in force in June 1939, for example, were: engineering 48; draughtsmen 17; biochemists 13; architects 2; quantity surveyors 1.[1]

[1] J. E. Collings, *Principles and Practices of Organization and Classification*, Commonwealth Public Service Board Assistant Secretaries Conference, 1956, Document No. 836, p. 8.

Overall, by 1938/9, professionals had come in or were coming in the following ways: 200–300 as ex-servicemen, 236 by Leaving Certificate, 11 as graduates under s. 36a, and 253 as clerical transfers. There had been 78 s. 47 appointments and there were 81 cadetships in force. S. 36a had been introduced as a very limited way of direct graduate recruitment in 1933, as exclusive ex-service recruitment had ceased in 1932: these were signs of a change. The third important change was in 1936. The Public Service Arbitrator then determined a separate scale for the base grade professional officer as such. That may be said to have re-instituted what is virtually, for some purposes at least if not for others, a separate professional division. It was part of one important chain, consisting of the original professional division and the 1917 arbitration award leading to the 1961/2 Engineers' Awards and summed up in Gardner's doctrine. Egalitarianism has, in fact, never been more than one of two fairly continuously held values in Commonwealth Public Service history.

6. THE POST-WAR CHANGES

Wartime and post-war expansion have made great changes in the service, and never more than currently. Yet, in an important sense, the two values of egalitarianism and professionalism remain together the dominant facts. The twin advantages of the professional, in conditions and in status, have not been at all lessened. Some changes in the Commonwealth public service have affected professionals only as a part of the service generally. An example was the introduction of the present promotion appeals system in 1945 as an implementation of the 1944 Bailey report. Other changes have had a more particular relevance. The introduction of full-time, as well as the old part-time free places by the Public Service Board in 1953 was one case. More important has been the award since 1945 of overseas post-graduate scholarships. In 1964/5, for example, twelve were granted; all may be regarded as having been given for work of a professional or specialized character.[1]

A general summary of the post-war changes would not quite immediately reveal any surprises: an increase in the number of

[1] Commonwealth Public Service Board, *Annual Report*, cit., p. 31.

departments from eleven in 1939 to twenty-five in 1956 and more additions (like Housing) since then; 47,000 in the Service in 1939, 150,000 by 1950s and 200,000 by 1960s. Against that setting the position of professionals has, of course, been affected. To take one example among many: the decision of the High Court in the 1959 Professional Engineers' Case meant that Commonwealth wide associations—like the Association of Professional Engineers—could now get Commonwealth awards covering officers employed by State as well as Commonwealth bodies. That was, of course, an enormous strengthening of the negotiating position of professionals in the public service. In calling the decision, somewhat regretfully, a landmark, the Chairman of the NSW Public Service Board in a 1959 paper[1] emphasized that the judgment made it clear that it applied to professionals and not to others in the public services. The Chairman also recognized that an improvement in graduate professional salaries would be a marked feature of the public service situation thereafter (i.e. after 1959).

How, overall, have changes of this sort affected the professionals? In the first place, there has by any standards of comparison been an improvement in their salaries and conditions since the end of the war. That has come about because there has been in various ways a wider and a sharper recognition. There has therefore been a more ready support for improvement. The tone of public statements has somewhat altered. There are many examples and many consequences. The opinions of people in controlling positions, and what they were prepared to say, have been changed. Some of the rules have, accordingly, been altered. For example, the NSW chairman recognized two particular problems. One was in the teaching service (part of the responsibility of his Board) where the differential between the two-year trainees and the four-year graduates was insufficient to encourage the students to take the longer course. The second, since the Murray report on Australian universities, was the more competitive position of university salaries. Thus NSW professional salaries had to be radically improved to meet the competition, and altered to provide appropriate differentials.

Even in the Australian tradition of recognizing professionals, that meant the possibility of important changes and improvements: better starting points, for example, and accelerated

[1] Canberra, 1959, pp. 8–9.

promotion. Certainly the 1959 decision in the Professional Engineers' case was important. Amendments to the Public Service Arbitration and Conciliation and Arbitration Acts also made it possible now for joint sittings of the Public Service Arbitrator and the Arbitration Commission to be convened by the President of the Commission. Some changes peculiar to professionals occurred. In 1956 the Public Service Board introduced a structure of 'sub-professional' grades specifically to establish a clearer division between work requiring professional qualifications and other technical work. Certain *ad hoc* grades were also, accordingly, absorbed into the new sub-professional grades of Technical Assistants 1 and 2, or Officers 1 and 2, or Senior Officers 1 and 2.[1] Similarly, over a period from 1955–8 conditions of appointment to and advancement in professional grades were thoroughly revised.[2] Commencing rates for whole ranges of professional officers were organized into two categories, one for engineers, scientists, etc., and the other for education officers, valuers, etc., at a slightly lower rate. All were determined by certain categories of qualifications: diplomas, three-year degrees, four-year pass or three-year honours degrees, and so on. These reorganizations were a very large factor in determining the advantageous outcome of the 1961 Engineers' cases.

It is changes at the top of the service that are most interesting. In war it was true that crisis, expansion of scale and new functions had found the service, after its years of domination by ex-service recruitment, wanting. Changes in demand were particularly significant below the level of permanent head. The number of departments and therefore of heads had, as we have seen, greatly increased. But whereas there was a need for more than twice as many permanent heads, there was also a need for more than five times as many assistant secretaries. The pre-war Commonwealth Service had a fairly minimal administrative structure; by the 1950s this was no longer true. However, it is just as important to see that that great development meant a more stable specialization. For example, the pre-war Attorney General's Department had only two assistant secretaries; by 1948 there were five functional divisions or subdivisions. In other words: the growth and radical improvement of the service had particularly come to mean a better status for professional expertise

---

[1] Commonwealth Public Service Board, Memorandum 16.11.1956.
[2] Ibid., Circular 1955–8, 1.8.1955.

precisely in and as the dominant part of the bigger and, no doubt, better top levels. And that included the recognition of new types of expertise, notably for economists in departments like Treasury and Trade. But there was nothing in the Service inherently inimical to changes of that sort. The most interesting thing about the service since the war has been, in a way, not simply that it has changed but, more precisely, what changes have been and what have been much less acceptable and successful, particularly in relation to the top.

The pre-war Service did not succeed in filling its top ranks from regular examination recruitment: only 18 per cent of permanent heads, 1901–39, had entered in that way. The major explanation was the combination of poor clerical recruitment, especially after the First World War, and relatively successful non-examination professional recruitment. Wartime solved the crisis at the top of the Service by a temporary recruitment of outsiders, many of them graduates and professionals. There was something of a conflict between those new entrants and the older pre-war entrants. The calibre of the top certainly improved, as the Australian-born political scientist, K. C. Wheare, observed in 1950. It is well known and accepted that the pre-war top was inadequate but, also, that things have changed greatly for the better. That is one central fact about the service. The question is whether such changes had needed, would lead to, or would go on to allow, the emergence of anything along the lines of an administrative class in Australia.

There have been those who looked to something like such a step. This was particularly true of the report of the Boyer Committee 1957/8 and its main author, Professor R. S. Parker: notably in the recommendation for direct non-professional graduate recruitment into a reconstructed 2nd Division. The arguments for the recommendation are scattered through the whole text of the report, which was altogether an unusually distinguished and exciting public document. If the recommendation had been followed it would have amounted to a complete change in the significance of the 2nd Division. The Division would have become at once more nearly homogeneous, more exclusive and functional for the central processes and policies of recruitment. Secondly, a recruitment method based quite explicitly on the British administrative class Method II would have been employed. Thirdly, these graduates would have been

F

brought into a new grade ('Officer in Training—Administrative') as the base of a new career (starting as 'Officers—Administrative').

There is no doubt at all that this was a courageous and provocative series of proposals based on such an appreciation of the concept of the generalist administrator as was quite new in any Australian official document and rare in any Australian political thinking. It was an irony that it should be expressed at a time when some British thinking was less than satisfied with the concept itself. At any rate the recommendations were not implemented. In due course two other related things did happen. In the long run the importance of Parker's work on the Boyer Committee may come to be seen partly at least as a provocation of possible changes in consequence of recommendations which themselves lay beyond the possible. It has to be put down, then, as a factor in somewhat altering what could be discussed.

The first change was that the Public Service Board introduced in 1963 an experiment with a graduate trainee scheme for administrative recruitment.[1] In its first year only seven out of sixty candidates were accepted. The main point was surely that without any radical alteration in the formal conditions and public rules of the service itself, a relatively isolated, cautious and well-designed new provision had been made. It was evidently popular with graduates, as the degree of competition showed. The actual training programme was very carefully arranged, spread over twelve months and included a period of attachment to a 2nd Division officer. It will not alter the whole service, and is not designed to do so. No more than fifteen trainees will be taken in a year. It is an intriguing step which may well come to provide some competition with the customary intellectual domination of the service by professionals.

A very different instance is the 2nd Division review, as it has been called, started by the Board in 1964. In some situations this is presented by Board spokesmen as a major change in policy, and as the centre of the position both for professionals and for the top level in the service. But what is said in fact

[1] F. H. Wheeler (Chairman, Commonwealth Public Service Board), *The Administrator in the Public Service: responsibilities*, Royal Institute of Public Administration, South Australian Group, 1964. J. C. Conway, *Training for Generalist Graduates in the Commonwealth Public Service Board*, Administrative Studies Seminar, Canberra, 1963. Commonwealth Public Service Board Graduate Training Programme Bulletins.

varies (unlike the message of a single document like the Boyer Report) and what has been done is, in any case, another matter. However, the Board did claim on occasions that what it was doing was an attempt to develop a new policy for the 2nd Division which would make some sense of the divisional structure.[1] It has, however, throughout been difficult for the Board to say consistently and precisely what its aim was, how new its proposals were or what precisely the extent of the alteration (as distinct from what was in any case already going on) would be. In this at least like the Boyer Committee it did appear sometimes to hanker after, apparently, some more purely 'managerial/administrative' 2nd Division, while not resolving the many problems, among others, of that very hyphenated concept: 'A primary purpose of our review is to foster the continuing improvement in the "top administrative and/or management" sector of the Commonwealth Service.'

The review itself was largely completed by 1965 and quite complete by 1966. The first occasion on which it was tested was, according to the Board, the unsuccessful claim of the POA to the Arbitrator in 1964/5 for the raising by one level the classification of each 2nd Division position in the Department of External Affairs and the Officer of Education. The claim failed. The test, such as it was, from the Board's point of view had been passed.

Like the 1963 experiment, the review was, at least in practice, very cautious indeed. The change was always described, whatever else was said about it, as 'evolutionary'. It was quite explicitly adopted while recalling, and therefore intentionally avoiding, any of 'the difficulties presently being debated in the British Civil Service'. Nor did it actually claim to be or in effect amount to a challenge to any important tradition of the service. The review would not imply, for example, any change in recruitment. It would not imply uniformity in the 2nd Division. The truth behind that hyphen seems to be that the review was very much adopted partly because an opportunity for some change did seem to exist and partly, on the other hand, because of a concern with the managerial duties and demands imposed on some senior officials. There was no adoption nor any readiness precisely to argue for a concept of a policy-advising function separate from both management and from professional, special or technical expertise: it is just that concept which is the essence

[1] Wheeler, op. cit., pp. 5 ff.

of the position of the British administrative class. Further, the road to the top of the service is still both diverse and wide and, in the Australian tradition, trod easily by professionals.

So far, indeed, the review has produced few results. A typical consequence was the decision not to classify in the 2nd Division senior officers of the School of Public Health and Tropical Medicine; even that decision, on such an extremely obvious case, as one might have thought, was taken only 'on balance'. The review cannot come to mean more, then, than some tidying up in classifications, not at all a change in the traditions of promotion or, therefore, in the nature of the actual top of the public service hierarchy. It would be a complete mistake to suppose that the service is turning towards a recognition of a complete, guaranteed and separate career for the specially recruited generalist administrator, moving into dominant positions of policy-making and advice, with the professionally qualified over to one side. The review is a limited approach to a new way of acting about classification (including broadbanding) in some parts of the service. Hence the Board saw a classification claim as a test of what it was doing. The review may also, at the most, be a new way of looking at the work to be done at the top. It is not a new way of actually recruiting and promoting the men at the top, including the top managers. To put it at the highest: there are two questions about a service. One is how it looks at the top work and the other is how it recruits and promotes people to do it. To an observer the review seems to have some potential about the first question; it has nothing to do with the second.

It is interesting to compare the Boyer Report with these actual changes. The report was a public document produced by a committee of some prestige and going to a wide and undifferentiated audience. It was a message sent to many hearers. Its radical content, as was likely, granted the structures in which the opposed interests were organized, was greeted with a vast hostility.[1] No countervailing support was available. It was an example of communication, not of policy-making. Its direct results lay in limited and technical directions, like the introduc-

---

[1] *E.G. Federal Public Service Journal* (Journal of the Administrative and Clerical Officers' Association), April 1959, p. 7, for the views of the High Council; and pp. 19–26, for the views of the Association Executive Council. This and subsequent numbers of the Journal also reports the generally hostile views of branches.

tion of the Commonwealth Selection Test, a battery of eight tests. Lateral professional recruitment under s. 47 has, in fact, been eased.

The experiment with the recruitment of some administrative trainees was never announced as an important public change and it was adopted without requiring much alteration in rules or formal systems. Hence those who heard about it were, on the whole, those who were likely to be sympathetic or, at least, understanding. The degree of support it needed was much less. It was minimized by the approach used. It was the sort of support which was just what the Board itself could provide. The 2nd Division review, on the other hand, may be spoken or even thought of by the Board in one way. On the other hand, it is actually, as we have seen, a slow and limited thing. The actual national policies about the top of the service can scarcely be said to have been revolutionized. What is said about the review varies from audience to audience. There are gaps between what is said and what has in fact happened. Support for a decision in favour of a radically different policy is lacking, partly because the need is lacking, too.

The three cases complete a significant picture of what can be and tends to be done and what can be said about changes in public service systems.

It is not, then, that the service has not changed. A very important step has been the introduction of positions reserved for graduates, especially in the use of the research officer classification. There has been a general increase in the percentage of graduates in the Service. The 1963 experiment with graduate recruitment shows, precisely, just how it is possible to handle a particular need without the introduction of a separate class of administrators running right through a service. Whatever the 2nd Division review is, it is not even an intention to do that.

The immense emphasis on training in the service's personnel management since the war has also had a lot to do with the continued reliance on professionals for top administrative movement. On the whole, Scarrow's answer is still true for the Service and recent changes have not made it less true: 'Is the Service designed to encourage the youth with a general university education, or are the opportunities now for the graduate trained in one of the special fields for which the Service has immediate use? Evidence suggests that the latter interpretation is the correct one.' Research officer positions stress specialist qualifications. Specialist officers are still dominant in graduate recruitment, overwhelmingly so if economics is included, as in the Australian setting at least it ought to be. The Service's bias towards the immediately useful qualification is still strong. What has happened is that its understanding of what is valuable in that way, and what to do about it, has greatly widened. The 1963/4 changes do not alter that; rather they show ways of coming to terms with it. The whole personnel system would have to be scrapped before things could be otherwise. There is neither need nor support for that.

7. CONCLUSION

The system is deeply rooted in Australian history. It is also rooted equally in its contemporary values and its needs. The Boyer Report was, amongst other things, one sign of the existence of a new sort of audience for political change which was interested in and sensitive to the problems of management. It is to that audience that some of the things said, for example, by the present chairman of the Public Service Board are addressed. The reactions to the report also showed the limits of that audience and the persistence of others. The public service is not insulated from its society. Its changes are, on the whole, typical of changes in the society as a whole. What can be done with it does depend in part on what that society wants of it and what it is prepared to see going on within it. Sometimes that may be jobs for ex-servicemen. Sometimes it may be more professional management. The Australian service is in particular characterized by a peculiarly powerful structuring of the rights, opportunities and organizations representing the employed personnel themselves. That has to be taken into account in any estimate of the possibilities of change.

The actual history both of the general political society and of those public service structures themselves is very much part of the present reality of the service. One aspect, then, is an egalitarianism. But that always has been and is still only one part; it is now valued widely but is only one of a series of held values and perceived needs. What has always gone along with it and still does is a positive respect for specialized skills and their appurtenances: various signs of professionalism, including examinations, diplomas, training and hence, if only by extension, education. The rest may not do so well. That fitted fairly easily into the felt wants of one sort of colonial and later one sort of developing society. The colonial origins of the Australian public services were different from the ICS or the colonial administrative services with the omnicompetent district officer, the generalist model familiar elsewhere and later. They were based on the technical bits and pieces required in a society governed always from capital cities not through scattered satraps. Public works and the railway age were the key conditions for the services later in the last century together with high degrees of patronage and representativeness. Technical needs had to be and were met; the rest could be left to patronage, representation and equality. So from the beginning the educated officer was not the non-specialist but, on the contrary, the technician. That was inevitable and acceptable. The other officers could be very different, for the most part, and, certainly, they were seen as very different, perhaps beyond their deserts.

That is part of a whole history of Government organization in Australia in the nineteenth century which was very different from the British. Different needs, conditions and policies meant an early use of non-Ministerial organization and only a late and limited use and understanding of Ministerial organization. Partly as a consequence of that, and in a similar way, public service personnel history has been very different also. That is neither surprising nor a deficiency. The administrative class in Britain emerged along with, as a condition of and as a response to the Ministerial form. Australian practice and needs have been quite different.

An important part of the difference has been a proper and easily understood respect for the professional element in further education, in separate organization and in certain marks of prestige: for the railway engineer, for example, and throughout the history of the public service, the post office engineer. Combined with the actual functions of the early Commonwealth service, limited as we saw them to be, that came to mean that the position of the post office engineer and similar groups was the first widespread exception in the Commonwealth service to a straight egalitarianism. The exceptions surprised the first commissioner, but they should not surprise the student. It was on that stock that any changes needed would have to be grafted. As it happens, that has proved to be quite possible. To put it in another way: it has always been possible to provide recognition in the Australian services for certain special groups sharing certain rights and characteristics. Ex-servicemen were one; professionals were another; the socially and educationally selected administrative generalist was not. Other groups and characteristics can be added. Professional management has come to be an example. Seen in that light, the confines but also the extent of the tradition and the attitudes become clear. They might, it could be thought, have more relevance to the needs of other developing societies than the British domestic or other colonial traditions. Further, it may be of general significance that the recognition of technical, specialized and professional groups has succeeded in going along with what has been called a clerical egalitarianism: it has gone along with a much narrower span between minimum and maximum awards than exists in other systems.

The egalitarian and the professional traditions were, then, never really opposed but easily reconcilable; what was unacceptable, in fact, was something quite different: the notion of a wholly and separately favoured complete career for the generalist. That was what the Boyer proposals seemed to threaten. It is on the other hand what the recent changes have avoided. It is what changes like a wider interpretation of professional, special or valuable qualifications, and like post-entry managerial training and executive development for the specially qualified have shown to be unnecessary during a period of quite dramatic improvement in the top of the service.

The functional changes that the service has been involved in have demanded more training. That has been met one way or another. One of the ways has been to recruit still more professional and technical workers. It is those sectors, in fact, in a changing and increasing service, which have obviously increased and possibly changed most of all. In part, that is a feature of the Australian society as a whole. There are, inevitably, some differences as between the wider setting and the service itself. The extraordinary increase in society in medicine and architecture is less important in the service. On the other hand, the percentage of professionals in the 3rd Division has more than doubled since before the war. The same seems to be true in the States. Further, it is the most professional parts of the Commonwealth machine which carry the most prestige and have increased the most. A good example is the CSIRO, which has increased ten times since before the war.

That is well within the Australian tradition. Meanwhile, less known at large (though the Press gives occasional tantalizing if misleading hints of it, to the titillation but not apparently to the annoyance of the public) the top of the public service has been changed. It is much younger and much better educated than it used to be as a whole. The old top was either professional recruits (as in Health or Works) or clerical (as in Customs and Excise). The new top is, and will be, either professional or other further, and now usually university, educated recruits; it is peculiarly those who can hold their own in these changes, and the graduate increase includes professionals and new sorts of specialists like economists, statisticians and psychologists.

It is in that light that the increased recognition for the demands for management are seen in Australia: in the 2nd Division review, or in training, for example. That may cover both management and, also, policy functions. That is to say, the increased respectability of the special demands both of management and of policy-advising too in Australia at any rate now comes precisely from the increased professionalization of management and of policy-advising techniques and aids. That is marked in the development of specialized post-entry training, for example, for O and M, ADP, computative and other officers, personnel and training work, and so forth; for management and for other functions. In that sense, more recognition for management in training, in promotion and (as in the review) in classification do not mark a break. The fact is that they fit in, also, perfectly well with how management generally (if not in the U.K. Civil Service) is seen.

So the top of the service is tending to consist of some technicians; graduates including new professionals; managers, seen as professionals, and often recruited from other professionals; and policy-advisers seen as technical and professional experts and, again, recruited from their ranks or trained to that level. It is the policy ranks which have tended to be relatively thin. A policy department like the Prime Minister's which has grown up since the war, has been very small, and more of a co-ordinating than an advisory machine. External Affairs has always had a special position. But the most interesting developments, and those which have grown and are growing much the most promisingly, are precisely those where specialists and special techniques are required and provided. Trade was the first and best, and Defence has become another example. In general, just as the Australian system has been extended to a recognition of professionalism in management, so it is also peculiarly able to recognize the policy advice function, where a professionalism of specialized techniques is relevant, and can be shown to be so. The Department of Trade is a good example, again, since it has been virtually the creature and the possession of the Country Party, which would not normally be thought of as especially sympathetic to intellectual claims.

Wartime and post-war developments presented great problems for the Service. It has, in fact, in many ways overcome them. The record of the top public service seems to have been more impressive than that of the politicians themselves. As Professor R. N. Spann has said, 'The administrative system seems to have been more adaptable than the political system to the increasing complexity of modern government.' He added that 'its very adaptability has concealed (or made up for) political shortcomings'.[1] That has a good deal to do with the ways in which it has been possible to use the potentials of the Australian tradition to extend the public service's use of professionals, to recognize new sorts of professionals' groups and so, amongst other things, to improve the top level and to accept its increased importance. Not surprisingly, then, the bulk of the changes has improved the conditions of professional officers. At the same time the increased understanding and acceptance of the special importance of the top level of the service has been assisted by its coincidence in Australia with increased understanding and acceptance of the importance of research (as in the CSIRO), of the graduate professional (as in the enormous improvement in the position of Australian universities), and the relation between these resources and the demands of the top levels of the Service. Those levels are, to say the least, expected to be at least as professional as ever they were if the content of that professionalism has widened. The consequential demands are acceptable precisely because they are seen as professional.

[1] In H. Mayer, op. cit., p. 454.

The Commonwealth itself has been in a much better financial position to deal with the relatively costly results in the public service, the universities and research organizations. A Cabinet Committee has paid regular attention to top public service salaries. It is an Australian tradition to respect professional qualifications, beginning originally in the Service with something as specific as a postal engineer. In that tradition Australia has found one of its most viable ways of dealing with its new problems.

The sort of need and demand expressed by the contemporary institutionalization of management (as in business schools) has not merely been recognized but has also been fitted into the range of status and conditions which the public service can provide. There is no reason to suppose that another tradition would have done better in that respect or, even, about the more difficult problems raised by the development of policy-making techniques. There is, then, no need or possibility for suddenly converting the Australian into a different system. That is true for the changing structure of the service; it is also true for the distribution of rewards, in salaries and conditions. The radical improvement in the top of the service is one of the most striking changes in Australia; the emergence to real importance of the Federal Council of Salaried and Professional Associations is at least one sign of a parallel and equally striking change. The service's traditional combination of respect for professionals with what may be called an open-ended structure has proved remarkably flexible in meeting those changes.

FRANCE

1. BACKGROUND

It is instructive to compare the role of the 'professionally qualified' civil servant in France and Britain and it may be possible to learn something from such a comparison. A simple juxtaposition of facts, taken out of context, may nevertheless mislead. The position of the 'professional' must be seen within the general structure of the Civil Service.[1] This, in turn, must be seen within the framework of the administrative system as a whole and in terms of the functions that civil servants have to perform. To understand why 'professionals' play a different role in the two countries, one must consider even wider factors. A 'confrontation of cultures' is beyond the scope of this account but reference will have to be made to certain aspects of French life which impinge on the Civil Service though they are not always thought of in this context. These differences of background do not destroy the usefulness of the comparison: they simply indicate that Civil Service reform should not be considered too narrowly.

The scope of Central Government Services
The modern British Civil Service was first organized when the prevailing belief was in liberalism, private enterprises and local self-government. The background to the Northcote-Trevelyan report was the 'nightwatchman' theory of the State. This, no doubt, is a simplification but it is a useful one. Much has changed since then but one can argue that the character of the British Civil Service is still shaped by the emphasis on regulatory and supervisory functions. France, on the other hand, has a long tradition of State intervention in all spheres of national life. The notion of the active state, responsible for the actual provision of services, was merely reinforced when Napoleon laid the foundations of the modern administrative system. The French Civil

[1] F. Ridley and J. Blondel, *Public Administration in France*, London, 1964; F. Ridley, 'French Technocracy and Comparative Government', in *Political Studies*, February 1966.

Service was thus established against a background of very different assumptions about the role of the State. Responsibility for the management of services, many of a technical or specialized nature, led to different criteria of recruitment. The two countries are now much closer in their ideas about the proper function of government. What is interesting in the comparison, however, is that these were already partly accepted in France when its Civil Service was being shaped. To that extent it does not have some of the problems of adaptation now facing Britain.

At the same time, it is still true that central Government is responsible for the administration of a much wider range of services in France than in Britain. Police, education and public works are only three examples. The Ministries of the Interior, Education and Public Works & Transport have field administrations parallel to those, more familiar in Britain, of the Ministries of Finance and Posts & Telecommunications. The French Civil Service is thus much larger than the British (even excluding the large component of schoolteachers). Many serve in the very complex network of 'external services' of central Government departments. In Sweden, Ministries are small policy-making bodies with no executive functions; in France they manage numerous ground services. Britain stands somewhere between the two: its Ministries are rather more concerned with policy and control, or with decisions of an 'office work' sort, than with technical operations in the field. This is an important point of comparison.

What it means, in fact, is that the French Government is responsible for many services run by local authorities in Britain. Many French civil servants therefore occupy posts similar to those filled by local government officers in Britain. This partly explains the need for large numbers of professionals (teachers, doctors, civil engineers, weights and measures inspectors, etc.). Though France is often thought of as a centralized State, there is considerable 'administrative deconcentration'. Senior staff is thus found in the provinces. And as they are responsible for the actual management of specialized services, they are themselves specialists. The position is not unlike that of the local government service in Britain, with its professionally qualified chief engineers, architects and medical officers. Many of these 'external services' are the responsibility of specialized Civil Service corps. It would be very difficult to direct them from the centre except through senior members of the corps concerned. This helps to explain why key posts in many sections of the Ministries are also filled by specialists.

Educational System and Career Patterns

There are marked differences between the French and British systems of higher education. The French State has always had a more direct responsibility in this field. It has also more often prescribed the qualifications necessary for the exercise of professions. Higher education has thus probably been more career-oriented than in Britain. More important is the fact that most higher Civil Service careers require study at Civil Service schools which now form an important part of the educational system. Some very specialized groups, such as laboratory scientists, doctors and architects, may have only university qualifications. But these are exceptions and tend to be less involved in administration. Members of the 'generalist' classes will have read similar courses in law and/or political science at the university before entering the National School of Administration. There are specialized post-entry schools attached to most Ministries, often at the postgraduate level. There are schools to train tax officials, Government statisticians, hospital, social security and school administrators, and their number is increasing. The State has long accepted responsibility for the general education of its servants (as distinct from mere job training). One consequence is that the members of any class of the Civil Service are likely to have a similar educational background. The limited number of relatively small institutions strengthens their *esprit de corps*.

The higher education of the most important specialist classes takes place entirely outside the university system. France has a system of technical colleges which run parallel to the universities, giving a training which originally could not (and to some extent still cannot) be obtained in the science faculties. The Ecole Polytechnique, founded by Napoleon to train military engineers, now gives a general scientific education (roughly equivalent to a B SC). Its graduates go on to one of the postgraduate 'schools of application' for more specialized training (mining, civil engineering, aeronautical engineering, telecommunications, etc.). Their students are in the main Civil Service cadets though a proportion of private students is taken. Their prestige, and this is an important point, is generally higher than that of the university faculties.

While the universities are open to all who matriculate, these schools recruit a fixed number of students each year by competitive examination and then train them for specific careers with guaranteed Civil Service posts at the end. Many of the higher level professionals in the French Civil Service (the engineers in particular) will thus have received their entire higher education on a post-entry basis. Because of the schools' prestige and the ease with which their graduates can move to private enterprise later on, they attract many of the best students in the country. There is thus little difficulty in finding recruits, though there may be difficulty in keeping them. The system means, however, that there is only limited scope for students to opt for the Civil Service at the end of an undirected university career as in Britain. The young Frenchman has to make his choice rather earlier.

At the same time there is a sense in which career patterns are more flexible than in Britain and this is really more important. France has never had the separation between careers in public administration, business management and technology that one has tended to find here. The Civil Service has always placed engineers and other specialists in key administrative posts; private enterprise has long recruited civil servants. There are historical reasons for this which need not be elaborated. In the past (and to some extent still today) there has been a tendency to think differently in the two countries about the sort of abilities required to fill various positions. In Britain one has often assumed that these are different fields, requiring different sorts of men, with different gifts of character or different training. In France, perhaps because of a tendency to measure all things in terms of intellectual ability, this has been less true and there has consequently been greater movement: careers have, on the whole, been more varied.

The educational system is one of the factors that makes this possible. The technical schools provide more than a technical education. They are less concerned with practical training than with a general understanding of science and technology, combined with some knowledge of law, economics and (now) management. They recruit students who, on the whole, do not intend to remain specialists and they educate them as all-rounders on that assumption. They are thus rather different from our science and engineering faculties. The sort of men who enter the specialized classes of the French Civil Service are thus potential administrators from the start.

2. THE DEFINITION OF 'SPECIALISTS'

France does not really have 'professional' civil servants in the sense that the term is used in Britain. There are Civil Service corps whose members have roughly similar qualifications. But there is a problem of definition. In Britain it is not too difficult to distinguish the general from the specialist classes, roughly identifying the latter with professionals. The distinction is less easy in France. The following points may thus be useful before we describe the actual structure of the service. Although this will involve some repetition, it will also help to pinpoint some fundamental differences. These will not vitiate our comparison but will clarify what is being compared.

The specialized classes in the British Civil Service can be distinguished from the general classes in a number of rough and ready ways, none of which has a ready parallel in France.

(a) In Britain the general classes are recruited on the basis of general educational qualifications. No specific training is prescribed. Members are 'generalists' in background. Most specialist classes are recruited with reference to specialized qualifications. In France virtually all higher civil servants have prescribed qualifications. The nearest equivalent to our 'generalists' are those who have read law and political science at the university and studied at the National School of Administration. One may talk of the 'administrative' and the 'technical' corps of the French Civil Service. But the 'administrators' have received a specialized training, while the 'technicians', for their part, tend to have wider than technical qualifications at the higher levels.

(b) Members of the specialist classes in Britain are often members of nationally organized professions. Their status depends on non-Civil Service qualifications (certain university degrees, membership of certain associations, etc.). The situation is different in France. Some professional qualifications are awarded by universities (medicine, for example). Most specialists (particularly engineers, the largest and most important group) receive their training in post-entry Civil Service schools. Their qualifications are Civil Service qualifications. Men outside the service are likely to have the same or similar qualifications, but there is little to compare with the British pattern of self-organized professions of which Civil Servants form only a small part. Members of the French technical corps are thus perhaps more likely to think of themselves as Civil Servants than as professionals.

(c) In Britain the general classes are interdepartmental. They are 'generalists' in that sense also. In France this is only true of the lowest ranking of the senior corps (that of the 'civil administrators'). Most corps, whether 'administrative' or 'technical', are linked to a Ministry and have primary responsibility for a defined sector of public administration. This does not exclude the fact that in both cases members tend to be posted to a wide range of posts outside their own corps' proper sphere of competence. The British Civil Service is organized through the Treasury. In France, though there is a Civil Service Directorate in the Prime Minister's Office, management of the service is more departmental. The only useful distinction in this context is between recruitment through the National School of Administration and through the great technical schools.

(d) In Britain it is the general classes which form the ordinary administrative hierarchy and are responsible for administration in the wider sense. Members of the Administrative Class fill policy-making and 'directorial' posts. Specialists tend to be advisers or have technical functions; where they hold administrative posts, these tend to be in specialized branches. This is not the case in France. Members of both the 'administrative' and the 'technical' corps are appointed to administrative positions. Again, it is worth making a point that will be stressed later. In general, the highest posts in the service are open to all. In practice there is a tendency to regard certain positions as the preserve of certain senior corps. The success of the prestigious Finance Inspectorate in obtaining many key posts is an example of this. The great technical corps have established a claim (not always honoured) to the directorial posts in the fields for which they have a general responsibility (industry, public works,

G

transport, etc.). Other posts, usually at the deputy head of division level, are supposed to be filled by the corps of general administrators.

But there is no underlying theory that there are two sorts of people, specialists and generalists, suited by their different backgrounds for different sorts of career. There is nothing in the structure of French administration comparable to the separation found in Britain between administrators and advisers. There are few advisers at all in our sense. Heads of divisions are generally assumed to be capable of being their own experts with the help of their staff. Members of most senior corps are likely to spend some time in 'managerial' posts (e.g. in the field services), in policy-making and directional posts at the centre, and in posts involving research, planning and inspection (i.e. in both line and staff functions). In this respect there is little difference between the 'administrators' and the technicians.

The professional classes of the French Civil Service are members of a profession in a different way from their British counterparts; they are recruited and trained differently; they perform a different range of functions and occupy a different place in the system as a whole. The fact remains, however, that there are qualified engineers, architects, doctors and the like in the French Civil Service.

3. STRUCTURE OF THE SERVICE

Classes
The Civil Service is divided horizontally into four classes, known as categories A, B, C and D. These levels are only roughly parallel to those set in Britain by the Administrative, Executive, Clerical and Messengerial classes and their equivalents. The functions of category A are defined as policy and direction, of category B as the application of general principles to specific cases. Recruitment is tied to different levels of education. Virtually all civil servants with some form of higher education (including post-entry training) fall into category A; those who have completed sixth-form education fall into category B. This partly explains why distribution between the classes is very different from Britain.

A	8 per cent	Higher Education (degree or equivalent)
B	40 per cent	Grammar School leavers (GCE 'A' levels)
C	32 per cent	Ordinary Secondary School leavers (GCE 'O' levels)
D	20 per cent	Primary School leavers

Categories A and B are both much larger than in Britain, both absolutely and relatively. One reason for this is the extended nature of the Civil Service (teachers form a large component). But it is also important to note that category A includes many civil servants who in Britain would fall into the Executive Class and its equivalents. Virtually all professionals are thus in category A.

A consequence of this is that all civil servants in the same category do not enjoy the same status (i.e. there are promotion barriers). Within category A there is a fairly clear division between higher and secondary corps (which, in Britain, would rank at Executive Class level). On the whole this line reflects different levels of higher education. Members of the higher corps have generally passed through the university and the National School of Administration or the Ecole Polytechnique and one of the postgraduate post-entry schools associated with it. Members of the secondary category A corps are likely to have only a university degree or to have entered the Civil Service as school leavers and passed through a post-entry technical school at undergraduate level. The functions of the latter are often described as aides to the former.

Corps

More important than the class is the corps. All civil servants are appointed to corps within which their normal career lies. They may be posted to positions other than those normally filled by their corps but in that case they are usually in 'detached service'. It is their corps membership, however, which determines their place within the Civil Service and it is through the corps, on the whole, that their careers are organized. A corps is defined as a group of civil servants governed by the same regulations and qualifying for the same grades (i.e. by routine promotion). There are generally examination barriers between corps. Each is governed by its own statutes which specify entrance qualifications, methods of recruitment, numbers and ranks, length of service required for promotion and other matters.

These statutes may also define the corps' 'mission'—the general field of State action for which it is responsible. This applies particularly to the most prestigious, generally the oldest. The great technical corps (mining engineers, civil engineers) have their own spheres of competence, defined less in terms of Civil Service positions than sectors of national life (the rural engineers, for example, have a very wide range of functions in agricultural areas). Others, however, have their 'missions' defined in more administrative terms: the civil administrators, for example, are supposed to fill such posts as deputy heads of divisions (i.e. act as administrative deputies to technical directors).

Services

This brings us to the fact that the Civil Service is organized on a vertical as well as a horizontal basis. The organization of Government services can only be understood by reference to this vertical structure. The field of public works may be taken as an example. The Corps des Ponts et Chaussées (the higher category A civil engineers) has a general responsibility for much of the whole field of public works: highways, public transport, navigable waterways, harbours and airports, urban infrastructure, water supply, drainage, electricity distribution, town planning (though its spheres of competence have been encroached upon by other, more specialized, engineers). It is supported by a secondary corps of category A engineers, category B technicians and other personnel in categories C and D. Together these form the Service des Ponts et Chaussées. This system unifies the field services and the relevant policy-making top management divisions in Paris.

The drawback is that some Ministries are internally less unified than they might be. This has been true, for example, of the Ministry of Agriculture which has had a number of higher technical corps, each covering the country with its own services (rural engineers, water and forestry conservators, agronomists, etc.), each tending to form its own empire within the Ministry. There is another side to the picture, however. As the spheres of competence of some corps tend to be wider than the responsibilities of the Ministries to which they are attached, they provide for links between Ministries and help to unify the public service as a whole. The corps of civil engineers works for a number of Ministries in addition to its own (Public Works & Transport), as well as for local government. The fact that members of such prestigious corps are frequently posted to a wide range of positions outside their service has the same effect.

Grades
Within each corps there are often a number of grades to which specific titles are generally attached. In the corps of civil engineers these are Engineer General, Chief Engineer, Engineer and Student Engineer. These titles are like army ranks and are not the same as the titles of positions. An Engineer General may also be the Inspector General of the external services in a region, a Chief Engineer may be the head of the services in a county, but both may equally well hold the post of director of a division in the Ministry itself. There is a clear distinction between the rank in one's corps and the post occupied. There is, however, also a relationship. The head of the external services in a county must have the rank of Chief Engineer. More often, it is laid down that higher posts can only be held by persons of at least a specified rank in a number of corps. Appointment to a more responsible post is thus likely to bring promotion of rank, and vice versa, promotion of rank (e.g. through seniority) will often establish a claim to a more responsible post.

The important point to note here is that careers in the Civil Service are organized on a corps basis. Salaries are generally attached to the grade rather than to the post filled. In the long run the civil servant's position in his own corps may be more important to his career than the work he does at any one time. Even while on 'detached service' in some other branch of the administration, he acquires seniority in the corps to which he belongs.

4. SOME GENERAL PRINCIPLES

Recruitment
Category A and B civil servants are generally recruited on the basis of competitive examinations. There may be separate examinations for new entrants with prescribed educational qualifications and for staff already in lower corps with prescribed periods of service. Such barriers exist not merely between categories but also between higher and secondary corps within the category. Exceptionally, entry may be by way of professional tests or even by simple promotion. In general only unestablished

civil servants with individual contracts are recruited purely on the basis of the qualifications they already possess. There is considerable attachment to 'objective' procedures (written examinations) and little demand for recruitment on the basis of qualities of character or technical expertise and proved ability. Examinations for even the technical corps tend to be theoretical in content, designed to test the candidate's intellectual abilities rather than his practical experience. The emphasis, moreover, tends to be on general scientific education rather than on theory oriented to practice.

Recruitment to the higher corps in category A is usually a two- or even three-stage procedure: admission to the postentry schools and graduation from them. There are two broad paths, through the National School of Administration and through the Ecole Polytechnique (there are other paths for certain specialized corps, e.g. through the National Agronomic Institute). Admission to the Ecole Polytechnique is by a highly competitive examination for advanced sixth-formers with a heavy emphasis on mathematics. Its best students graduate (on the whole in their order of merit) to the postgraduate specialized schools, then to the corps associated with the latter. Although the Polytechnician is already a cadet civil servant, the student of the Ecole des Ponts et Chaussées a cadet engineer of the corps, these examinations are important hurdles.

Promotion

Promotion within the corps is by 'steps' and by grades. Promotion by 'steps' is based largely on seniority, though an element of merit may enter at certain levels. It leads to a salary increase. Promotion to a higher grade is a more formal procedure and at the same time one in which there is a greater element of discretion (it is often limited to names inscribed on promotion lists vetted by special committees). Regulations always specify the minimum number of years service necessary. It not only gives rise to a salary increase but generally entitles the civil servant to occupy a range of more senior posts.

Regulations may also ensure that civil servants who show the required ability have facilities for study so that they can sit the competitive examinations necessary for promotion to a higher corps (either by admission to one of the Civil Service schools or by direct transfer). The theoretical character and high standard of most of these examinations, and the consequent preparation required, makes these a very serious barrier. There is nevertheless little demand for the replacement of these 'objective' procedures by promotion between corps on the basis of past record alone.

Salary Scales

Salary scales are extremely complex. A grid has been established and, on the basis of rank and seniority, each civil servant is given either an index number (on a scale running up to 1,000) or, for the very highest ranks, an index letter. There are additional residence allowances to compensate for the higher cost of living in certain parts of the country, and family allowances additional to those of the ordinary social security system. These are generally given at a flat rate and may account for a substantial part of the actual pay a civil servant receives, particularly at the lower end of the scale. Translated into monetary terms the index figures may therefore be misleading. Comparison between groups in terms of their indices is thus generally more useful, showing as it does their relative status.

Even then, there are complications. Certain members of the technical corps may receive additional remuneration, notably those in the external services who are working for local authorities as well as the central Government. Others may have found it more profitable to transfer from their corps of origin to the position of a contractual civil servant at a salary negotiated on a less rigid basis. This applies mainly to those who have acquired qualifications in new and highly specialized fields (e.g. computer techniques).

Broadly speaking, the salary scales for the senior corps in category A run from 370–1,000 and on into the letters. Some run to higher letters than others, and thus to considerably higher salaries, but these apply to relatively few men at the top. The 'administrative' corps as such, however, are not better placed than the 'technical'. Councillors of State, Finance Inspectors, Mining and Civil Engineers can all attain high letters on the grid, Civil Administrators, Town Planners and Public Health Doctors stop at letter A. But this does not limit the salary prospects of the latter: if they are appointed to the post of deputy director or director of a division in the Ministry they are also placed higher on the letter grid. This is an exception to the rule that salaries depend on rank in one's corps. It may nevertheless mean that men in equivalent posts are receiving different salaries as some may still be entitled to a higher place on the grid by virtue of their corps rank.

Secondary category A corps include the Administrative Attachés who run from 340–865 and Public Works Engineers who run from 300–765. In category B the Administrative Secretaries have a range from 210–545 and the Public Works Technicians from 235–545. There is thus a considerable overlap between each level.

5. THE ENGINEERS

The point has been made that most civil servants who would be regarded as professionals in Britain are members of category A corps. Take first the engineers and the services they direct, in fact the major technical services of the State. The engineering corps have the highest prestige and the widest responsibilities. Together they constitute an important part of the Civil Service. A list of these corps is given opposite. The senior corps are those recruited through the Ecole Polytechnique or the Agronomic Institute. They are responsible for policy and management. The secondary corps are their aides, responsible for the more practical aspects of work.

The members of all these corps (with one minor exception) are entitled to call themselves engineers. This underlines the point that this title has a rather wider meaning in France than in Britain. The title 'Ingénieur du corps des Ponts et Chaussées' indicates more than membership of a Civil Service corps; it is also the professional qualification of the senior civil engineers. The secondary engineers are generally called Works Engineers, e.g. 'Ingénieur des Travaux Publics'. These titles largely replace the British qualifications (university degree or membership of a professional association).

It will be noted that the list is relatively short. This reflects another important point. It must be remembered that the corps are not organized primarily on the basis of specialized qualifications but on the basis of responsibility for sectors of public administration. To some extent, therefore, both the engineering profession and the engineering classes of the French Civil Service are organized on different lines from those found in Britain.

CATEGORY A: ENGINEERS

Ministry	Senior Corps	Secondary Corps	Field
Agriculture	Eaux et Forêts* Génie Rural* Services Agricoles	Travaux des E. et F. Travaux ruraux Travaux agricoles	Water and forestry conservation Public works in rural areas Agricultural advisory services
Industry	Mines Instruments de Mesure (Engineers)	Travaux Publics de l'Etat (Mines) Instruments de Mesure (Inspectors)	Mining Weights and measures
Interior	Services des Transmissions	Travaux du Ministère de l'Intérieur	Communications (of the Ministry)
Posts & Telecommunications	Télécommunications	—	Telecommunications
Transport & Public Works	Pontes et Chaussées Géographes Navigation Aérienne Météorologie Nationale	Travaux Publics de l'Etat Travaux géographiques Travaux de la Navigation Travaux météorologique	Public works, highways, etc. Cartography Air traffic Meteorology
Armed Forces (Armaments)**	Fabrications d'Armement } Télécommunications Poudres Air Génie Maritime	Travaux d'Armement et des Télécommunications Travaux de Poudrerie Ingénieurs chimistes des Poudres Travaux de l'Air Travaux de construction et d'armes navales. Travaux maritimes	Armaments and military communications Explosives Aeronautical engineering Maritime engineering

* Amalgamated.
** All corps amalgamated: Armament Engineers.

6. MINISTRY OF PUBLIC WORKS AND TRANSPORT

A closer look at the services of the Ministry of Public Works and Transport will perhaps help to illustrate the position of engineers. The Corps des Ponts et Chaussées is the oldest and one of the most prestigious of the technical corps (second only to the Corps des Mines), one of the largest and, above all, one with the widest range of responsibilities.

The Ministry

The Ministry is essentially a Ministry of Transport (not Public Works in the British sense). The term 'public works' comes from earlier days when the State was primarily concerned with road building. The Corps des Ponts et Chaussées (literally 'Corps of Bridges and Roads'), founded as early as 1716, tended to acquire responsibility for new technical services. Despite its name, it came to be considered a general corps of civil engineers. It was not until 1870 that a separate Ministry was established. This gradually shed some of the duties originally allocated to it because of the wide competence of its technical corps (public works in rural areas, public buildings, fuel and power). In some cases the more specialized technical corps of other Ministries took over (e.g. the Rural Engineers of the Ministry of Agriculture), in other cases the corps continued to work for them (e.g. the supervision of electricity for the Ministry of Industry). In so far as the Ministry was concerned with transport before the war, this was largely a matter of land transport (road, rail and waterways). Since then there has been an attempt to unite responsibility for land, sea and air transport. This has only had limited success and there are at present two sub-Ministries for Shipping and Civil Aviation within the Ministry.

Three divisions of the Ministry are in fact the old 'public works' services directly associated with the Service des Ponts et Chaussées. The Land Transport division is the tutelary authority for the national railways. Road transport is largely in private hands and co-ordination is thus more difficult. Some of the Ministry's powers depend on traffic regulations which come under another division. It is also responsible for transport workers, particularly railwaymen. The Roads and Road Traffic division was previously called the Roads division and the change of name reflects a growing preoccupation with traffic problems. The title of the Ports and Waterways division is largely self-explanatory. The three divisions are concerned not only with transport policy but also with the 'infrastructure' (the roads, canals, bridges and harbours). The Ministry is concerned with a good deal of construction, either directly or through supervision of local authorities. There is also a number of 'horizontal' divisions (a common services division for personnel, accounts, etc., and another for economic and international affairs).

The Service des Ponts et Chaussées

The Service des Ponts et Chaussées forms the main external service of the Ministry. Its responsibilities are wider than those of the divisions it primarily represents. The functions of technical services can be divided according to sectors of the economy or according to the type of work involved. While the division of functions between Ministries, and between vertical divisions within the Ministry, tends to be based on the first principle, its external services are based on the second. This reflects the fact that the service is headed by a corps claiming professional competence in virtually all fields of civil engineering.

The external services are responsible for the field work of the technical divisions in connection with such matters as road construction and maintenance and rail transport. They deal with problems of traffic control. They are responsible for navigable waterways, docks and harbours, lighthouses and airports (for the Civil Aviation side of the Ministry). They are concerned with urban 'infrastructure', including water supply, drainage and sports facilities. They have duties with regard to school and hospital building. They co-operate with the Ministry of Agriculture which has similar responsibilities in rural areas and with the Ministry of Construction in questions relating to housing and town planning. They supervise the distribution and production of electricity on behalf of the Ministry of Industry. Reference may finally be made to their work for local government. At county level all officials are now members of the national Civil Service. Many act in dual capacity as agents of the central Government and as agents of the local authority. While the Prefect has his own staff for general administration, the technical services of the county are generally the external services of the Ministry.

The service is staffed by engineers of the two category A corps, cateogry B technicians and category C personnel. Many members of the senior corps will be serving elsewhere. The service itself is organized at several levels. In each county town there is a chief engineer of the Corps des Ponts et Chaussées with his office. Below him there are districts and sub-districts. In addition to these administrative areas, the country is divided into regions for purposes of inspection and co-ordination, each under an Inspector General based in Paris. There are specialized services for ports and navigable waterways with their own areas.

7. THE CORPS DES PONTS ET CHAUSSÉES

Functions
The corps is therefore responsible for a wide range of functions. As a class of the Civil Service, it also acts as a pool of highly qualified engineers for service elsewhere. It thus attracts men interested in many different aspects of engineering. The functions of the corps, moreover, are only partly technical. Engineers have managerial, financial and even political responsibilities (in their relations with elected local authorities and other local interests). They enjoy considerable independence in their areas and participate actively in the life of the county, with a wide range of contacts and considerable discretion. They participate in the work of economic planning and regional development committees. Those who wish may pursue scientific research in the laboratories of the service or teach in its school. They are likely to spend some time in the policy-making sections of the Ministry and can aspire to the highest directorial posts. It is worth noting that the 'vocation' of the corps is officially described as covering technical and scientific functions on the one hand, functions of an administrative, economic and social nature on the other. There are also excellent opportunities for transfer to the highest managerial positions in public or private enterprise. This wide range of opportunities gives the corps considerable appeal. As members are likely to be involved in a mixture of technical and administrative work from the start, it tends to recruit men who already have administrative ambitions rather than those who may develop such ambitions in mid-career (as tends to be the case in Britain).

Recruitment
There are several methods of recruitment to the corps:
1. New entrants to the Civil Service are admitted via the Ecole

Polytechnique and the Ecole des Ponts et Chaussées. Admission to the Polytechnique is by competitive examination. Candidates must be between 17 and 21, must possess the baccalaureat in mathematics or mathematics and technology, and must not have sat more than once before. The examination (written and oral) covers mathematics, physics and chemistry, technical drawing, French composition and a foreign language. It is usually necessary to come in the top third of the 200 students who graduate from the school each year to go on to the Ecole des Ponts et Chaussées. Students are allowed to choose their corps (and thus postgraduate school) in their order of merit, within the limit of places available. Two-thirds of the places in the corps as a whole are reserved for polytechniciens.

2. Engineers of the secondary Public Works corps may also be admitted to the Ecole des Ponts et Chaussées by competitive examination. They must have at least four years' service and be under 32. Only three attempts are permitted. Up to a quarter of the places at the school may be allocated in this way.

3. Public Works engineers may be promoted directly to the corps if their names are inscribed on an 'aptitude list'. For this, they must have served at least twelve years and obtained satisfactory results in a professionally oriented examination which they may not sit more than three times. The number of places available is limited by what has been said above.

4. If one-third of the places in the corps have not been filled by methods 2 and 3, Public Works engineers with at least twenty years' service may be promoted. They must be chosen from names inscribed on another 'aptitude list' drawn up on the basis of their past record with the approval of a special committee.

In recent years the average intake has been thirty-five by method 1, two by method 2 and six by methods 3 and 4. Polytechniciens thus obtain more than the two-thirds of all places guaranteed to them. The difficulty of the examinations no doubt explains the low intake by method 2, an indication that such promotion possibilities are often more theoretical than real.

Training
The Polytechniciens receive a two-year general science education as cadet civil servants. Though the baccalaureat is a minimum qualification for entrance, they will already have done one or two years' post-sixth-form work at grammar school. Cadet en-

gineers enter the second year of the three years' course at the Ecole des Ponts et Chaussées (the full three-year course is taken by the eighty non-Civil Service students who enter as school-leavers). There are specialized courses in the construction, maintenance and management of roads, railways, canals, dams and hydro-electric stations, harbours and airports and their installations, as well as in administrative law and economics. Their teachers are often practising civil servants. In addition students do practical work: they prepare plans, draft reports and serve a term in the external services, the railways, the nationalized electricity corporation or private enterprise. If they obtain satisfactory marks they graduate as full 'engineers of the corps' (non-civil servants graduate as 'civil engineers of the School').

Grades and Salaries
The corps has three grades. The following table shows the distribution of members between the grades (the ratio is laid down in regulations) and the numbers in each (these figures refer only to those serving in the Service des Ponts et Chaussées itself). It also shows the number of years required to reach the top of each grade by routine promotion and the minimum number of years service necessary for promotion to a higher grade. Index numbers on the salary grid are given together with approximate annual salaries (at fourteen francs to the pound).

Grade	Ratio per cent	No.	Years Service	Index	Salary Francs	£
Student						
Engineer	—	78	—	355	12,500	890
Engineer	60	345	2 yrs student	390	13,800	980
			15 yrs in grade	885	31,300	2,230
Chief Engineer	30	174	8 yrs service	735	25,900	1,850
			11 yrs in grade	A	42,400	3,030
Engineer						
General	10	51	15 yrs service, 7			
			as Chief Engineer	B	47,700	3,385
			5 yrs in grade	D	58,300	4,150

1. The numbers in each grade exclude those in detached service retaining their corps rank and promotion rights. At the higher level, there are a considerable number of these.

2. There is a considerable overlap between grades, i.e. one may be promoted to a higher grade before reaching the top salary position in a lower one. It is theoretically possible to reach the highest salary position in twenty years. Other figures show that the average age of promotion to Chief Engineer is 40, to Engineer General late fifties.

3. Promotion within grades (relatively automatic) is by 'steps' (=salary increments). These are roughly biennial.

4. The career grade is Chief Engineer. Promotion prospects within the corps are better than one might expect from the ratio between ranks. A fair number leave the corps for public or private enterprise in mid-career. This (a) provides promotion opportunities for those below and (b) reduces competition for promotion among peers.

5. Salary figures exclude residence and special family allowances. An engineer at the bottom of the scale, stationed in Paris and with three children, will receive an additional £280. Ordinary family allowances, to which civil servants are also entitled, are substantial and form an important part of all salaries in France. Engineers may receive additional remuneration for local authority work.

6. Student engineers receive a full salary.

Career Prospects

Engineers of the corps serve in a variety of posts in the central and external services of the Ministry at different times in their career. It may be interesting to list some of the key posts in the Ministry of Public Works & Transport filled by them. Heads of divisions are directly responsible to the Minister. Engineers General: 'High Official charged with Defence Questions', 'High Official charged with International Relations', Commissioner General for the Public Works and Building Industries, Secretary General for Civil Aviation, Director of Roads, Director of Ports and Navigable Waterways, Director of Airports, Director of the Lighthouse Service. Chief Engineers: Director of the division for Personnel, Accounts and General Administration, Head of the Economic Affairs Service, Head of the Railways Service in the Land Transport division.

Engineers General serving in similar key positions in other Ministries include the following directors of divisions: Electricity and Gas (Industry), Building and Housing (Construction),

Equipment (Education). Until recently the Planning Commissioner was a member of the corps.

Members of the corps represent the Government on the boards of public enterprise, electricity and gas, railways, shipping, petroleum, etc., and sit on other important bodies such as the Transport Council and the committees of the Planning Commissariat.

Others have been appointed to key posts as Directors General or Directors in public enterprise, including the electricity and gas corporations, the railways, Air France, Paris Airport Corporation and the Rhône Development Corporation. Among those who have moved to private enterprise is the chairman of the Federation of Road Industries.

8. THE CORPS OF PUBLIC WORKS ENGINEERS

Functions

This is the secondary corps of category A civil engineers. It has some 4,000 members. 3,500 are in the Service des Ponts et Chaussées and participate in the whole range of technical and administrative functions, mainly in the external services but also in the Ministry itself. It is an all-purpose corps and, like its senior, officially described as having interministerial character.

Recruitment

Student engineers are recruited to the Ecole d'Application des Travaux Publics de l'Etat by an annual competitive examination. Papers include mathematics, physics, technical drawing and French. The level is considerably lower than that of the senior corps.

(*a*) 85 per cent of the places are reserved for new entrants to the Civil Service, aged between 18 and 25.

(*b*) 15 per cent of the places are reserved for category B technicians with four years' service. The maximum age is 35 and they may only have three attempts at the examination. Technicians are allowed a preparatory year of study before they sit this examination if they pass a preliminary test (which may not be repeated). Both groups take the same examination. There is no provision for direct promotion from category B to category A on the basis of merit alone, or even on the basis of non-competitive tests.

Training

There is a two-year course. The first year consists of a mixture of general education and general technology with some practical work, the second of specialized courses with a good deal of practical work. The final level is below that of a British degree.

Grades and Salaries

There are two grades: Engineer and Divisional Engineer. The salary scales overlap. Normal promotion brings the engineer to the top of his scale after twenty-three years but he may be promoted to a higher grade after a much shorter period. It takes twelve years to reach the top of the divisional engineer grade. Salaries overlap with those of the senior corps but do not reach anything like the same heights; promotion is, on the whole, much slower.

Grade	Ratio per cent	Years Service	Index	Salary Francs	£
Student					
Engineer	—	—	300	10,600	760
Engineer	90	2 yrs student	340	12,000	860
		23 yrs in grade	685	23,250	1,660
Divisional	10	13 yrs service,			
Engineer		10 in corps	545	19,300	1,380
		12 yrs in grade	765	27,000	1,930

Career Prospects

Divisional engineers may head district services or section in county offices. Little prestige attaches to the corps and there is not much movement out. Possibilities of promotion to the senior corps (rare) have been mentioned.

9. PUBLIC WORKS: CATEGORIES B AND C

The corps of Public Works Technicians is the category B corps of the service. It consists of three distinct groups, separately recruited. There is no post-entry training.

1. Technical Assistants work in the offices of the engineers as their aides. Recruitment is by competitive examination at 'A level' mathematics standard for 90 per cent of the places (70 per cent new entrants, 10 per cent clerks and 10 per cent foremen from category C). Foremen under 40, with at least ten years' service, may be appointed to the remaining places after passing a qualifying test.

H

2. Technical Secretaries may be in charge of accounts sections, transport pools, etc., or supervise clerical and other staff. There are two competitive examinations, with an equal number of places for new entrants between 18 and 25 and for clerks under 35 with five years' service.

3. Technical Draughtsmen are similarly recruited, with separate examinations for new entrants (60 per cent of the places) and for drawing assistants in category C (40 per cent).

There are three grades. The two higher grades (common to all three groups) are Section Leader and Chief Section Leader. Promotion to these depends on obtaining a number of certificates. Section leaders must hold two certificates in two of the following groups of subjects: basic techniques, specialized techniques, administrative techniques. Chief section leaders must have four certificates, including one in each group.

Grade	Years Service	Index	Salary Francs	£
Technical Assistant	⎫	205	7,500	550
Technical Secretary	⎬ 26 yrs in grade	360	12,700	900
Technical Draughtsman	⎭			
Section Leader	4 yrs service	250	8,900	640
	20 yrs in grade	390	13,800	990
Chief Section Leader	10 yrs service	280	9,950	710
	20 yrs in grade	420	14,800	1,060

A word may be said about the category C corps of Public Works Foremen to indicate their relative salary position. Eighty per cent are recruited by competitive examination between the ages of 21 and 30 (60 per cent from new entrants, 20 per cent from within the service); 20 per cent are promoted from below (qualifying tests open to those under 45 with eight years' service). This corps has a single grade. The salary scale runs from Index 205 (Frs. 7,500/£550) to Index 330 (Frs. 11,700/£840).

10. ARCHITECTS AND TOWN PLANNERS

There are some 300 architects in the service of the central Government, though only a part are full-time established civil servants. Their training is that of ordinary architecture students and does not take place in Civil Service schools. Work is usually more specialized and they are relatively less involved in the administrative system as a whole. Some combine public and private practice. Some (even among those employed full-time) receive fees rather than a salary. They are divided between several small, quite specialized corps and for this reason too they do not qualify for the same wide administrative careers as the engineers. Several Ministries have their own architectural services and a few architects are found in most of the remainder. Architects in private practice may be employed on an *ad hoc* basis, especially in the design of new buildings. General responsibility for public buildings rests with the Architecture Division of the Ministry for Cultural Affairs which is staffed by administrators at the centre. The external services, on the other hand, are headed by architects. The seventy Architectes des Bâtiments de France are established civil servants recruited by competitive examination open to registered architects. They are responsible for the great palaces and for the maintenance of other public buildings. They also act as technical representatives of the Ministry, e.g. advising on new buildings in their area. The forty Architectes des Monuments de France are fee paid but, that apart, are full-time civil servants. The 200 Architectes des Bâtiments Civils may continue in private practice. They are called upon in the case of major works.

The existence of a strongly entrenched corps of civil engineers, with wide claims of competence, has inhibited the growth of a major corps of architects. Many senior posts in the Ministry of Construction are held by these engineers who are often also responsible, at county level, for the supervision of local authorities and private builders.

A corps of town planners has been established, comparable in status, though not in prestige or influence, to the great technical corps. It is attached to the Ministry of Construction. Members exercise administrative and technical functions in the fields of town planning, infrastructure development and building. They may be charged with the preparation of plans to be executed by public authorities, the supervision of private contractors, the drafting of regulatory schemes defining priority development zones and similar matters.

Ninety per cent of the members of this corps are recruited by competitive examination as student planners and receive a year's specialized post-entry training. Four-fifths of these places go to new entrants with a degree in architecture; one-fifth are reserved for the staff of the Ministry (under 35, at least five years' service in category A). The examination has a relatively technical character (planning, architecture and building), with oral questions on law

and administration. Extra credit is given for the University
Diploma in Town Planning or other qualifications which would
permit the holder to sit the entrance examination for the National
School of Administration. The small size of this corps at present
is indicated by an intake of ten in 1964. The remaining 10 per cent
of the places are available for the promotion of civil servants
with at least ten years' service who have passed a qualifying test.

There are two grades. Promotion within grades is by regular
increments. The top of the scale falls below that of the great
engineering corps, but members would come on a higher scale
if appointed to the directorial posts for which they are qualified.

Grade	Ratio per cent	Years Service	Index	Salary Francs	£
Student Planner	—		355	12,500	910
Planner	67	1 yr student	390	13,800	990
		15 yrs in grade	835	29,500	2,110
Chief Planner	33	8 yrs service	735	25,900	1,850
		11 yrs in grade	A	42,400	2,030

The higher ranks may be entrusted with general missions of
enquiry or with regional co-ordinating functions. They qualify
for appointment to directorial posts, though the Town Planning and Building divisions of the Ministry are at present headed
by a finance inspector and a civil engineer. The lower ranks may
head the external services in a country. The problem of the corps
is that of a newly emerging profession trying to insert itself in a
system in which others already have established claims. There
are signs, however, that it is coming to be recognized as the field
of work increases in importance.

11. DOCTORS

Medically qualified staff is employed in various branches of the
administration and there are a number of separate corps. An
example is the medical inspectorate of the Ministry of Labour.
The most important, comparable in structure and functions to
other category A specialists, is the corps of public health doctors
attached to the Ministry of Public Health (there is a parallel
corps of 'generalist' administrators with legal training).

The corps was established in 1964 by the fusion of two groups:
health inspectors and school doctors (who previously came under
the Ministry of Education). It has some 800 members (500 more,

mainly school doctors, are employed full-time on a contractual basis). To understand their functions it is necessary to remember that the external services of the Ministry staff many local authority services and that school services are the responsibility of the central Government. Either as administrators in the Ministry or its external services, or as inspectors, they are involved in a wide variety of work covering the whole field of public health (preventive medicine, sanitation, child welfare, school health, control of public and private hospitals and laboratories, supervision of medical practice generally, etc.). Higher ranks may be appointed as directors of external services, as heads of municipal public health bureaux or as technical advisers to the directors of education. They may be employed in detached service in other branches of the administration, in hospitals or in research.

Established members are recruited by competitive examination from qualified doctors. As with most senior corps, there is a period of post-entry training at a Civil Service school (a year's course with various specializations possible). A tenth of the places are reserved for contractual staff with ten years' full-time service in the schools. Members enter the corps at a point on the salary scale which takes account of previous experience.

There is no regular pattern of movement to the Ministry as with the engineers. Approximately forty category A level posts in the central administration are filled by men with medical qualifications though only half of these are members of the corps. Some, moreover, occupy specialized or advisory posts (and some of these, again, tend to remain within the Ministry throughout their careers). Relatively few doctors are appointed to the key positions. Appointment at the head of division level is at the discretion of the Government. The present Director of Public Health has medical qualifications but is not a member of a Civil Service corps (nor is he a 'real' doctor, in the sense that he has never practised medicine). He is assisted by two Medical Inspectors.

Members of the corps nevertheless tend to have administrative-type careers. The school medical service is an exception but it is largely staffed by contractual personnel and even they do not give treatment. Most are recruited into the public service at the beginning of their careers and thus have little experience of medical practice. As heads of external services they perform functions similar in part to those of the Medical Officers of British local authorities, in addition to functions as local representatives of their Ministry. The corps is a new one and its position is not firmly established yet. The tendency, however, seems to be to free doctors from administrative work by the establishment of new groups of specialized administrators with legal backgrounds in various health fields (a similar pattern is developing in education).

12. ACCOUNTANTS

Much of the work that is done by auditors in Britain is done in France by members of two prestige corps. Public accounts are subject to 'the verification of the Finance Inspectorate and the jurisdiction of the Court of Accounts'.

The Finance Inspectorate is attached to the Ministry of Finance and its members are directly responsible to the Minister. They are charged with the supervision of all external services of the Ministry (and these handle most Government receipts and expenditure), other financial services of the State (e.g. post offices) and local authorities. Teams of inspectors hold audits at selected offices without prior notice. Though concerned primarily with the accuracy of accounts, they may also investigate the efficiency of administration generally. While this relatively routine, relatively technical work is the *raison d'être* of the corps, it plays a second and more important role as a pool of highly qualified administrators who can be called upon to fill senior posts. It is probably the most generalist of all the corps of the French Civil Service. Members are usually engaged in the work of audit only in the early stages of their career, acquiring familiarity with many branches of the public service in the process. They are subsequently posted to a wide variety of key positions. The corps has acquired a vested right to most of the directorates in finance and economic affairs. Its members frequently move to managerial positions in public or private enterprise.

The Court of Accounts is responsible for the end-of-year audit of all public accounts. As its name implies, it is a judicial body and its members have the status of judges. They are often posted to other positions, though perhaps less frequently, and they are more likely to return to their original functions.

Members of both corps are recruited from the graduates of the National School of Administration. Their high prestige and excellent career prospects mean that only the top candidates have a chance of being accepted. This, in turn, means that they are likely to be ambitious young men with an eye on administrative careers rather than in the real work of their corps. Though they will have studied economics and administrative law (which includes the rules of public finance), there is nothing in their training and little in their subsequent experience which qualifies them for the more technical aspects of accountancy.

Responsibility for the actual keeping of accounts lies with other civil servants, mainly of the Ministry of Finance. But this is relatively routine work and the corps concerned do not have a particularly high status. Their members have a certain amount of technical training but little theoretical background. They are essentially book-keepers. It is now suggested that this leaves a marked gap in French administration. This is another example of how the existing structure of the Civil Service may inhibit the growth of important new specializations.

13. LAWYERS

What has been said above is even more true of lawyers. All the generalist classes who have graduated from the National School of Administration have received a training in administrative law. They will have done a fair amount of public and private law in their previous studies (most are likely to hold law degrees). Members of some of the secondary category A corps may also have degrees or diplomas in law. It can be argued that such a background is more necessary for administrators in France than in Britain. The administrative process is regulated by law to a far greater extent and a far wider range of decisions is subject to appeal in the administrative courts. The assumption is that no special class of lawyers is necessary. To an extent this is true. Adequate expertise for the drafting of laws and regulations is available. But the administrators lack experience in private law and legal practice. It has been suggested that this is another gap in the Civil Service, though a minor one.

14. SCIENTISTS

Most Ministries have become involved in scientific research in connection with their work. This is sometimes farmed out to universities or private industry. But it has long been recognized that research and policy-making are closely linked and there is a strong tendency to expand research within the administration. This may take place in laboratories which form an integral part of the Ministries concerned or in the growing number of public corporations with 'administrative character' (a technical term to define corporations financed almost entirely by the State and subject to most of the rules of public administration: their staff has quasi-Civil Service status). Examples of the latter are the Atomic Energy Commissariat, the National Office for Aeronautical Research, the Institute of Applied Chemical Research, the Bureau for Geological and Mining Research, and the Scientific and Technical Centre for Building. The most important of these institutions is the National Centre for Scientific Research which doubles as a division of the Ministry of Education and as a public corporation. It is responsible for a wide variety of pure and applied research in the natural and social sciences, much of which would be done within the universities in Britain. It has numerous laboratories and a very large staff. Senior members (directors of research) have full Civil Service status, others are usually employed on contractual terms (all may also be involved in university teaching).

It is impossible to describe the range of careers open in this way. Some laboratories tend to be staffed by members of the corps of the Ministries concerned. The central laboratory of the Ministry of Public Works & Transport, for example, is very much the preserve of the corps of civil engineers and provides openings for its more scientifically-minded members. On the other hand, the laboratories of the Ministries of Agriculture and Health tend to be staffed by career scientists, graduates of the science faculties, who are recruited on the basis of their university qualifications. The Ministry of Finance has a laboratory branch for the taxation and customs services which also tests alcohol and assays precious metals. It recruits 'engineers' into a specialized corps by competitive examination at science degree level and also employs specialized personnel at lower levels.

All these are 'specialists' in the narrower sense and do not take part in administration. This reinforces a point made earlier. Many administrative careers in the French Civil Service require specialized higher education of a professional nature. But if a young man decides to pursue purely scientific studies and graduates with no more than a university science degree, he is likely to find himself debarred from them.

15. GENERAL IMPRESSIONS

The following impressions are based on a series of interviews with senior civil servants in a variety of posts in Paris. Most of the points have already been touched upon in the more descriptive account above and it is inevitable that there should be a certain amount of repetition. This procedure may nevertheless help to summarize some of the characteristics of the French Civil Service, and some of its problems, in so far as these affect the role of professionals.

Career Orientation

At the higher levels French education is more specialized and yet wider than in Britain. The explanation of this apparent paradox is simple. Studies tend to be career-oriented: in most cases it is not possible to enter the higher levels of the Civil Service after taking an undirected arts or science degree. But the courses of the great technical schools are more widely based than those of our science faculties: they are not really designed for those who intend to remain specialists. They produce administrators who understand engineering problems rather than working engineers.

This sort of education is excellent for a relatively small élite. But the very fact of their 'open competence' means that they lack the more practical training which is required at a slightly lower level. This is provided by the less prestigious technical schools and there is consequently a gulf between the graduates of the two, seriously hindering internal promotion prospects.

The decision to pursue a Civil Service career in the great technical corps has to be taken at least at sixth-form level as it involves post-sixth-form preparation for the very difficult and highly competitive examination of the Ecole Polytechnique (and it is necessary to have entered the maths stream much earlier). The examination is heavily biased towards science and the Polytechnique itself gives a general science education. It is hard to generalize about the motives of candidates. A number probably have no clear idea about their future nor, indeed, fully understand what is involved in a choice between scientific and managerial careers. The best in the form may sit on the advice of their teachers ('it's worth trying'), others may simply know that it is a sure path to good positions and high salaries. It seems clear, however, that the majority know from the start that they are opting for administrative careers (and a proportion are thinking even then of a subsequent transfer to high managerial posts in private enterprise). This is even more marked during their period of study. It is the students' associations which are pressing for a widening of the syllabus to include more economics and relevant social sciences. The Polytechnique nevertheless prides itself on the 'scientific culture' it instills in its students and this probably remains part of their intellectual baggage throughout their lives. There are opportunities for the more scientifically or technically minded to remain in specialized posts.

The situation is rather different in the case of the more specialized non-engineering corps such as doctors, architects and town planners. These pursue ordinary university studies and may make their career decisions much later.

The choice of those who enter the lower ranking corps is also likely to be made later and is more likely to be a matter of chance. Their qualifications resemble those of young men who enter public or private enterprise and the work in which they will be involved is not dissimilar. Security of employment is an obvious attraction. There is relatively little movement out of the service at these levels. This may be due to a lack of demand for their services at sufficiently attractive salaries (except in the case of certain specialists in short supply). But it also seems to indicate that once they are established they quickly develop a public service orientation.

Professional Allegiance
France has a large number of professional associations but they are relatively weak. They act as learned societies and promote rather superficial contacts between members. The allegiance of the specialist civil servant is to his corps, particularly where it is linked to a Civil Service school. Where his qualification is that of such a school, the profession to which he belongs can be said to be his corps. The social links between '*anciens élèves*' are certainly stronger than any others. The engineer thus has little sense of belonging to a wider profession. There is a marked difference of outlook between engineers in Government service and those in industry. Members of the great technical corps 'are

aware of themselves as representatives of the State power'. When they transfer to the private sector, they move to managerial rather than technical posts. There is little scope for the movement of engineers in the other direction.

A stronger professional sense tends to be found among other specialists such as the doctors and architects mentioned above. Their student-day ties are with the university and the majority of their fellow graduates will be in private practice. The fact that these are newer corps, less well placed in the administrative system, also means that their members may be less able to think of themselves as sharing in 'State power'. They nevertheless see themselves as civil servants first.

Specialists as Administrators
The technical background of members of the great corps tends to be of a fairly general nature. That is not to say that members cannot become real specialists if they so desire. It may be possible for an engineer to concentrate his activities in a particular field in which he acquires the reputation of an expert (e.g. a rural engineer may develop a special interest in food refrigeration). He may undertake further studies (e.g. a civil engineer interested in hospital building may take a year's course at the School of Public Health in mid-career). But this is a matter of individual choice.

On the whole, most professionals are concerned with the management of broad technical services right from the start. This involvement in managerial functions is true even of the secondary corps of Public Works engineers. The chief engineers at the head of external services have even wider administrative functions. They are responsible for legal, financial and personnel matters. Their contacts with elected local authorities and other local interests gives their work a political character as well. As they move up the hierarchy, they reach the policy-making levels of central Government.

It is sometimes suggested that French civil servants are specially trained for administration. This is only partly true of the graduates of the National School of Administration (a necessary grounding in administrative law, practical exercises, a period of observation in the field). 'Administrative science' is not taught. The specialists receive virtually no training in administration as such. They learn the art of management in the same way as British administrators: through practice. It is only fair to add that a different sort of person may have chosen to enter these corps in the first place from some British science graduates who enter a specialized class. Those whose gifts do not lie in that direction will either not reach the top ranks or they will be employed in more specialized activities for which they are better fitted (e.g. research).

It is rarely suggested that professionals do not make as good administrators as members of the 'generalist' corps. Criticism may come from those whose own career prospects are likely to be frustrated (the civil administrators). Interestingly, it is in the field of public enterprise that more criticism has been heard. Some public corporations have been accused of engaging in over-ambitious schemes, technically successful but economically unsound, under the direction of engineers for whom finance is a secondary consideration. It is easier to test the efficiency of nationalized industries than of Government departments and, on the whole, these have done very well over the years.

Another suggestion is that the present system is a waste of specialized talent. The great technical corps recruit some of the most brilliant men in the country (certainly in so far as examinations are any test) and these could be more usefully employed in really specialized tasks. This may be true but the choice is their own and it would probably be impossible to divert them away from the real centres of power.

The Choice between Specialists and Generalists
At all but the highest levels, particularly in the external services, it is usually obvious what work requires administrators with a technical background and posts are usually clearly earmarked for generalists or specialists. Regulations often specify the actual qualifications necessary (membership of certain corps, seniority). At the highest levels, the nature of work tends to change somewhat, losing its technical side, and posts become more open. There are few rules (seniority apart) about the specific qualifications of civil servants appointed to posts in the central administration of the sort filled by the Administrative Class in Britain (deputy heads of divisions are an exception: see below). Nor is there any real theory about the relative suitability of specialists and generalists for particular posts at this level.

It is rare for a French Ministry to have the equivalent of a

Permanent Secretary (i.e. a single civil servant head). The most interesting posts, therefore, are the directorships of division. Appointment to these is in fact at the complete discretion of the Government. There are patterns of appointment, however. It has been estimated that there are some 120 such posts and that between a third and a half of these are held by members of specialist corps. Good arguments can be advanced for their choice. Specialist knowledge is one; experience another. The former may be important because of the absence of a separate advisory hierarchy. The latter is perhaps even more important. Many central divisions are not only responsible for policy-making, they also manage field services. Familiarity with their work and close links with their personnel are an obvious help. Indeed, friction that can arise if members of the great technical corps are forced to work under a 'stranger' is a consideration that cannot be ignored. Tradition itself is an important factor. The great corps have established claims in their own fields and these are reinforced by the loyalties which lead the most senior members to arrange for their succession by their colleagues. An example may be the Liquid Fuel Division of the Ministry of Industry, traditionally headed by a mining engineer. It is true that oil drilling lies within their province (the corps is in any case the major technical corps of the Ministry), but the extensive and growing State intervention in the petroleum industry makes this division a centre of economic policy rather than of technical control.

These traditions can be broken. The present Director of Road Transport in the Ministry of Public Works & Transport is a finance inspector and he is quite likely to be appointed Director General of Transport should such a co-ordinating post be established. In the last resort there is no clear rationale to the highest appointments. Specialized knowledge and past experience are factors. So are corps pressures. Increasingly, however, it seems that personality is decisive: initiative and managerial ability. Patterns of appointment are becoming more fluid (though this must not be overstated) and there are more cases of the 'best man available' being appointed, regardless of corps. In many cases a specialist will in fact have been the best administrator available. Even where corps membership is considered a necessary qualification, the individual will have been selected for his administrative rather than his technical ability.

It is nevertheless still possible to see different patterns in the staffing of different Ministries at the higher levels. The Ministry of Finance is largely directed by finance inspectors, graduates of the National School of Administration and thus 'generalists' in one sense though, as suggested earlier, specialists in another. The Ministries of Public Works & Transport, Agriculture and Industry, on the other hand, are largely directed by technicians. The Ministry of Posts & Telecommunications is unusual in that it has separate hierarchies based on separate schools. Newer Ministries, such as Public Health and Construction, are not built on corps in the same way and the specialist corps they subsequently establish do not enjoy the same prestige. Their senior appointments are thus more varied.

Administrators as Advisers

Most central departments are organized on the assumption that it is impossible to distinguish technical and advisory functions within the Ministry from administration (advisory committees are, of course, attached to them). Though the Civil Service is organized in parallel corps, the Ministries themselves are not structured to separate specialists or advisers from the ordinary administrative hierarchy.

It is true that there are line and staff posts. The line of command (management functions) goes from the Minister to the heads of divisions and their subordinates and from the heads of divisions to the heads of the external services.

Certain inspectorates, the Minister's private office and the counsellors attached to some directors may be thought of as having staff functions. But all these posts are filled by ordinary civil servants (members of the generalist or technical corps) who serve in line and staff functions at different stages of their careers. There are also sections in every Ministry which are more concerned with 'studies' (information, research, planning) than with the actual management of services, but the same applies to their staff.

The heads of divisions are in fact their own chief advisers. They are also the Minister's chief advisers (a function that may be shared with Inspectors General, usually the most senior members of the Ministry's specialized corps). There is no Chief Scientific Officer or equivalent. The organization of advice poses few problems, either on specific technical issues or on longer-term policy. Much is interspersed in the ordinary administrative process. Hierarchical barriers to communication are eased by the strong corps spirit that links junior and senior members of the élite corps (a feature of the system, not mentioned earlier, is the sense of equality between ranks and generations that it promotes).

The situation is slightly different in a few cases. Relatively few doctors serve in the central administration of the Ministry of Public Health (though certain directorates are traditionally held by them). Long-term policy proposals are thus more likely to come from the powerful advisory committee attached to the Ministry or, on the economic side, from the Planning Commissariat. A partial explanation is the absence of a strongly entrenched corps with wide claims of competence. This helps to underline the extent to which the latter have influenced the organization of Government work elsewhere.

The Case for Administrative Deputies

There is really only one corps of senior civil servants that can strictly be called a corps of general administrators: the civil administrators. In practice, it is the lowest ranking of the corps recruited from graduates of the great post-entry schools. It is the only one which does not have specific responsibility for a defined sector of State activity.

Regulations provide that the positions of Deputy Director and Under-Director in the central administration should normally be filled from its ranks. There are many exceptions but the underlying thought is that much of the work at this level is best done by those specialized in administrative business, taking this in a rather narrow sense: the 'technical' aspects of administration common to all departments (e.g. personnel, accounts, legal matters). The lower ranks are also likely to be appointed to those sections of the Ministry where work is not marked by a strongly departmental character. It is useful to have legally trained administrators near the top (the extent to which French administration is regulated by law has already been noted). They relieve the professional civil servants of work for which they may not be qualified and of a good deal of work which is largely routine. Unlike the British Administrative Class, they play only a minor role in policy making. Office management is as good a description of their functions as any.

It is now argued that a similar division of labour might be useful in the external services. At present chief engineers have no administrative assistants of category A status. The suggestion is that an inter-service corps of administrators might be established with one or two members serving under the directors of the external services of each Ministry at county level. They too would be concerned with the more 'technical' and routine aspects of administration, especially legal and financial, and would free the directors from part of a growing burden of work. This is likely to become necessary as recent reforms have meant the transfer of responsibility for a good deal of such work, previously done in the Prefect's office, to the various specialized services. A rather similar development has in fact taken place in the field of education where the large number of establishments has made it worth setting up a specialized corps of educational administrators. It is not suggested, however, that there should be a division of responsibility: such administrators would come under, not rank with, the technical directors. Where dual responsibility has been tried, as in hospitals, it has not always worked well.

Corps Rivalries
There is little serious conflict between the great generalists and technical corps. At the lower and middle levels of administration, their respective spheres are fairly well defined. Rivalry is more likely to occur near the top, where the pyramid narrows and posts become more open. But this is limited by the mutual recognition of established claims (a 'truce situation'). In any case, the most ambitious generalists tend to steer away from the more technical Ministries, knowing in advance that their career prospects are poorer there, and this helps to prevent conflicts developing.

The tendency for the School of Administration's best graduates to avoid these Ministries does little harm as they already have their fair share of talent in the best graduates of the Polytechnique.

Some rivalries may occur between adjacent corps with 'frontier disputes' about their respective sectors of responsibility: e.g. between the civil and rural engineers or between engineers and town planners. Where one Ministry has several technical corps (e.g. Agriculture) the establishment of separate 'empires' may have bad effects on internal co-operation. Both these problems can be eased by the fusion of corps into larger, even less specialized groups. Such a reform was recently initiated in the Ministry of Agriculture; another example was the amalgamation of public health and school doctors.

The most serious conflict is not between generalists and specialists as such but between the civil administrators and the rest (with the finance inspectors their target of complaint as much as the engineers). Because this corps has no defined sector of responsibility, and thus no divisions it can call its own, it tends to recruit the poorer graduates of the School of Administration (a relative term as all are highly qualified). They have to compete against members of the more prestigious corps who carry the stamp of success from the start. The provision that they should be appointed deputy heads of divisions is a way of improving their promotion prospects, thus enhancing the prestige of the corps. It is still relatively new and, as more members work their ways up and the corps establishes an 'old boy network' of its own, this situation may ease.

What is interesting at present, however, is that grievances in France are the reverse of those in Britain. In France it is the true generalists who complain that they are underprivileged. It is not a matter of functional segregation, however, but simply of poorer promotion and salary prospects. Civil administrators tend to earn rather less than members of the other senior corps. This may be true even where they occupy the same positions. As Under-Directors, an engineer and a civil administrator should be at the same point on the grid (civil servants appointed to directorial posts are detached from their corps and its scale for salary purposes). But a chief engineer will already be earning more in the external services (taking into account additional remuneration from local authorities) and will thus have to be paid extra to induce him to move to the central administration.

Underprivileged Professions

The existence of some strongly organized corps with extensive bases and wide claims has the effect of inhibiting the growth of other professions. The service is relatively weak on accountants. Even when new corps are established, they are likely to find themselves hemmed in. The town planners are the example quoted. To an extent they are trespassing on civil engineers'

I

ground. There is a fairly clear distinction between two groups of specialist corps. The first, older, engineers in the main, have defined responsibilities, Ministries or at least divisions which are their domain, and well-established career structures. Their post-entry schools are an important base. The other corps are in a much weaker position. Doctors, architects and town planners have received the greater part of their training outside the system. They are not members of the Civil Service 'establishment' in the same way. This not merely reduces their promotion prospects as far as directorial posts are concerned, it may also reduce the impact of the services they do staff.

Both points are serious. It is relatively difficult for some professions to find a place within the system and, when they do find it, it may still be difficult for them to play an equally power-ful role. As in Britain, Civil Service structure may influence the activities of the State as well as reflect them. In the French context the solution would seem to lie in strengthening the newer corps by making them less 'professional', i.e. by integrat-ing them more fully in the post-entry training system.

Promotion Possibilities

Promotion within corps is a relatively routine matter though there are certain 'efficiency bars' and the career grade is below the highest levels. The real problem is that of mobility between corps. The chance of a really successful career hinges on this question for all but the favoured few who are recruited directly into the élite corps.

The extensive nature of category A and its consequent division creates some difficulty. Members of the secondary corps are theoretically recruited into the highest class of the Civil Service but will rapidly discover that this is not so. They will have received university level education and may have been diverted to a secondary corps by their failure in the stiff com-petitive examinations for the more prestigious corps. They will then find it much more difficult to cross the barrier than gradu-ates diverted into the Executive Class in Britain. There are thus some causes of grievance. It is almost impossible for them to reach the top, even less possible for those in category B. The French Civil Service is probably more élite-conscious than the British, with élites defined in terms of intellectual ability as proved in student examination results. Top posts are no more open than in Britain, they are merely reserved for a rather different group of civil servants.

It must be added, however, that a good deal of emphasis is placed on provisions which should theoretically encourage promotion between corps. Regulations specify the proportion of places to be reserved in competitive examinations for civil servants in lower categories (though this is also a way of reserving the majority of places for new entrants). 'Social promotion' (the French term for upward mobility by adult study) is perhaps organized most effectively in the Ministry of Posts & Telecommunications where difficulties of external recruitment on the scale required are a factor. In theory a man can rise from the bottom to the top. To do so he must pass a series of competitive examinations. Most are of a theoretical rather than practical nature, testing intellectual ability rather than knowledge acquired by experience. Usually the candidate has to prepare for these in his spare time (only for the highest examination is study leave granted; special courses are more often organized). This imposes a heavy burden on the ambitious civil servant. There are even more limited possibilities of promotion on past record, sometimes with qualifying tests, and these are 'formalized' (inscription on lists as eligible for promotion after vetting by special committees).

The structure of the French Civil Service is probably more closely linked to educational levels than the British, and the barriers to inter-category promotion are probably greater. The fact that an age limit is usually set (often 35) is also important. The system is not one in which civil servants can hope to climb gradually up a ladder if they are efficient in their work. It is more a case of jumping hurdles early enough in life. The lower levels of the French Civil Service are thus more closely confined than the higher. This is true not only of movement upwards but also of movement sideways. It is relatively difficult to transfer from a lower technical corps to an executive post. The principle of 'general competence' is largely reserved for the élite.

Yet there is relatively little demand for promotion between corps on past record. Fears of favouritism, or even political bias, are a partial explanation. But it is also important to remember that France is a country which traditionally places even greater weight on examinations and intellectual ability than

Britain. It is also a country which tends to believe in formal procedures as a means of ensuring fairness. Attachment to objective tests open to all candidates, as against personal assessments and discretionary decisions, is linked with attachment to the principles of equality and legality.

Movement In and Out

Movement out of the Civil Service is very common in the more prestigious corps, particularly after fifteen or twenty years' service. Many enter with this possibility already in mind. Private enterprise seeks them out because it knows that the great corps will have recruited a high proportion of the most promising students in the country and because it has a high regard for their training. The system is also self-perpetuating: those already in the private sector will naturally look with favour on members of their old corps. It is true that this pattern involves the State in expensive training and a steady loss of senior staff in mid-career. On the other hand, as these possibilities are one of the major attractions of the great post-entry schools, it is also easier for the Civil Serivce to recruit really good students than would otherwise be the case. Useful links are moreover established between Government, nationalized industries and private enterprise. These are an important characteristic of the French economy. Common background and ties of friendship go much of the way to explaining the success of the French planning system.

Movement out at lower levels is less common. It is more likely to occur where the Civil Service has trained staff in new techniques which are in short supply for the time being and this may cause greater problems.

Movement into the service in mid-career is extremely rare. A certain number are employed on a contractual basis, usually in specialist posts with few administrative functions. In general the service prefers to train established staff as new specialist needs arise. There are few academic economists; polytecnichians in the statistical services and School of Administration graduates in the financial services have turned themselves into econometrists. The Ministry of Posts organizes its own courses to meet the need for computer experts. The situation is slightly different in those professions which are not recruited through post-entry schools. It is easier to bring in doctors and architects in mid-career, for example, because those already in the service will have the same educational background as those in private practice and because the corps are not strong enough to establish a monopoly for their members. The Civil Service unions are hostile to outside recruitment and lay great weight on adherence to the rules regarding competitive examinations, age limits and the limitation of contractual personnel. This is most marked at lower levels where, on the face of it, the intake of specialists should be easier because there are fewer differences in the nature of the work involved.

It is almost impossible to say whether one Civil Service system is better than another. 'Better for what?' is an obvious question. The Civil Service plays different roles in different countries. In the present day one might be tempted to ask whether one is more effective in promoting economic development than another. There is no way of measuring this, nor indeed of isolating the contribution of the Civil Service from other factors. Some may nevertheless feel (and it is no more than a feeling) that the French system is more effective than the British in this respect and that the role of specialists is an important factor.

A simpler question perhaps (though not much simpler) is to ask which system works more smoothly. All have their own internal problems and the author has not disguised those of the French system. On the other hand, the French Civil Service seems to have avoided some of the problems facing the British at the moment, particularly those relating to the place of professionals. What lessons can be learnt is another matter. The extent to which Civil Service systems must be seen against a wider background has been stressed, so that it is impossible to isolate and copy particular aspects. What can be said, however, is that it appears possible to have a system in which there are few theoretical problems about the relationship between generalists and where the latter play a major part in the administrative process.

WESTERN GERMANY

1. INTRODUCTION

The modern professional public service is to a large extent a German invention. Its emergence in the eighteenth century is associated in particular with the consolidation of the Prussian State. Here an administrative service was developed, designed not merely for the maintenance of law and order, but also for the management of important aspects of social and economic life. In the encouragement of agriculture and forestry just as in the establishment of a national system of education the Prussian State took initiatives which were unknown in the *laisser-faire* climate of Great Britain. For such purposes a bureaucracy was required which even in the second half of the eighteenth century had some of the characteristics of contemporary professional Civil Services. There was emphasis on professional skill and competence, recognition of the desirability of securing officials with technical qualifications appropriate to their functions, and an effort to develop a coherent administrative organization reaching to all parts of the State.

In the early part of the nineteenth century the idea of a professional Civil Service on the lines of that being evolved in Prussia struck root throughout Germany. Even before unification confirmed the political preponderance of Prussia, the methods and style of administration throughout the German States had been harmonized to a large extent. Consequently, by the beginning of this century Germany had acquired a highly developed and homogeneous public service, respected for its technical competence, and enjoying high social prestige and a secure status.

This is not the place to discuss the role of the German bureaucracy in the political development of modern Germany, nor the extent to which, in virtue both of its functions and of its social origins, the public service became a conservative force of formidable influence. What is relevant for the discussion which follows is that the professionalization of the public service was fully established at a relatively early date, and the State accepted a measure of responsibility for ensuring that the higher educational system produced people with the various professional qualifications needed in the public service. For general administration a training in law became the normal requirement. But the activities of Government also called for officials with technical qualifications, particularly in various branches of civil engineering, mining engineering and forestry, and these took their place in the public service alongside those qualified in law. Germany has not known either the complicated structure of general and specialist classes familiar in Britain, nor the specialized and élitist corps of France. Instead, even though the political structure was federal and administration was not organizationally integrated, there developed at all levels a more or less uniform public service, founded on the principle that all those in it must be appropriately qualified for whatever career within it they aspired to. Despite the crises of the twentieth century which have shaken and finally split the German State, there is no mistaking the continuing influence of these traditions on the public service of the Federal Republic.

2. THE CONTEMPORARY INSTITUTIONAL CONTEXT

When discussing the German Civil Service it is important to stress at the outset the fact that Western Germany is a federal State. There is a large amount of administrative decentralization, from the Federal Government to the Laender Governments (of which there are eleven), and from the latter to the local authorities. In addition both Federal and Laender Ministries make use of a technique of deconcentration which involves the relegation of executive work—whether this be routine administration or technical services—to subordinate agencies known as *nachgeordnete Dienststellen*. These are responsible to their parent Ministries, but generally are set up on terms which allow them a wide measure of operational independence.

The consistent pursuit of decentralization in the provision of public services, even though it takes place within an overall structure in which the sense of hierarchy is strong, makes the analysis of German administration and of the German Civil Service very complex. Certainly it is risky to approach these matters with the preconceptions imposed by British experience in mind. There is nothing in Western Germany like the huge centralized British Departments with their vast range of executive functions; in the distribution of functions at different levels the Germans have not been so inhibited by the distinction between policy and administration which has played such a big part in the structural development of British Ministries; nor has the distinction between general administration and technical advice, which has influenced so much British discussion of the relations between general administrators and technically qualified staff, been drawn so sharply.

The Federal Government structure is on a fairly modest scale. Federal Departments are for the most part much more concerned with establishing the broad framework of policy and with expressing this in statutes and regulations than with executive functions. Apart from Defence, Finance and Foreign Affairs few Departments undertake much executive administration. Even those which do, such as Finance and Transport, decentralize such functions, in the manner already referred to, to organizations separate from the central Ministry.

The total non-industrial staffs employed by the Federal Government numbered about 190,000 in 1967. This excludes the Post and Railways, both of which are Federal agencies, and it also leaves out of account those in uniform in the armed forces. Of this total about 85,000 are in the Ministry of Defence, nearly 38,000 are in the decentralized organization of the Ministry of Finance corresponding to the British tax-collecting departments, over 20,000 are in the border police coming under the Ministry of the Interior, and 12,000 are in agencies coming within the sphere of the Ministry of Transport. These figures underline the fact that the central Civil Service apparatus is far smaller than it is in Britain. But relatively the higher grade of the service is quite large: of those employed by the Federal Government about 15,500 are in this grade, and thus come within the scope of this chapter.

3. SCOPE AND SIZE OF THE PUBLIC SERVICE

One cannot properly speak of the 'Civil Service' in Western Germany in the sense in which this term is used in Britain to refer to the civil employees of the Central Government. No sharp distinction can be drawn between those who work for the Federal Government and those who work for other public authorities, e.g. the Laender Governments, local authorities, public law institutions, etc. People in all these categories of employment are civil servants.

The figures given below refer to the whole public service, the scope of which is wider than in Britain. Not only are local authorities included, but teachers and judges, to mention but two examples, come within the scope of official statistics relating to the public service.

There were, in 1965, 2·9 million people in the German public service. These were distributed as shown in the following table. The horizontal entries list the principal public authorities, the vertical entries refer to categories of employment in the public service.[1] Military personnel in uniform are excluded, but the second column (*Beamten*) does include judges, the majority of whom are employed by the Laender.

PUBLIC SERVICE EMPLOYMENT IN WESTERN GERMANY, 1965[2]

	Totals	Beamten (Officials)	Angestellte (Employees)	Industrial Staff
Federal Government	265,656	73,477	91,326	100,853
Laender Governments	1,004,470*	584,331	315,525	106,614
Local Authorities	600,487	124,899	281,989	193,599
Industrial Corporations†	174,905	11,612	41,211	122,082
Federal Railways	461,649	241,359	7,112	213,178
Federal Posts	393,343	248,615	42,344	102,384
Grand total, all categories of staff	2,900,510			

* This figure includes teachers and police.
† Known technically as business enterprises without public law corporate status.

It is very difficult to break down these figures any further in a manner which will illuminate the issues under discussion here. Of those in the service of the Federal Government in 1967, excluding Posts and Railways, 12,566 were officials (*Beamten*) in the higher grade of the service, and 2,913 were 'employees' at the same level. Thus we can say that approximately 12 per cent of officials belonged to the higher Civil Service, and about 3 per

[1] The law relating to the public service recognizes three categories of employment—officials, employees and industrial staff. For further remarks on the distinction between officials (*Beamten*) and employees (*Angestellten*), see page 144 below.

[2] *Stat. Jahrbuch 1966*, Staff count at October 2, 1965.

cent of those in the employee category.[1] Comparable proportions cannot be given for the Laender since there are no co-ordinated statistics available, but it is known that in local government about 15 per cent of officials and 5½ per cent of employees were in the higher grade in 1963. Although these proportions must be treated with caution, it appears that throughout the Federal Republic the higher grade must amount to between 12 per cent and 15 per cent of the officials employed in the public service. This is probably a higher proportion than is found in the United Kingdom at this level. It is, of course, in this category that those classed as 'professional civil servants' are to be found.

When we come to consider the proportion of the higher grade which can be regarded as equivalent to professional, technical and scientific civil servants in the British sense of these terms, there are serious problems arising from the absence of appropriate statistics. An investigation published in 1963 indicated that in the Federal service 32 per cent of the higher grade officials had a legal training.[2] This means that just under 70 per cent must have had other specialized qualifications. But it is impossible to determine whether all these can be treated as equivalent to professional civil servants in Britain, and there is no way of breaking this group down into its component professions. Moreover, the distribution of different types of official is obviously important. In most Federal Ministries the number of higher grade officials not trained in law is small, and general administration is for the most part in the hands of lawyer-administrators. This is true, for example, of the Ministry of the Interior and the Finance Ministry. But in may of the subordinate agencies of the Federal Ministries the technically qualified official predominates. Examples are the Waterways and Shipping Directorates (external services of the Ministry of Transport) and the Federal Physical and Technical Standards Institute. In the Laender lawyer administrators have a major role in the Ministries, but technical and scientific specialists are strongly represented in the running of all those services which demand their skills and experience, e.g. road construction. In local

---

[1] These percentages are related to total employment figures given in the Ministry of Finance Annual Report for 1967 which differ somewhat from those in the table on the previous page.

[2] See 'Juristen im Öffentlichen Dienst', *Wirtschaft und Statistik*, Heft 7, 1963.

government the technical specialists, particularly in engineering, are numerous, since local authorities undertake a great deal of building for various purposes as well as running public service utilities to an extent now unknown in Britain.

4. THE STRUCTURE OF THE PUBLIC SERVICE

The structure of the German public service and the conditions of employment in it are determined in great detail by law. The current statute dates from 1953, as amended in 1957, 1961 and 1965, and as amplified by regulations. The legislation of 1953 referred to the Federal service, but similar provisions have subsequently been extended to the public service at regional and local levels. There is, therefore, a considerable degree of uniformity in the public service of the Federal Republic in such matters as structure, staffing, qualifications, conditions of service, etc. Even salary scales are in principle standardized, although public authorities other than the Federal Government have scope for varying these, and at the local level may offer various inducements such as housing on favourable terms. All this has tended to make public service away from Bonn, the Federal capital, more rewarding than it is in a Federal department.

The law relating to the public service defines four grades or careers—lower, middle, upper middle and higher (the *einfacher, mittlerer, gehobener* and *hoeherer Dienst*). The simplest clerical work, messengerial duties, shorthand and typing, etc., falls within the scope of the lower grade, and to some extent of the middle grade. The middle level is responsible for much of the work done by the lower-to-middle range of the executive class in Britain, and by the clerical class. The upper middle grade corresponds to the upper range of the executive class, and includes many people with technical qualifications who in Britain would be in technical/professional classes roughly equivalent to the executive class, but below the Scientific Civil Service or the Works Group of Professional and Technical Civil Servants. The higher grade corresponds to the administrative and scientific/ professional classes in the British Civil Service.

For each grade of the public service the qualifications for entry correspond to different levels of education and professional training. For the lower and middle grades the entry requirements are roughly schooling to the age of 16; for the upper middle level schooling to the age of 18 for posts in general administration, and for more specialized posts the completion of courses in the German equivalent of technical colleges; for the higher grade it is necessary to have completed a university course and to have had the appropriate professional training and/or practical experience. At most levels there are provisions for internal training, and in many cases for examinations before the applicants can be confirmed in the grade which they have entered. Each grade of the public service provides, in principle, a self-contained career, but promotion from one grade to another is possible, often subject either to completion of a minimum period in one level or to the passing of a promotion examination. As the figures already given have indicated, the higher grade of the public service in Germany is wider in scope than its counterparts in Britain. It is a fairly large and diversified group, including, for example, those responsible for general administration in central and regional government departments, a wide range of officials with scientific, technical and professional qualifications, of whom many are in non-Ministerial agencies and independent special-purpose public bodies, all the chief officers of local authorities, secondary school teachers, university staffs, the top levels of the revenue administration and so on. In short, the higher grade can best be defined as that segment of the whole public service which is responsible for the more important functions carried out by the State, and for which a higher education is deemed to be a necessary qualification. The rest of this chapter refers only to the higher grade.

5. QUALIFICATIONS AND TRAINING FOR THE HIGHER GRADE OF THE PUBLIC SERVICE

When considering entry requirements it is important to distinguish between careers in general administration, and those of a specialist character. Although there are no separate classes in the German public service, the law on the Civil Service does recognize different entry requirements for different types of career. It defines first the general entry qualifications for an administrative career in the higher grade, and then indicates that where appropriate applicants must provide evidence of 'the necessary technical or professional qualifications for particular careers, and these must be in addition to or instead of the general requirements [for the higher grade]'. Normally this means 'instead of'. The general requirements for the higher grade are a training in law, or as a result of recent amendments, in economics, other social sciences or public finance. For those careers calling for other specialized knowledge and training candidates have to show that they have acquired the relevant qualifications which are demanded instead of those applicable to careers in general administration. The content and level of these 'technical qualifications' are defined in numerous Federal and Land regulations.

Specialized careers in the higher grade fall roughly into two categories. There are those for which recognized State qualifications exist, which means that after completion of an academic education there is a period of at least two-and-a-half years further training under supervision by some public authority. Civil engineering, mining engineering, architecture, agricultural science, forestry, veterinary medicine, and a number of other disciplines come within this category. Then there is another group of careers for which no State examinations exist, and for which the qualifications for entry into the public service are, broadly, a university training and a minimum of four-and-a-half years professional experience outside the public service. Most careers calling for qualifications in the natural sciences, mathematics, archaeology, geology, etc., come into this group.

This method of relating university training and professional qualifications to particular careers in the public service has, of course, led to an extremely complicated situation as the number and variety of specialists required has increased. In practice it has meant that as soon as a new specialism is called for—let us say psychologists or physical geographers—a new 'career' is defined and the appropriate authorities (either the Federal Government or the Laender Governments) determine what qualifications and training must be obtained by those wishing to work in this specialist field in the higher grade of the public service.

The whole system of entry qualifications cannot be understood unless one appreciates that the State has exerted a much greater influence on higher education, and on professional training and qualifications than in Britain. The idea that the State has a responsibility to establish the standards which must be attained for entry into particular professions, to ensure that the necessary institutions for attaining such standards are provided, and to see that examination provisions and methods are uniform, is deeply rooted in German educational development. Consequently a significant part of higher education is more closely tied to vocational requirements than in Britain, and many students can see more clearly to what careers, public or private, their courses will lead them.

Private corporate bodies play little part in professional training. The first step in such training is normally a course of academic study at a university or technical university. Some university courses, notably law, lead not to a university degree but to what is known as the first State examination. For those wishing to enter the higher grade of the public service (whether as administrators or as judges) there is prescribed a further period of training of two-and-a-half years, after which the second State examination is taken. If successful in this the applicant is fully qualified, and can apply to any public authority for admission to the higher grade of the public service. State examinations exist for other disciplines. For example, in medicine five-and-a-half years of university study is required, leading to a State medical examination. Confirmation to practice can be given only after a further two years' experience as a medical assistant. For the public service doctors would have to specialize in the relevant fields, e.g. public health, and produce evidence of their experience and advanced qualifications when making application for a post.

In a subject like engineering the position is slightly different. The various branches of engineering are studied in technical universities, usually in a four-year course which leads to a Diploma. This is not formally a State examination, but on the other hand the universities are not free to follow their own wishes in deciding the content and standard of it. There is State supervision. The Diploma would enable its holder to apply for posts in private industry, but if a career in the public service is desired it is necessary to undergo a period of from two-and-a-half to three years supervised training, followed by a State examination, before the applicant is fully qualified for entry to the higher grade of the public service.

Similar provisions requiring a university qualification plus two or more years' further training apply to many other professions represented in the public service—architecture, surveying, agricultural science, mining engineering, etc. This further training does not take place in a university, nor is it like 'in-training' inside the public service such as is known in Britain. What happens is that applicants are attached on probation to a branch of the public service, and during this time have to complete a course of practical and theoretical training (including private study) which is determined by the State educational authorities in conjuction with the interested branches of the public service. Those undergoing such training have a recognized status and receive a small salary.

The content of this training is determined in separate regulations for each professional career or discipline. The courses are carefully organized and it is ensured that those taking part spend several months on all the main aspects of their subject and in each of the principal sectors of the organization which is responsible for the training. In many cases those in training will be seconded to a number of different organizations in order to widen their experience. (This reflects to some extent the influence of the law training model which has always included periods with the more important branches of the administration and judiciary.) Many public authorities participate in training, particularly if they are large and have a continuing need for recruits. The Federal Railways, for example, are highly esteemed for their training of certain types of civil engineer, and such people can readily find posts in many branches of the public service.

For specialisms for which there is no State examination and no official training period, as has already been mentioned, candidates must have completed a university course and have a minimum of four-and-a-half years' relevant experience before they are acceptable for permanent employment in higher grade posts. Often such people will have taken the doctorate at a university, done some research, and may even have gone as far as the 'habilitation', the qualification which formally entitles its holder to a university chair. These conditions apply particularly to those specializing in theoretical science, and who, if they enter public service, will be engaged in research work. But it must also be remembered that the number of such posts in research establishments directly managed by the Government is fairly small, and that a large part of research effort in Western Germany is concentrated in specialized institutions which are partly publicly-financed, but independent of Government control. The Max-Planck-Gesellschaft is a notable example of this.

As these remarks on some aspects of qualifications and training imply, entry to the public service is by application and interview, and not by competitive examination. There is no centralized recruiting agency to which applicants can turn. Those who have the requisite initial academic qualifications and who desire a public service career will apply to that agency or department which interests them, and if they cannot get a post in one preferred agency they are perfectly free to try their luck with another.

6. EMPLOYEES

So far we have been referring to persons who wish to become career officials, *Beamten*. An official under German public law corresponds roughly to a permanent established civil servant in Britain. But many people in the public service have a rather different status, corresponding in some respects to unestablished service in Britain. They are known as 'employees' or *Angestellten*. There is no need in this context to go into the legal differences between the status of officials and that of employees. Broadly speaking, the latter have less security of tenure and their pension rights are regulated in a different manner. In practice the conditions of service of employees have steadily been approximated to those of officials, so that the distinction between the two categories has become somewhat unreal. A considerable number of professional public servants (i.e. in the British sense of professional) are in the employee category. At the Federal level there are about 3,000 employees in posts equivalent to the higher grade of the public service (as opposed to just over 12,000 officials), although it is not known how many of these employees have specialized qualifications other than law or the social sciences. As far as qualifications go, there is very often no significant difference between the two kinds of staff: the employee working at the higher level will have similar training and education to the permanent official. On the other hand, the employee status is not so closely tied to legally enforceable conditions of entry as that of the official: it is possible for the Federal Personnel Commission to take a more flexible view of what training and qualifications will justify the appointment of employees than would be possible with regard to officials. Moreover, the employee status may be more suitable for specialized staff who are required for relatively short-term assignments, and who will afterwards return to some form of private employment.

7. THE FUNCTIONS AND ROLE OF SPECIALIST OFFICIALS

The Germans do not, as a matter of doctrine, make a distinction between administrative work directed to policy-making, and other more technical and advisory functions. This reflects to some extent the belief that for all aspects of administration relevant specialized knowledge and training are necessary. It reflects too one of the organizational principles which is applied in German public administration. This is that all functions should be broken down into distinct subject areas, and then individually or in small groups they are entrusted to an organizational unit known as the *Referat*. Literally this means 'report', but in the organizational sense means a branch or section with responsibilities defined according to subject-matter and function. The person in charge of a *Referat* is the principal authority on all questions and work falling within the terms of reference of his branch. In large Federal departments there may be up to 100 such branches, whilst in smaller departments and at the level of the Laender Ministries the number might fall to thirty or less. These branches are in turn grouped into sub-divisions and divisions, the heads of the latter being the most senior officials immediately below State Secretaries.[1]

The essential point about this organization is that it produces a distribution of business according to subject and function with no distinction in principle between work which involves policy-making and that consisting mainly of technical advice or management. The officials in charge of branches will have whatever qualifications and background appear most appropriate to the activities in question. In departments with a high proportion of regulatory and policy work (e.g. Interior, Justice, Finance, Economic Affairs) most branches and nearly all divisions are headed by lawyer-administrators. But if the work

---

[1] The position of State Secretary is nearer to that of Deputy Minister than of Permanent Secretary. It is a political appointment, but usually from the career service.

K

requires scientific or technical knowledge then the branches in question will be in the hands of specialist staff. There will be no 'policy' branch alongside keeping an eye on issues of policy which might arise.

The situation can best be illustrated by quoting a few examples. The Federal Ministry of Transport has nine divisions. Of these the Waterways division and that looking after Road Construction are headed by engineers. The one concerned with internal shipping is headed by an economist. The rest are led by lawyer-administrators. Within the divisions many of the branches are headed by engineers, for example, that concerned with new autobahn construction. Those branches with functions of general administration, budgeting, the drafting of regulations, etc., are under legally trained administrators. Turning to the smaller Ministry of Scientific Research one finds that there are only four divisions. The central division (staff, finance, etc.) and that responsible for the general support of scientific research and higher education are under traditional administrators. The other two, one for nuclear research and the other for space research, are headed by officials qualified in pure science and engineering respectively. Of the twenty-four branches in these two divisions as far as can be ascertained at least twenty are headed by technical and scientific civil servants. Finally, to quote a different area of administration, that of the Ministry of Economic Affairs, about 40 per cent of the staff in the higher grade are trained in economics and public finance as opposed to law, although it has to be stated that relatively few of these are in leading positions. Most of them are concerned with economic advice and appreciation rather than with the making of policy decisions.

What has been said so far underlines the fact that the German public service does not know the British distinction between policy and technical functions. There is no system of parallel hierarchies with a different type of staff in each hierarchy. There is one pyramid in which, at various levels, there are different types of higher grade staff in accordance with the demands of the work. This situation is found not only at the Federal Government level. It is typical too of most other branches of public administration, and in those agencies which have highly technical functions it is normal for the specialist staff to control the bulk of the directing posts.

8. GENERAL ADMINISTRATION AND POLICY-MAKING

It would, however, be misleading to conclude that the absence of formal distinctions between administrators and professional staff means that the latter are generally in a position significantly different from that of their opposite numbers in Britain. It is an inescapable consequence of the scale of modern government that many of the functions which have to be discharged are mainly concerned with determining how technically certain services can be provided, with the scientific and technical assessment of problems to be overcome, with the continuing management of technical services, and with research and the analysis of information. On the whole all these functions are within the German system of administration entrusted to people with the appropriate professional qualifications, i.e. in pure and applied science, in a technology, and in many other specialized disciplines. But these functions must be carried out within a framework of general policy and legislative regulation. For a long time the formulation of policy at the higher levels, the translation of this into binding regulations or law, the management of expenditure, and the work imposed by attending to the demands of the political environment, have been mainly the province of administrators trained in law. There are provisions for people educated in the social sciences to enter general administration, but so far they have made little impact.

A legalist approach to administrative activity is a dominant characteristic of the German tradition of government, and there is so far little sign of fundamental change in this respect. Indeed, political and constitutional changes since 1945 have strengthened this tradition rather than weakened it. It means, therefore, that whilst officials in professional careers (in the British sense of 'professional') are not in any formal sense subordinate to their colleagues trained in law (who to the German way of thinking are just another species of professional), they do in fact in many areas of administration have only limited influence on the determination of major issues. To put it another way, their policy-making role is often marginal. This situation is found also at the level of the Laender administrations, and even in local government, where the structure is not dissimilar from that in British local authorities with their specialized principal officers, it is normal for the leading positions to be held by people with law qualifications.

It follows from what has just been said that the promotion prospects of non-legal specialists are not on the whole as good as those of the lawyer-administrator. Admittedly this is a generalization for which no statistical evidence is available. But it does appear that the technical official has more limited opportunities for rising above the position of head of a branch than his lawyer colleagues. Within Federal and Laender Departments relatively few of the sub-divisions and divisions are headed by technical specialists, and it is only in the decentralized agencies of the Ministries that such people have really good prospects of getting to the top positions. On the other hand, it has to be remembered that a few State Secretaries have been technically qualified specialists, and it is not unknown for Ministers too to rank as specialists in their own field.

Even if the majority of professional civil servants have less chance of occupying the leading positions than the lawyer-administrator, there is so far little evidence to show that they suffer from a sense of grievance on this account. There has in recent years been some complaint from scientists in universities and in independent, publicly financed research institutes about the frustrating effects of regulation and control imposed by Government Departments: this expresses to some extent the belief that the lawyer-administrator fails to understand the conditions in which research work must be carried out. But it is also worth noting that scientists have played a relatively modest part in the German public service since 1949. There is nothing corresponding to the Scientific Civil Service in Britain. This reflects the fact that in the post-war years the employment of scientists by and on behalf of the Government has been on a relatively small scale. Expenditure on research and development, particularly for military purposes, has been much lower than in many other countries. The absence of a large aircraft and guided-missile programme is just one example of this. Thus the problems involved in the large-scale employment of scientific manpower by the Government have so far claimed little attention in the Federal Republic. As the Government expands its support for civil and military research work, the technological need for which is now emphasized more frequently, so the problems of ensuring fruitful co-operation between scientists and administrators may become more acute. But up to the present time there are no obvious grounds for concluding that the non-legal professional civil servants as a body are seriously discontented with their situation. Certainly there has been no widespread and public complaint about the neglect of technical considerations by general administrators unfamiliar with the problems faced by their technical colleagues.

9. CONCLUSIONS

The professional and technical staffs in the German public service are fully integrated in the higher grade of the public service. There is nothing resembling the splitting-up into separate classes and groups with which we are familiar in Britain.[1] Nor is there any formal distinction drawn between people who have mainly administrative functions and those who have more specialized work for which the appropriate technical or scientific qualifications are required. As already noted there are no differences in all the basic conditions of service, including salaries: all these matters are standardized throughout the public service, subject to certain local variations and additions. Thus, for example, a civil engineering director in the Ministry of Transport, a general administrative officer of similar rank in the Ministry of the Interior, and a Counsellor in the London Embassy might all be at the same point on a standardized salary scale, subject to variations with respect to local allowances, foreign service allowances, housing facilities, etc.

At what can be called the working level—and this is to a large extent outside the sphere of the Federal Ministries—the technical and professional official carries considerable weight. There is a very strong commitment to subject specialization, and full recognition of the need to use specialized knowledge and skill wherever the services to be provided call for it. Indeed, so strong is the commitment to subject specialization in the training of staff, that there is little doubt that in all branches of the higher grade of the public service it leads to a certain neglect of training in management methods, personnel relations and new operational techniques. The system is in some respects too narrowly professionalized.

[1] It is worth noting that there is nothing like the host of separate Civil Service trade unions which have grown up in Britain. Effectively there is one German Civil Service Union, the powerful Deutscher Beamtenbund which civil servants (*Beamten*) of all ranks and professions may join.

But in assessing the position of specialists one should not underestimate the prestige and influence of the administrator trained in law. At the Federal level he remains dominant, controlling the bulk of the key posts in Federal administration. At many other levels he is also in a powerful position, particularly in posts with functions of co-ordination and general direction. In local government, for example, despite the fact that technical staffs have a big part to play, the head of local administration is nearly always a lawyer by training, whether he be a permanent official or an elected chief executive.

In fact the Germans would probably be perplexed by the British preoccupation with the relations between non-specialist administrators and public servants with scientific, technical or other professional qualifications. In the German context all higher officials can be regarded as specialists of one kind or another, their knowledge and training being related to the kind of service they are providing and the type of functions they have. That the lawyer-specialist bulks so large in general administration reflects a particular view of the terms on which public authorities should act. There is a political explanation for his role, just as there is a political explanation for the presence of the non-specialized general administrator in Britain.

SWEDEN

1. INTRODUCTION

At first sight, the Swedish Civil Service could well appear to consist *entirely* of professionals. Leafing through the *Sveriges Statskalender*, the enquirer notes some professional tag to almost every name. In practice, however, the distinction between professionals and generalists is readily understood. The Federation of Civil Servants stresses, for example, that its membership includes not only 'salaried employees with purely administrative functions' but also 'officials with exacting duties in the technical field' such as highways, research and public building.[1] The generalists have hitherto been mainly recruited from graduates in law—the jurists, as they will be called in this report. 'For general administration a legal training has on the whole always been preferred.'[2] This gives the Swedish legal profession a completely different structure from that of Great Britain. The young jurist has three main careers to choose between: the Civil Service, the judiciary, and private practice. The first of these is numerically the most important.

TABLE 1
STRUCTURE OF THE LEGAL PROFESSION IN SWEDEN, 1960[3]

Civil Service	3,383
Judiciary	1,518
Private practice	1,435
Other employment	1,575
Total	7,911

Just as civil servants predominate in the legal profession, so do jurists dominate the Civil Service.

[1] *A Guide to the Federation of Civil Servants in Sweden and its Activities*, Stockholm, 1964.

[2] N. Andren, *Modern Swedish Government*, Stockholm, 1961, p. 126.

[3] *Folkräkningen den 1 November 1960*, Statistiska Centralbyrån, Stockholm, 1964, Table 54; *Statistisk Årsbok 1965*, Statitiska Centralbyrån, Stockholm, 1965, Table 335; *Tjänstemän inom Statlig och Statsunderstödd Verksamhet År 1964*, Statistiska Centralbyrån, Stockholm, 1966, Tables 12a & b.
N.B. The Civil Service figure relates to 1964.

TABLE 2
DISTRIBUTION OF CIVIL SERVANTS BETWEEN SALARY SCALES A AND B, OCTOBER 1, 1964[1]

Professional group	Salary scale A			Salary scale B			Total	
	No.	Percentage of salary scale	Percentage of professional group	No.	Percentage of salary scale	Percentage of professional group	No.	Percentage of salary scales A+B
Jurists	2,271	2·2	68	1,088	25·1	32	3,359	3·2
Technologists (including graduate engineers and architects)	2,469	2·4	72	937	21·6	28	3,406	3·2
Doctors	1,468	1·4	76	458	10·6	24	1,926	1·8
Economists	533	0·5	86	84	1·9	14	617	0·6
Others	94,698	93·4	98	1,773	40·8	2	96,471	91·2
Totals	101,439	99·9		4,340	100·0		105,779	100·0

[1] *Statistisk Årsbok* 1965, Tables 234 and 235; *Tjänstemän inom Statlig och Statsunderstödd Vertsamhet År* 1964, p. 31.

Scales A and B comprehend the great majority of established, salaried civil servants, scale B being the more senior. It is noteworthy that, whereas the jurists constitute only 3·2 per cent of both scale-groups, and hold only 2·2 per cent of the relatively junior scale A posts, they fill almost a third (32 per cent) of the more senior scale B positions. There is some justification for this, both historical and functional. In the past, law was the only suitable course for the would-be administrator. Moreover, administrative work in Sweden consists largely in 'finding out what is valid law and deciding on administrative appeals'.[1]

In recent years graduates in other fields have been more to the front, particularly social scientists.

TABLE 3
ACTUAL AND ESTIMATED PROPORTIONS OF JURISTS, SOCIAL SCIENTISTS AND ECONOMISTS WITHIN MINISTRIES (OTHER THAN THE MINISTRIES OF JUSTICE AND FOREIGN AFFAIRS), 1950–80[2]

Professional Group	Number				Proportion per cent			
	1950	1960	1970	1980	1950	1960	1970	1980
Jurists	192	219	259	304	84	71	67	65
Social scientists	30	45	78	112	13	15	20	24
Economists	5	45	50	51	3	15	13	11

Even allowing for the tenfold increase in the number of economists during the period 1950–70, it is clear that jurists will remain the most important single group in the Swedish higher Civil Service during the foreseeable future.

Professional civil servants in Sweden might be defined, as in Great Britain, as members of professions serving in the central administration on duties closely connected with their special qualifications. The main groups are much the same in the two countries: architects, engineers, draughtsmen, doctors, economists, scientists, land and quantity surveyors, etc. They are employed both in administrative and in advisory positions.

2. RECRUITMENT

In recruiting their civil servants, 'European countries fall neatly into two categories; those which recruit personnel by competitive

---

[1] N. Andren, op. cit., p. 126.
[2] *Tendenskalkyler över det Framtida Behovet av Jurister, Samhällsvetare, Civilekonomer*, Arbetsmarknadstyrelsens Prognosinstitut, Stockholm, 1964, Tables 2.4 and 2.5.

written examinations, and those which recruit them by a comparison of the paper qualifications already possessed by the candidate.'[1] Britain does not, in practice, fit neatly into either category. Whilst most generalists have hitherto been recruited by the former method, she uses the latter for professionals. This makes for easier comparison in the present context with Sweden, which uses the second method for both groups. The normal procedure is for Ministries and boards to advertise vacancies as and when they occur, specifying any particular qualifications required. Qualifications and references are studied, and selected candidates may be interviewed. Under this system, the successful candidate need not necessarily come from a lower level in the hierarchy. He may not even be a civil servant.[2] But in some cases, the requirement that posts should be advertised is held to be satisfied by an announcement in the internal staff bulletin, which is, of course, only seen by civil servants. This promotes movement between one administrative body and another but does not bring in outsiders. Some very senior posts—e.g. heads of bureaux in the Board of Building Works—are not advertised at all, but filled directly by promotion.

This pattern of recruitment smacks somewhat of a buyers' market, implying as it does a passive role on the employer's part. But in Sweden, as elsewhere, there is in fact a sellers' market in professional labour. Qualified people may approach Ministries and boards even if no vacancies have been advertised. Public bodies themselves approach individuals, prompting them to apply for posts. Such measures are necessary because really promising candidates find the Civil Service less attractive than in the past. It may be true that 'State service has . . . the traditional advantage of giving a certain social prestige'[3] but that prestige is constantly declining. Social benefits, such as longer holidays and higher pensions, are still better in the Civil Service than in private employment, but the gap is continually diminishing. Security of tenure loses some of its appeal in an age of full employment, especially if the price that has to be paid for it is a lower income.

The recruitment system outlined here may seem to carry with it the risk of favouritism to certain individuals, as compared with competitive examinations. A special feature of Swedish govern-

[1] B. Chapman, *The Profession of Government*, 1959, p. 83.
[2] Op. cit., p. 168.
[3] N. Andren, op. cit. p. 128.

ment exists, however, which reduces this risk to the minimum. There is a provision in the constitution that public documents are to be open for public inspection, except where considerations such as national security are involved. This principle provides a guarantee against arbitrary appointment. Unsuccessful applicants for a post can inspect the documents in the case, and appeal against the decision if there appear to be any grounds for doing so. 'In the great majority of cases the appeal is unsuccessful, but this is largely because the knowledge that publication and appeal is possible means that there are very few indefensible decisions.'[1]

3. PAY

A system in which each Ministry and board recruits its staff separately might seem to destroy any possibility of unity in the service. Before showing why this is not the case, it is worth pointing out the advantage the system can have to the recruit—provided he is well qualified and full employment prevails. Since he is not dependent on one central body for his chance to enter the Civil Service, 'he is free—if he can—to play off one Ministry against another; a candidate with good qualifications should have little difficulty in finding a post suitable to his talents'.[2] However, that is rather by the way. What brings unity in diversity is the common pay scale. Of the two prevailing European patterns,[3] Britain adheres to one with classes common to the whole service, while Sweden exemplifies the other, with posts classified according to pay scales common to the entire service. This is shown in Table 4. It should be borne in mind that the exchange rate is 14·4 Swedish kronor to the pound. The existence of these common scales creates a strong bond of interest between professionals working in one board with their opposite numbers elsewhere in the public service—and indeed with other civil servants generally.

Professionals may also be paid on contract terms, usually for a period of five or six years. Some hundreds of graduate engineers, and a number of doctors, are at present serving on these terms. Officials employed on contract lack the status of a civil servant—

[1] B. Chapman, op. cit., p. 84.
[2] Op. cit., pp. 83–4.
[3] Op. cit., p. 75.

TABLE 4
SALARY SCALES APPLICABLE TO SWEDISH PROFESSIONAL CIVIL SERVANTS AT JANUARY 1, 1966[1]

Point on scale A	Salary scale A Monthly salary with regional variations			Point on scale B	Salary scale B Monthly salary
	3	4	5	B	
A	kr.	kr.	kr.		kr.
1	866	921	975	1	4,040
2	911	967	1,025	2	4,255
3	960	1,022	1,079	3	4,480
4	1,009	1,074	1,136	4	4,717
5	1,066	1,129	1,196	5	4,967
				6	5,230
6	1,122	1,190	1,262	7	5,508
7	1,181	1,255	1,327		
8	1,240	1,318	1,395		
9	1,306	1,388	1,470		
10	1,378	1,465	1,550		
11	1,450	1,540	1,633		
12	1,534	1,629	1,718		
13	1,627	1,718	1,808		
14	1,722	1,813	1,906		
15	1,820	1,913	2,005		
16	1,928	2,020	2,112		
17	2,038	2,130	2,223		
18	2,159	2,251	2,341		
19	2,284	2,374	2,465		
20	2,417	2,506	2,596		

Point on scale A	Salary scale A			Point on scale C	Salary scale C Monthly salary
21	2,559	2,646	2,733		
22	2,709	2,793	2,877		
23	2,867	2,949	3,029	C	kr.
24	3,029	3,110	3,191	1	5,616
25	3,206	3,282	3,360	2	5,897
26	3,391	3,466	3,538	3	6,251
27	3,590	3,658	3,725	4	6,689
28	3,800	3,859	3,923	5	7,224
29	4,017	4,073	4,131	6	7,873
30	4,250	4,299	4,350	7	8,661
31	4,493	4,534	4,580	8	9,613
32	4,750	4,784	4,822		

[1] Data supplied by the Swedish Confederation of Professional Associations.

e.g. security of tenure—but enjoy higher salaries. For example, an architect holding a B6 post in the Board of Building Works transferred to contract at point C1 on the salary scale in 1965. The whole trend reflects the need of the Civil Service to compete actively with private employers, and with private practice, for the best staff. Contract service is increasingly popular, and the number of professionals employed on such terms is likely to grow.

Superannuation

Thirty years' service qualifies a civil servant for full pension. The scheme tends to obstruct mobility of professionals in and out of the Civil Service. A man who leaves for private employment after, say, twenty years, is at a disadvantage when the time comes to fix his pension on retirement. However, the difficulty is declining year by year, since a reform of 1960 brought the pension arrangements for all workers up to a level close to that which civil servants already enjoyed.

4. TRAINING

The professional civil servant needs training for two distinct purposes. Firstly, he must keep abreast of new developments in his special field. If he fails to do so, he will gradually cease to be, in any real sense, a member of his profession. Year by year it will become more difficult to move out into private employment or private practice, should he wish to do so. With rare exceptions, the Civil Service takes no responsibility for training its professionals in this sense. Where, however, appropriate courses are arranged by professional associations or universities, professional civil servants may be given the opportunity to attend.

Secondly, the professional needs training in every aspect of his Civil Service job. Without it, he is likely to be at a disadvantage as compared with his generalist colleagues when it comes to promotion. Training in this sense has hitherto been the responsibility of each Ministry or board, so far as its own staff was concerned. Recently, however, a start has been made in providing centralized courses, and the trend seems likely to develop. This kind of training has mainly benefited the less well qualified professionals—e.g. technical and scientific assistants—who are enabled by its aid to qualify in considerable numbers for promotion to posts which would otherwise be filled by graduates. The graduates themselves are less well catered for, and there seems to be a real need for training of this kind at an appropriate level.

5. THE PLACE OF PROFESSIONALS IN THE SWEDISH CIVIL SERVICE

Swedish central administration has a unique character. It is based on the 'Ministry and board' pattern. Traces of this system still exist in Britain—for example, the Treasury and the revenue boards—and as late as the early nineteenth century it was of considerable importance here. The only exception to the rule in Sweden is the Ministry of Foreign Affairs. That apart, the staff of the typical Ministry (*departement*) is very small—normally less than 100—with a group of attached boards, whose staffs run into thousands.

TABLE 5

STAFFS OF SWEDISH MINISTRIES AND BOARDS, 1964[1]

Ministry	Ministry staff	Staff of attached boards
Justice	112	5,981
Defence	69	41,238
Social Welfare	77	24,173
Interior	62	15,025
Communications	82	8,880
Finance	197	6,588
Church and Education	102	26,377
Agriculture	49	6,229
Commerce	75	1,564
Civil Service Affairs	64	274

Swedish Ministries function almost entirely as policy-planning staffs. Only exceptionally do they handle routine administration. The staff of the Ministry constitute a small group of advisers to the Minister. Although boards draft their own budgets, only the Ministry can present the estimates to Parliament. The Ministries have a similar monopoly of introducing legislative proposals.

The main task of the boards, on the other hand, is to deal with routine administrative work, including inspection and control of subordinate offices, local agencies and officials. They are free within wide limits to interpret the statutes and decrees for whose

[1] *Tjänstemän inom Statlig och Statsunderstödd Verksamhet År 1964*, Statistika Centralbyrån. Stockholm, 1966.

application they are responsible. Some of the boards act as administrative courts of appeal.[1]

Broadly speaking, the Ministries are staffed by generalists. It is in the boards that professionals are mainly to be found. It is natural to ask whether the latter feel aggrieved at their exclusion from the Ministries. Generally this does not appear to be the case. There seems to be some difficulty in appreciating the importance of advisory posts in the British scheme of things. If the Minister *wants* advice, it is assumed he will turn to an appropriate advisory council, or to the interest groups in relevant fields. If, on the other hand, an interested group wants to urge advice on a Minister, it seems to be taken for granted that it will always be able to gain his ear. There seemed to be a near universal confidence that expert views would always be heard and given due weight. An extreme case is that of the nursing profession. There is no post comparable with that of Chief Nursing Officer in the British Ministry of Health. But the consultative status held by the nurses' association is such that they feel certain that they will be informed of every relevant development in public policy and given the chance to express their views before action is taken. The one exception to this was the engineering profession, whose spokesmen considered there should be more technologists in the Ministries, because politicians cannot understand the technical considerations on which policy decisions now so often depend.

6. COMPARISONS

The Swedish Civil Service is not so different from that of Britain as to make comparisons impossible, nor so much like it as to make them easy. To simplify matters, four groups have been chosen for special study, namely doctors, graduate engineers, architects and economists. Salary comparisons with Britain would be complex and probably not very fruitful; it would be necessary to take into account such factors as the difference in the cost of living, and the impact of taxation in the two countries. A more profitable line of enquiry is to investigate how the salaries of professional civil servants compare firstly with those

[1] These two paragraphs are based on: N. Andren, op. cit., pp. 113–20; B. Chapman, op. cit., pp. 18–19 and 49–51; and D. A. Rustow, *The Politics of Compromise*, Princeton, N.J., 1955, p. 176.

of other civil servants and secondly with the salaries and incomes of members of their professions outside the Civil Service. Information on these points is contained in the discussion which follows.

Doctors as Professional Civil Servants in Sweden

At October 1, 1964, there were 2,042 doctors in the Civil Service, as compared with 7,398 economically active doctors in the entire population in 1960.[1] But differences of classification make comparisons with Britain difficult. More than half the total are on the staff of a number of State hospitals. Doctors serving in positions analogous to those held by professional civil servants in this country are not more than a few hundred.

The central administration of health in Sweden is indicated in the following diagram:

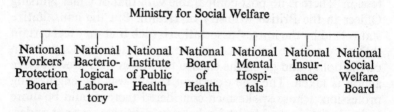

Ministry for Social Welfare

| National Workers' Protection Board | National Bacterio- logical Labora- tory | National Institute of Public Health | National Board of Health | National Mental Hospi- tals | National Insur- ance | National Social Welfare Board |

In 1964, there were twenty-six jurists and no doctors among the forty-two senior members of staff of the Ministry for Social Affairs. In the National Board of Health, on the other hand, the General Director and four of the ten heads of bureaux were doctors. (The Deputy Director and three heads of bureaux were jurists.)[2] However, a new pattern of central health administration is expected to come into effect shortly, in which the Board of Health is to be merged with the Social Welfare Board. In the new system, doctors would as a rule be ousted from administrative posts and become advisers. They would be subordinate to the chief administrative officers.[3]

The salaries of higher Civil Servants in Sweden have been rising steadily in recent years, as is shown in Table 6.

[1] *Tjänstemän inom Statlig och Statunderstödd Verksamhet År* 1964, Statistika Centralbyrån, Stockholm, 1966, Tables 12a & b; *Statistisk Årsbok* 1965, Statistiska Centralbyrån, Stockholm, 1965, Table 335.

[2] *Sveriges Statskalender,* 1964.

[3] 'Medicinal och socialstyrelserna sammanslas till ett verk', in *Fran Departement och Namnder,* Vol. 27, 1965, p. 368.

SWEDEN 161

AVERAGE MONTHLY SALARY OF SWEDISH HIGHER CIVIL SERVANTS, OCTOBER 1957–OCTOBER 1964*

Year	Number of Individuals	Average monthly salary (Swedish kronor)	Index
1957	19,873	2,116	100
1958	21,125	2,177	103
1959	21,956	2,215	105
1960	23,147	2,377	112
1961	24,351	2,505	118
1962	26,002	2,767	131
1963	27,802	2,881	136
1964	29,947	3,014	142

Although they have shared in the general trend, doctors in the Civil Service have done less well than other comparable groups. Table 7 illustrates this point.

TABLE 7
INDEX OF MEAN SALARIES OF SELECTED GROUPS OF HIGHER CIVIL SERVANTS IN SWEDEN, 1957–64*

Profession	1957	1958	1959	1960	1961	1962	1963	1964	Average annual increase per cent
Jurists	100	103	107	117	124	140	147	154	6·4
Doctors	100	99	100	107	114	124	130	135	4·4
Engineers	100	104	107	115	124	140	146	154	6·4
Economists	100	103	107	117	124	139	148	156	6·6
All groups	100	103	105	112	118	131	136	142	5·1

What the difference has meant in cash is shown in Table 8.

TABLE 8
AVERAGE MONTHLY SALARIES OF DOCTORS IN THE SWEDISH CIVIL SERVICE, COMPARED WITH OTHER SELECTED GROUPS, OCTOBER 1957–OCTOBER 1964*

Year	Doctors		Jurists		Higher civil servants generally	
	Individuals in sample	Average monthly salary kr.	Individuals in sample	Average monthly salary kr.	Individuals in sample	Average monthly salary kr.
1957	977	2,428	2,821	2,228	19,873	2,116
1958	1,257	2,403	2,890	2,296	21,125	2,177
1959	1,361	2,429	2,871	2,379	21,956	2,215
1960	1,383	2,607	2,914	2,603	23,147	2,377
1961	1,537	2,769	2,987	2,763	24,351	2,505
1962	1,648	3,021	3,062	3,112	26,002	2,767
1963	1,742	3,156	3,110	3,268	27,802	2,881
1964	1,924	3,277	3,147	3,441	29,947	3,014

* Data supplied by the Swedish Confederation of Professional Associations

L

The decline in the differential enjoyed by doctors over other higher civil servants a decade ago relates only to basic pay. In addition, the great majority receive special allowances, which have risen considerably over the last few years.

Engineers as Professional Civil Servants in Sweden
At October 1, 1964, there were 3,452 technologists (including graduate engineers and architects) in the Civil Service. This figure may be compared with the total of 15,659 economically active technologists in the entire population in 1960.[1] Within central Government, the most important employers of graduate engineers and architects (the two professions are usually lumped together for statistical purposes) are: Land Survey Administration (361), National Power Administration (274), National Road Board (220), National Telecommunications Administration (207), National Patent and Registration Office (162).

As an example of a central Government department concerned with technology, the Ministry of Communications may be taken.

Ministry of Communications
(*Kommunikationsdepartementet*)

| National Commission for Road Transport | Swedish Geotechnical Institute | National Board of Shipping and Navigation | National Road Research Institute |

| National Board of Building | Local Pilotage and Lighthouse Organization | Swedish Meteorological and Hydrological Institute | National Road Board |

Of forty-five members of the senior staff of the Ministry in 1964, twenty-seven were jurists as against two who were engineers: though admittedly one of these headed one of the four bureaux into which the Ministry's work was divided. In the National Road Board, on the other hand, they provided the Deputy Director and five of the nine heads of bureaux.[2]

[1] *Tjänstemän inom Statlig och Statunderstödd Verksamhet År* 1964, Statistika Centralbyrån, Stockholm, 1966, Tables 12a & b; *Statistisk Årsbok* 1964, Statistiska Centralbyrån, Stockholm, 1965, Table 335.
[2] *Sveriges Statskalender*, 1964.

Graduate engineers are well paid in relation to other civil servants of comparable qualifications. This is brought out by their distribution within salary scale A.

TABLE 9
SELECTED GROUPS OF SWEDISH PROFESSIONAL CIVIL
SERVANTS IN SALARY SCHEME A[1]

Point on scale	Jurists	Doctors	Graduate Engineers and Architects	Economists
1–4	–	–	–	–
5–8	2	–	2	–
9–10	1	4	4	1
11–12	1	1	1	1
13–14	1	1	–	1
15–16	2	12	12	4
17–18	315	149	19	41
19–20	299	103	159	42
21–22	408	173	544	53
23–24	432	614	377	173
25–27	810	411	1,351	217
Totals	2,271	1,468	2,469	533

More than half the graduate engineers (including here architects also) were at the top three points of the scale, as compared with only 36 per cent of the jurists. Less than 2 per cent of the former were below A19 on the scale, in contrast with 14 per cent of the latter.

It appears, however, that jurists secure a greater proportion of the highest paid posts (i.e. those on scales B and C), since if the incomes of all higher civil servants are analysed, and not merely those on scale A, the engineers' advantage is less striking.

Over a number of years, the Swedish Confederation of Professional Associations has conducted regular enquiries into the earnings of professional civil servants. The salaries of the engineering group may be compared with those of all higher civil servants in the sample, and with those of jurists.

It will be seen that the engineers maintained a lead (sometimes small) over the jurists throughout the period, and that they received at all times substantially higher salaries than the general run of higher civil servants.

By comparison with their professional colleagues in other

[1] *Statistisk Årsbok* 1965, Tables 234 and 235.

TABLE 10
AVERAGE MONTHLY SALARIES OF SWEDISH HIGHER CIVIL
SERVANTS, OCTOBER 1957–OCTOBER 1964[1]

Year	Jurists		Engineers		Higher civil servants	
	Individuals in sample	Average monthly salary kr.	Individuals in sample	Average monthly salary kr.	Individuals in sample	Average monthly salary kr.
1957	2,821	2,228	2,941	2,268	19,873	2,116
1958	2,890	2,296	2,954	2,354	21,125	2,177
1959	2,871	2,379	2,910	2,420	21,956	2,215
1960	2,914	2,603	3,030	2,612	23,147	2,377
1961	2,987	2,763	2,993	2,823	24,351	2,505
1962	3,062	3,112	3,058	3,180	26,002	2,767
1963	3,110	3,268	3,155	3,319	27,802	2,881
1964	3,147	3,441	3,374	3,485	29,947	3,014

forms of employment, on the other hand, Civil Service engineers are less well off. In August 1965, the Sveriges Civilingenjorsforbund[2] conducted an investigation into the monthly salaries of 7,214 graduate engineers, of whom 1,777 were in the Civil Service, 490 in local government service, and 4,791 in private employment. (No information appears to be available about the income of engineers in private practice.) The results show that, while newly qualified engineers start with much the same salaries whether in private employment or the Civil Service, after twenty years, the median salary of the former group is almost 30 per cent higher than that of the latter.

A professional association of engineers conducted an enquiry into the salaries received by its members in order to discover which employers of engineers paid best in 1965. The investigation covered sixty employers. It is notable that no public body appears among the first thirty-nine in rank order. Thereafter the sequence is as follows:

Rank order	Name
40	Board of Telecommunications
41	Air Force
47	Defence Research
50	National Road Board
56	Army
57	Navy
58	National Patent and Registration Office
59	National Land Survey Board
60	Geographical Survey Office

[1] Data supplied by the Swedish Confederation of Professional Associations.
[2] The term *civilingenjor* should be translated 'graduate engineer', not 'civil engineer'.

Admittedly, the greater security of public service, together with the pension provisions, longer holidays, etc., go some way towards making up for lower salaries. All the same, it is hard to see how enough engineers of a sufficiently high standard can be recruited against such strong competition from the private sector.

Architects in the Swedish Civil Service
The place of architects in the Swedish Civil Service may be illustrated by reference to the National Board of Building, one of the dependencies of the Ministry of Communications. There are no architects in the Ministry. Although the Director General of the Board was not, in 1964, an architect, the profession was strongly represented in the highest posts. The Board was split into two divisions, one headed by an architect, the other by a land surveyor. Six of ten chiefs of bureaux were architects, and one was a graduate engineer; only one was a jurist. In all, the Board employs 116 architects. The Board maintains an office, headed by an architect, in every seat of provincial government throughout the country.

Little information is available about the incomes of architects. It appears from Table 9, where they are classed with graduate engineers, that they are well paid in comparison with other civil servants, except perhaps in the very highest reaches of the service.

A qualitative assessment was offered by an architect holding a senior post in the National Board of Building. In his view, incomes from private practice were high in comparison with the Civil Service, but the salaries of privately employed architects were lower. A few years' experience in the Board was valuable to the young architect, since he got the chance to make useful contacts. Thereafter, many left to set up their own practices. Perhaps he was generalizing from his own experience. As a young man he was in the Board. Then he spent a number of years in practice, returning eventually to public service in the Stockholm city administration. Now he is back in the Board as deputy director of the Planning Bureau.

Economists as Professional Civil Servants in Sweden
At October 1, 1964, there were 649 economists in the Civil Service, as compared with 4,981 economically active economists

in the entire population.[1] Economists as a professional group in Sweden are fed from two distinct sources. On the one hand are those who graduate with degrees in Economics from the universities. On the other are the 'business economists' (*civilekonomer*) who have been educated in business schools of university rank. Discussion of their role in the Civil Service is complicated by the fact that some of the statistics refer to economists in general, and others to 'business economists' only.

Their status in the central administration may be illustrated by reference to the Ministry of Commerce and the boards attached to it.

Ministry of Commerce
(*Handelsdepartementet*)

Geological Survey of Sweden	National Institute for Handicrafts and Industry	National Institute for Consumer Information	Board of Trade
National Patent and Registration Office	National Price and Cartel Office	National Institute for Materials Testing	National Board Economic Defence

TABLE 11

AVERAGE MONTHLY SALARIES OF ECONOMISTS IN THE SWEDISH, CIVIL SERVICE, COMPARED WITH OTHER GROUPS
OCTOBER 1957–OCTOBER 1964

Year	Economists		Jurists		Higher civil servants generally	
	Individuals in sample	Average monthly salary kr.	Individuals in sample	Average monthly salary kr.	Individuals in sample	Average monthly salary kr.
1957	479	2,028	2,821	2,228	19,873	2,116
1958	495	2,088	2,890	2,296	21,125	2,177
1959	494	2,173	2,871	2,379	21,956	2,215
1960	534	2,373	2,914	2,603	23,147	2,377
1961	591	2,521	2,987	2,763	24,351	2,505
1962	604	2,825	3,062	3,112	26,002	2,767
1963	603	2,992	3,110	3,268	27,802	2,881
1964	638	3,159	3,147	3,441	29,947	3,014

[1] *Tjänstemän inom Statlig och Statsunderstödd Verksamhet År* 1964, Statistiska Centralbyrån, Stockholm, 1966, Tables 12a & b; *Folkrakningen den November* 1, 1960, Statistiska Centralbyrån, Stockholm, Table 52.

TABLE 12

SWEDISH CIVIL SERVANTS' SALARIES CLASSIFIED BY AGE GROUPS, OCTOBER 1965[1]

Age group	Jurists		Doctors		Graduate Engineers		Economists	
	Individuals in sample	Average monthly salary kr.	Individuals in sample	Average monthly salary kr.	Individuals in sample	Average monthly salary kr.	Individuals in sample	Average monthly salary kr.
20–29	487	2,279	395	2,453	684	2,690	100	2,496
30–39	805	2,997	738	3,089	921	3,293	152	3,071
40–49	807	3,782	453	3,671	837	3,785	214	3,329
50–59	757	4,001	257	4,077	687	4,004	151	3,403
60 +	291	4,215	81	4,270	245	3,949	21	3,464
Totals	3,147		1,924		3,374		638	

[1] Data supplied by the Swedish Confederation of Professional Associations.

The staff of the Ministry, thirty in number, included in 1964 ten jurists and one economist, while two others had a double qualification in law and economics. Eight economists, by contrast, were to be found among the thirty-eight officials of National Price and Cartel Office.[1] None of these held high places in the hierarchy, but this may reflect the relative newness of the profession of economist rather than any desire to keep such specialists in lowly situations.

It is clear that economists have improved their position in relation to higher civil servants generally during the last decade. In 1957, they were less well paid, but since 1961 have been steadily drawing ahead. As compared with jurists, on the other hand, their salaries were consistently lower throughout the period.

This disadvantage does not apply to all age groups, however. In the two lowest age groups, economists earn more than jurists. But between 40 and 49 the latter overtake them, and from 50 onwards jurists are very much better paid than economists—perhaps because the latter, belonging to a newer profession, have had less time to work their way up to the most highly paid posts.

Economists in the Civil Service are less well paid than those in the private sector.

TABLE 13
SALARIES OF ECONOMISTS (*CIVILEKONOMER*)
PER MONTH, 1965[2]

Age group	Civil Service		Private sector	
	Individuals in sample	Average salary	Individuals in sample	Average salary
20–29	93	2,600	540	2,824
30–39	134	3,423	1,051	4,433
40–49	167	3,792	674	6,075
50–59	94	4,063	252	6,825
60+	3	3,177	66	7,985
Totals	491		2,583	

Although the two groups start more or less level, those in private employment draw ahead immediately, and with each decade the gap widens. The very small number of civil servants in the highest age group presumably invalidates comparisons, but it is

[1] *Sveriges Statskalender, 1964.*
[2] Data supplied by Allmanna Tjanstemannaforbund: civilekonomsektionen.

noteworthy that their average salaries were less than half those of their opposite numbers in the private sector.

7. ORGANIZATION OF PROFESSIONAL CIVIL SERVANTS IN SWEDEN

Professionals in the Swedish Civil Service are organized on two contradictory principles, horizontal and vertical, which may be likened to the 'craft' and 'industrial' patterns among manual workers. The more highly qualified and best paid officials generally adhere to associations which are open to all members of their professions. Some of the most important of these from the present point of view, with their membership at January 1, 1966, are:

National Association of Swedish Architects	1,830
Swedish Association of Graduate Engineers	11,289
Swedish Federation of Jurists	7,442
Swedish Medical Association	9,084
Swedish Association of Natural Scientists	968

It is particularly interesting to note that jurists holding general administrative posts in the Civil Service belong to the same association as practising lawyers and judges. These associations, and many others, are affiliated to the Swedish Confederation of Professional Associations, SACO, which is, broadly speaking, a union of graduates of universities or other institutions of equal rank. The Confederation claims to have organized about 80 per cent of the potential membership, and the process is continuing. For example, the association of 'business economists' (*civilekonomer*) is at the present small, with 400 members at January 1, 1966. In spite of the name they give themselves in English translation, they are all in the Civil Service. The association believes, however, that it is on the point of breaking through into the much larger private sector of their profession.

SACO admits that the vertical principle of labour organization has in general replaced the horizontal, and that it is more suitable for manual and some white-collar workers. It maintains, however, that professional workers have different needs. The most natural and efficient way, they argue, for professional people to protect their interests is through associations whose members all have the same profession or the same university degree, irrespective of whether they are in private practice or are employed and irrespective of who their employers may be. Horizontal organization leads to solidarity and strength even in quite small professions. In a vertical union, on the other hand, graduates form only a small minority. In collective bargaining, there will always be a danger that the interests of that small minority will be sacrificed in order to reach agreement.

Professional workers, moreover, require their associations to be something more than trade unions. Over and above salaries and conditions of work, they must concern themselves with a great many questions, such as professional education at the under- graduate and postgraduate level. Clearly a horizontal union can serve these needs of its members far more efficiently than a vertical one. It is true that there could be dual organizations, one for professional matters, the other a trade union. But professional questions have an intimate connection with purely trade union questions. It is therefore natural and proper for professional associations to function as trade unions also.

Professional civil servants at a rather lower level, such as draughtsmen, architectural and scientific assistants, mostly belong to the Federation of Civil Servants, which is organized almost entirely on vertical lines. It sets out to organize all salaried officials irrespective of education and salary grade, maintaining that in order to gain influence, civil servants must display solidarity. It is opposed to any organization which bases itself on the belief that civil servants with a certain educational standard ought to protect their special interests in a separate grouping. Although the vertical principle of organization has had a good deal of success in some quarters—for example, the State Power Board—the Federation now seems to accept in practice that most professional civil servants of graduate level will adhere to SACO and that its own role will be to organize those of lower qualifications, along with salaried civil servants employed on general administrative duties.

The primary units of the Federation are associations—about eighty in number—the great majority of which represent the civil servants employed under one central authority, typically, one of the administrative boards. The Federation, in turn, is affiliated to the Central Organization of Salaried Employees, TCO. Within TCO, a special section exists to co-ordinate action between civil servants and other groups of State employees, such as primary school teachers and police.

Civil servants have long enjoyed the right to organize and to bargain collectively, although formally and juridically the decision on their salaries and terms of employment rested entirely with the Government. The sovereign employer was supposed only to hear the views and suggestions of the employee organization before making his decisions. In practice, the hearings became indistinguishable from wage negotiations, in which the Civil Service Minister represented the Government, and the results have invariably been confirmed by Parliament. In 1966, however, legislation came into force which gives civil servants a statutory right to negotiate and to strike similar to that of private employees. To supplement this development, a Basic Peace Agreement between the Government and the organized civil servants was provisionally concluded on September 3, 1963. This extends to the Civil Service wherever possible the pattern of freedom under responsibility which has been evolved in the private labour market and which has proved highly effective in maintaining industrial peace. On the side of the State, a new body, the Board for State Collective Agreements, has been set up under the Ministry of Civil Service Affairs, to carry on negotiations with the various associations of civil servants.

SACO itself negotiates annually with the Government on the size of the percentage increase in salary to be awarded in order to give its Civil Service members a share in the improved standard of living and to compensate them for the fall in the value of money. The constituent associations negotiate over such questions as changes of position on the salary scale, holidays, pensions and sickness benefits. No changes are made in the conditions of professional civil servants without their associations being consulted. Relations with the Government, as employer, have generally been good and it is usually possible to reach a compromise.

SACO has always maintained that these wage increases should take the form of a percentage of each individual salary. Other organizations have insisted, however, that the increase should take the form of a fixed sum which is the same for all employees or should be decided according to a sliding scale so as to give a higher percentage increase to the lower grades. This system had the result of reducing differentials. SACO has managed to get the percentage method more and more widely adopted. When salary scales for civil servants were revised in 1957, it was agreed that the difference between one grade and the next should always be 5·3 per cent of the lower salary, and that this difference should be maintained during subsequent revisions.

SACO is prepared to take a tough line when necessary in the defence of its members' interests. In 1951, it managed to reach an agreement with the Government which resulted in a considerable increase in salary for senior officials. The following year, when it was the turn of the middle grades, to which the majority of professional civil servants belong, it proved impossible for SACO to reach a satisfactory result by negotiation. Indeed, the Government would not even agree to unconditional negotiations without pre-arranged limitations. Strictly speaking, a strike of public officials was at the time illegal, but several hundred of them, including some professional civil servants, handed in their resignations as part of a co-ordinated plan. The State retaliated by announcing that the general salary increase of 15 per cent granted in 1952 should not be paid to members of an organization that had taken part in the campaign. SACO took counter-measures, including a blockade of all Civil Service posts.

Civil servants had to give at least a month's notice and before that time expired, the Prime Minister sent for representatives of SACO to discuss the matter. It was agreed that free negotiations should commence at once and that SACO's threatened measures should be suspended. After long negotiations, agreement was reached, the 15 per cent increase was paid and SACO's 'strike' and blockade was abandoned. The temper of Swedish professional associations can be judged by a quotation from an official handbook: 'It is always necessary to be well prepared for strike action, for, in the last analysis, it is the danger of a labour dispute that makes an employer disposed to make concessions.'[1]

The TCO Section of Central Government Employees, including a considerable number of professional civil servants, negotiates general salary increases for all its constituent groups, as well as changes in their general terms of employment including fringe benefits, and the revision of salary schedules through the upgrading of categories of posts. Unions of public employees have achieved considerable influence on the establishment of posts open for promotion and the principle governing promotion,

[1] *Swedish Professional Associations as Trade Unions*, SACO, Stockholm, 1959, p. 23.

thereby off-setting in part the rigidity of the salary system. The unions are regularly invited to discuss with the Ministries concerned any significant reorganization plans and devote on these occasions great attention to the establishment of new jobs for promotion. Similar efforts are made also in the annual revisions of the Government's salary schedules, which serve the primary purpose of upgrading categories of positions.

In 1954, TCO established a Statistical Committee to collect data which would be useful in wage negotiations. In central Government service, wage surveys had been compiled only occasionally at irregular intervals, but in 1961 regular wage surveys conforming with TCO rules were introduced by all unions belonging to the TCO Section of Central Government Employees, the unions co-operating in the preparation of a basic survey.

As in SACO, there is a latent strain of militancy in TCO. 'The unions feel that it is their preparedness for a possible conflict that determines their strength at the bargaining table.' Reserve funds stood at 399 kronor per member in 1961. The civil servants have been rapidly building up their reserves in preparation for their new legal status in which they now enjoy the right to strike.

In the autumn of 1966, the first Swedish Civil Service strike took place. Although it did not originate with professionals, some account of it may be of interest. Negotiations about teachers' salaries between SACO and the Board for State Collective Agreements broke down on October 7, 1966. Three days later, 1,200 teachers in universities and secondary schools went on strike. The Board replied with a lock-out of all teachers affiliated to SACO, amounting to more than 20,000. SACO's retort was to proclaim a general strike of all its Civil Service members for three days commencing October 24, 1966. A settlement was reached on November 5, 1966. SACO estimated the cost of the strike at 15 million kronor, whereas the gains should amount to 16·5 million kronor in the first year alone, quite apart from improvements in conditions to which it is not easy to give a cash value.

UNITED STATES

1. INTRODUCTION

The modern Federal Civil Service began with the passage of the Civil Service Act of 1883—the Pendleton Act. Agitation for the abolition of the 'spoils-system' of appointments to the Government service had, however, started at least two decades before this date, and the shock to the national conscience administered by the murder of President Garfield by a 'disappointed office seeker' resulted in the passage of the 1883 Act. The reformers had studied European Civil Service systems. The American consul in Paris reported, in 1863, on the French customs service and recommended that the u.s. adopt a similar system based on competitive examinations. The Joint Committee (of Congress) on Retrenchment produced a report in 1868 which reviewed extensively the Civil Service systems of China, England, France and Prussia. It included summaries of the opinions of over 400 American Government officials and it advocated reforms in the procedure for recruitment to the Government service. It condemned spoils and recommended that officers be selected after due examination by proper boards. The Committee's reforming Bill was, however, tabled. At the request of President Hayes (elected in 1876), Dorman B. Eaton prepared two reports, one on the British Civil Service, the other on the improvements which had been effected in the New York Customs House as a result of the introduction of competitive entry into that service.

By 1884, 10·5 per cent of the 131,208 Federal civil servants were under 'classified-merit" Civil Service rules. The percentage of employees thus covered continued to grow; 44·8 per cent of 208,000 by 1899; 60·6 per cent of 482,721 by 1914; 79·7 per cent of 559,579 by 1929 to 85·6 per cent of 2,527,960 by 1963. The progress has been steady over the years with only the early 'New Deal' years showing a substantial setback to reform. In 1932, 80·1 per cent were in the classified service, but in 1936 only 60·5 per cent of 824,259 were classified servants. The reason was the large number of spoils and temporary appointments made by Franklin Roosevelt to staff his new alphabetical agencies. Many of those appointed were 'blanketed in' in later years, so that when President Truman left the White House 86·3 per cent of 2,603,267 Federal civilian personnel were in the classified service.[1]

The open competitive system of selection provided by the Pendleton Act has been called the 'Americanization of a Foreign Invention' (primarily a British one). But the emphasis here should be Americanization, for the American variations on the model were more important than the model itself. The Congress which passed the Pendleton Act explicitly rejected the notion of a 'closed' career service with entry available only at the bottom. It also added an instruction that tests given for entrance should be practical in nature and related to the duties to be performed. These instructions undoubtedly reflected a fear of a closed bureaucracy, and the desire to maintain the democratic tradition in the Civil Service. The insistence on tests of a practical nature made it necessary for the Civil Service Commission, and in the present day for the departments and agencies, to write out detailed specifications of the nature of the duties to be performed by aspiring applicants for particular posts (and thereby to indicate what professional or technical skills are desirable); and to fill the posts so specified with those who have the professionally or academically appropriate qualifications and experience. A very great deal of effort is expended—in the opinion of some, far too much effort—on accurate job specification. A variety of tests, from general intelligence tests to the possession of a Ph.D in the appropriate field, are applied to make certain that the job so elaborately described is filled by the perfect applicant.

A general view which has frequently been advanced about the u.s. Federal Civil Service is that it is not a genuine Federal service, but a collection of departments, agencies, bureaux, programmes and activities, each of which seeks to find the most appropriate personnel for the attainment of its particular objectives. Though there may be a 'career' from the bottom (more likely the middle) to the top of a bureau, there is no career to the very top of an agency or department, for here the top 'civil servants' are still political appointees.

The insistence on 'lateral' entry, in addition to entry at the bottom, has at least two effects. It refreshes the bureaucracy

[1] All figures from *The Federal Government Service*, ed. Wallace S. Sayne, 2nd Edition, Prentice Hall Inc., 1965, pp. 41–3.

with new professional experience from outside; but it may well frustrate the career aspirations of those who see a 'lateral' entrant blocking their own promotion hopes. Also, it is doubtful what amount of refreshment results for the service as a whole. There is probably more personal advantage accruing to those who go in, out and in again than there is advantage to the service in stability and regularity of career expectation.

The Civil Service of the USA has not normally been the prestige occupation desired by the nation's best young graduates. In the 'New Deal' days it attracted many able young people; prospects in the private sector were dim, and for some there was too the excitement of being at the centre of great events. McCarthyism and low pay in the higher grades made the service highly unattractive in the 1950s, but the position is much improved today as a result of the Federal Salary Reform Act of 1962. There will always, however, be an inevitable ceiling set to the salary of even the highest civil servant, for Congressmen will not allow a bureaucrat nor even a Minister (with one or two exceptions) to be paid more than they pay themselves. This no doubt expresses their view of the relative importance of the people's representatives and the people's servants.

When one takes into account the services in the USA which the Federal Government does not administer, nor directly provide, it becomes clear that those that they do provide will, given the emphasis on practical tests, call upon the skills of very many who in other regimes would be called 'specialists'. The U.S. Government is not deeply involved in welfare matters and, Federal pensions apart, other important areas, e.g. unemployment benefits, are administered by State personnel. There is no national health service; education is not provided or supervised by the Federal Government; town and country planning is an aspiration as yet, and federally assisted housing activity is on a very modest scale. Much road building is federally assisted financially but States arrange for the actual construction. Inter-State air, rail, and bus transport is entirely private enterprise. The U.S. Government only produces and trades in electrical power in the Tennessee Valley. Natural gas and oil production are watched by Federal regulatory commissions, but the Government is not a producer. The inefficient postal services are entirely Federal but telephone and telegraph services are privately owned and operated.

What is left to the Federal Government service is by no means negligible, however. The Defence Department employs vast numbers of out-of-uniform personnel, in procurement, supply, storage, pay and personnel management, weapons evaluation, political analysis and general administration. The Department of the Interior is actively engaged in river and harbour improvements, water supply, hydro-electric installations, fish and wildlife and National Parks—to mention only a few of its activities. The Department of Agriculture is concerned with soil chemistry, seeds, farm prices and crop subsidies, farm machinery and agricultural education. The Forest Service (which has its own very tight merit system with *no* lateral entry) is a highly specialized corps of tree scientists and custodians of timber resources.

The difficulty has been to persuade Civil Service opinion that there is any place of importance for the general administrator with a non-specialized education or background in this well-established pattern of particular professional skills, but we must return to this theme later.

The picture of the higher Civil Service of the USA therefore is one of specialized, technically competent persons administering activities in which their specialist competence is regarded as a prerequisite to administrative efficiency. Where we come across 'generalist' administrators—those who do not claim or do not need special technical or scientific competence—we will find a large number of persons whose original, or postgraduate, training was in law.

2. THE U.S. CIVIL SERVICE TODAY

In June 1964, the Federal Government employed 2,126,570 persons all of whom had entered the service by some test or competition to assess their ability for the job they hold. Of this number 82 per cent were 'career' civil servants, i.e. they could if they wished stay in until they reached pensionable age; 13 per cent were 'career conditional', that is to say, a 'career' depends on the development of a particular programme, or of an agency or part of an agency; 5 per cent were temporary appointments. In addition to this figure of 2,126,570 some 217,709 persons are in government posts exempted from the provisions of Civil Service rules, e.g. temporary consultants and researchers on contract, advisers and aides to Cabinet and sub-Cabinet 'political'

M

Ministers, Chaplains, and 'Schedule C' appointees (those in confidential positions, as advisers, legal counsel—even chauffeurs close to Ministers or other politically sensitive persons). Some of these posts are 'spoils' appointments in the gift of the incoming President—and/or on the advice of his Cabinet colleagues. Two things should, however, be noted with regard to the extent and character of the modern spoils system:

1 Only about a 1,000 spoils posts are worthy of a President's attention.

2 The educational level of the politically appointed top Government servants is today marginally *higher* (as measured by MA's, Ph.D's and LL.B's) than that of the career bureaucrats they outrank. In respect of policy planning we must note, therefore, that the top career bureaucrat is unlikely to be anything like as influential in policy matters as is the British Permanent Secretary. The 'whiz-kids' from Harvard, MIT, the great law firms, the foundations, the business world, or from the President's actual or political 'family circle' are imported to make and if they can, implement new policies.

Below this stratum we find chiefs of the various bureaux in the Departments and Agencies of the Federal Government. Here is a deposit of the collective departmental wisdom which in the British pattern lies immediately beneath the Ministerial level. Bureau chiefs are administrators and it is here that we discover the importance attached by the American tradition to technical and scientific qualifications—and (because of lateral entry) to the technical experience gained outside the Civil Service.

A study of sixty-three bureau chiefs[1] undertaken in 1958 showed that twenty-six had been trained as engineers, scientists or technicians, nine were economists, eight were lawyers and the remaining twenty came from administrative or business careers. The study presented detailed biographical profiles of the sixty-three chiefs and the very clear conclusion, resulting from an examination of their education and experience background, against the work they were doing as bureau chiefs, is that with a few exceptions they were in jobs for which their education and experience were highly relevant. Eleven of the sixty-three had

[1] Michael E. Smith, 'Bureau Chiefs in the Federal Government, 1958', in *Public Policy*, Vol. 10, 1960, Graduate School of Public Administration, Harvard University.

backgrounds which did not seem *obviously* relevant, while a
further five seemed to have no qualifications at all for the
positions they held. (It must be added that a very small number
—not coinciding with the number of 'irrelevant' backgrounds
were political or 'Schedule C' appointees.)

To get a more general view of the 'specialist' nature of the
background of America's administrators we must turn to the
studies by W. Lloyd Warner and colleagues. Warner presented
a report on a sample (7,640) of career civil servants in the higher
grades.[1] Two-fifths of the sample were from G S 14; one-half
from G S 15, and one-tenth from G S 16–18.[2] The sample covered
approximately 20 per cent of all G S 14, and 50 per cent of G S
15–18. In 1959 the average age of the sample was 49½ years, and
the average length of service in the Federal Government seven-
teen years.

Seventy-eight per cent of Warner's sample were university
educated and of these one-third had studied engineering, one-
quarter the physical or biological sciences, one-sixth business
administration, public administration or education. About 9 per
cent had studied humanities, or pre-law or pre-medical subjects.

Approximately 10 per cent of the whole sample had law
degrees—often added to other academic qualifications and 10
per cent had PH.D's.

A further study by Warner *et al*[3] presents much the same
picture using somewhat different groupings of the university
education undertaken—viz. 9·3 per cent had studied humanities,
15·7 per cent the behavioural sciences, 23·4 per cent physical or
biological sciences and 47·6 per cent applied science (including
engineering).

David T. Stanley,[4] grouping the subjects studied by G S 15–18
civil servants, shows that 24 per cent were educated in engineering, 21 per cent in law, 14 per cent in the social sciences, 13 per
cent in physical sciences. The rest had studied agriculture,

[1] 'A New Look at the Career Civil Servant Executive', in *Public Administration Review*, Vol. 22, No. 4, December 1962.
[2] GS 14 . . . $14,680–$19,252 p.a.
GS 15 . . . $17,055–$22,365 p.a.
GS 16 . . . $19,619–$25,043 p.a. } GS=general schedule 1964 figures
GS 17 . . . $22,217–$25,325 p.a.
GS 18 . . . $25,382 p.a.
[3] Warner and colleagues, *The American Federal Executive*, Yale University Press, 1963.
[4] Stanley, *The Higher Civil Service*, Brookings Institution, 1964.

biology, medicine, mathematics, etc. Stanley's figure of 21 per cent trained in law is not necessarily inconsistent with Warner's findings, for the higher one goes up in the GS scale the more likely one is to find people trained in law in important positions. Many a Washington civil servant (whatever his initial academic training) sets out to acquire—often by evening study—a law degree, for, as Thomas Paine once said, 'in America the law is king'.

The man, often the not-so-young man, entering the U.S. Federal service as a graduate with or without professional experience sees himself typically as presenting himself and his qualifications to fill a particular job in a particular agency, or as participating in a particular programme. He will be placed in a GS grade; will hope to move up in the grade; may hope to be able to apply for a post later in a higher grade—or to have his own position 'upgraded'. He is in the service for the pay, pension (contributory and returnable if he leaves permanently), for the paid holidays and often for the experience and contacts he will make which will be useful when he leaves again for the outside world of private enterprise. A great advantage of being in the service is that one can at once look around and apply for a different post at a better salary within the service—a most attractive prospect for the ambitious man, but undoubtedly debilitating for the service as a whole. Movement within, and in and out of the service is a tremendous problem for the U.S. Civil Service Commission. In some post-World War II years as many as 400,000 civil servants per annum have been moving in or out. Scientists in particular, in the U.S., do not expect to make Civil Service employment their life career. As McCrensky observes,[1] 'In the U.S. Civil Service the position itself is the predominant consideration. The man intervenes only to occupy it. In determining the pay grade, his qualifications are subordinate to the aggregate of duties and responsibilities represented in the position . . . personnel are recruited at all levels to fill individual functional positions. . . .' And, McCrensky adds, ' . . . the British Scientific Civil Service is not regarded as an aggregation of employees who are given individual work assignments, but as an institution to which members have dedicated their careers in the service of the Crown'.

The most persuasive and well-informed writer on science and

[1] McCrensky, *Scientific Manpower in Europe*, Pergamon Press, 1958, pp. 150–1.

government, Don K. Price,[1] sums up admirably the differences and different strengths of the U.S. and U.K. attitudes toward 'specialists' in administrative positions. 'In Great Britain,' he writes, 'the scientific civil servants have always complained that they were kept out of positions of top authority by the administrative class. In the United States the complaint is more likely the opposite—that good scientists are ruined by being taken from laboratory positions and given administrative responsibilities for which they may be poorly suited.' Price continues,[2] 'On the other hand, I would argue with equal emphasis that the administrative personnel of all agencies ought to have a fair proportion of men with some training and experience in science and engineering. If administration is to serve as a useful layer in the pyramid of policy between the peak of political power and the base of science and technology, it needs in its composition an appropriate mixture of general competence and special knowledge. . . . The British Administrative Class is a great deal more efficient than its chaotic counterpart in the U.S. Government . . . but there is great merit in having many (administrating) members drawn from earlier experience in professional and scientific specialities.'

In another book,[3] Price states that, 'in the U.S., on the other hand, men trained in science and the professions based on science find it easy to move into higher administrative positions. . . . Scientists who become bureau chiefs in the U.S. service are of course no longer practising scientists; they are doing the work that in the U.K. would be done by a member of the Administrative Class educated in history or classics.'

Scientific opinion in the U.K. has not been unaware of the probable connection between U.S. productivity and the employment in management positions of men with a strong scientific and technical background.[4]

But are American observers wholly satisfied with their traditional pattern of fitting specialists into particular specified positions? ; with the increasingly widespread practice of devolving on departments and agencies the task of writing out the detailed job specifications and filling the posts? ; with the disappearing

[1] Don K. Price, *Government and Science*, 1954, p. 25.
[2] Op. cit., pp. 186–8.
[3] Don K. Price, *The Scientific Estate*, 1965, p. 59 and p. 62.
[4] 6th Annual Report of Advisory Council on Scientific Policy, 1952–3, HMSO Cmnd. 8874, p. 2.

image of 'the Federal Civil Service', as it gradually dissolves into its particular parts and its specialized activities? And is there not a place, and an important place, for career generalist administrators? The u.s. and the u.k. are rarely in step on this— as on other matters; for the evidence suggests that many in the u.s. feel that, overall, Federal administration would be much improved by the presence of a corps of powerful and respected generalist administrators. The political context of Federal administration is so different from that of the u.k. and the respect for the 'expert' so great that a generalist Administrative Class on the British model is not a serious possibility.

That the u.s. Government feels it needs more generalists in administration, young men, and senior men, whose life career will be *administration* is apparent from certain programmes and proposals of recent years.

The movement towards an administrative career in the Federal service for young college graduates began with the New Deal,[1] and it was an attempt at a reversal of tradition. It was a response to the increasing size of the Federal bureaucracy during the New Deal, World War II and the Korean War—and to the complexity and novelty of many Federal Government activities. The drive for a programme of positive career recruitment was strengthened by the report in 1935 of the Commission of Inquiry on Public Service Personnel. The Commission's recommendations for a true career programme were endorsed by the President's Committee on Administrative Management (1937) and by the First and Second Hoover Commissions (1949 and 1955).

The u.s. Civil Service Commission offered its first examinations for unspecialized college graduates in 1934—the Junior Civil Service Examiner examination; and the examination was held again in 1936. In 1939, the effort was resumed with the first examination for Junior Professional Assistants; this was designed to attract college graduates who had majored in particular fields and it offered twenty-two 'options', including one, for Junior Administrative Technicians, for students who had specialized in Public Administration or Political Science. The JPA examinations were given at intervals during the war years until 1947. The JPA programme was succeeded by the Junior Management Assistant examination, the principal vehicle for

[1] F. C. Mosher, 'Features and Problems of the Federal Civil Service', in W. S. Sayne, op. cit., pp. 181–4.

general university recruitment from 1948–54. The JMA differed from its predecessors in important particulars—its examining process was more thorough, and the successful entrants were subjected to a systematic training and career development programme after entry. (Perhaps surprisingly 'in-training' and 'executive develop' programmes have advanced rather slowly in the Federal service, until the great spurt of the last few years.) The JMA programme, while no doubt the most serious and potentially effective way of attracting the young college leaver into Federal administration, fell on hard times. The rapid decline in the prestige of public service occupations, McCarthyism, and the sluggishness of salaries in an era of rising prices, the effects of 'veterans' preference' in Civil Service posts, reduced the number of JMA applicants from 19,000 in 1951 to some 8,000 in 1953.

In 1954 the Civil Service Commission conducted an investigation into its whole college recruiting programme and in the following year launched its newest scheme, the Federal Service Entrance Examination (FSEE). The examination was to recruit college leavers and graduate students from a wide variety of educational specializations. The FSEE tests measured IQ and general knowledge and ability in the student's chosen academic field. It was supplemented by a test (and a programme) for Management Interns—the 'high-flyers' as discovered by FSEE. These Interns were started at higher salary levels than ordinary FSEE entrants and could anticipate rapid advancement to posts of high administrative responsibility.

The FSEE and Management Intern schemes are designed to compete with employers in the private sector for the best young talent. While not restricted to 'upper division' students they are clearly directed to them and they have made up the bulk of entrants. This is now the principal means of entry to the service from college—though some specialized examinations are still offered to 'majors' in physical sciences, engineering, accountancy and forestry. FSEE is one of the few examinations now wholly conducted by the Civil Service Commission itself. It is offered more than once each year, to synchronize with the rhythm of the academic year, and the results are impressive. In 1963, 230,000 applied for FSEE, 140,000 took it, 58,000 passed and over 8,000 were appointed to Federal jobs. The more difficult hurdle, Management Interns, is attempted mainly by graduate students.

In 1963, 23,000 applied for the tests, 2,500 passed, 700 reached the 'eligible' register and 300 were appointed. But there are still difficulties to be recognized. Informed opinion still doubts whether high academic ability in subjects other than those related to administration is sufficient; for the 'planned career system' with in-training ends too soon after its beginning, and then the young men and women must fend for themselves.

3. A SENIOR CIVIL SERVICE?

The Second Hoover Commission (1955) dealt, *inter alia*, with the need for a stronger generalist higher Civil Service, an expanded non-career political leadership and the relation between the two. Career administrators it said should 'be relieved by non-career executives of responsibility for advocacy or defence of policies and programs'. The political appointees should be confined to the departmental, as distinguished from the bureau, level. However, and perhaps with less than impeccable logic, the Commission also urged the creation of an inter-departmentally mobile corps of 'senior civil servants'. Appointment to this group, from among exceptionally qualified career civil servants would carry with it status, rank and salary 'in the man', i.e. regardless of the particular position he might be assigned to fill. 'The primary objective,' they urged, 'is to have always at hand in the Government a designated group of highly qualified administrators whose competence, integrity and faithfulness have been amply demonstrated, who will make it easier for non-career executives to discharge their responsibilities. . . . A secondary but related objective is to make the Civil Service more attractive as a career to able men and women.'

To the British reader no explanation or defence of this proposal need be made, for it is the image we have of our powerful Permanent Secretaries. In the USA, however, it did not receive overwhelming approval. The main objections were two: firstly from the civil servants themselves—who was to be chosen, and how chosen, for membership of this elite?; and secondly from the politicians, and the more politically minded Civil Service. Political (party) neutrality was accepted as a desirable ideal but *neutrality of commitment to a programme* was not acceptable. Congressional objections were along traditional lines—no civil servants should be allowed to assume, or be granted, 'superior' status.

President Eisenhower supported the plan, however. In 1958 he established by executive order a Career Executive Board, as an adjunct to the Civil Service Commission, to develop standards and procedures for the introduction of a Career Executive Service—a milder variant of a 'Senior Civil Service'.

A committee of the House at once asked him to stop the exercise. He refused. Congress then struck out of the appropriation for the Civil Service Commission the funds for running the Career Executive Board. The President had lost; his order was rescinded.

The most important recent development affecting the attractiveness of employment in the higher ranks of the u.s. Federal Service is undoubtedly the Federal Salary Reform Act of 1962. This act of the Kennedy Administration reaffirmed the principle of equal pay for substantially equal work and indeed extended it by declaring that 'Federal salary rates shall be comparable with private enterprise salary rates for the same levels of work'. Substantial pay rises were made therefore in the higher GS grades. And this was a most urgent need, for GS paid supervisors of Federal blue-collar employees were tied to the slow-moving GS rates, while those they supervised had their pay set by district wage boards which took into account the (often very high) union rates of pay prevailing in the district.

In 1963 the President's Advisory Panel on Federal Salary Systems proposed very high salaries for politically appointed and elected officers. ($60,000 for the Vice-President, the Speaker and Supreme Court Justices, $50,000 for Cabinet Ministers and $35,000 for Congressmen). But the panel did not recommend comparability with private enterprise for the career civil servant, for it held the two fields to be incomparable in terms of prestige, pensions, etc. The panel considered that a salary of $25,000 for the top GS grade (GS 18) was high enough to ensure competitiveness with private enterprise, and that recommendation was implemented in 1964.

It is not possible to say, in conclusion, how effective the attempt has been to create the 'image' of an attractive lifetime career in Federal administration. Those entering through FSEE and the Management Intern programme may perhaps become the powerful generalist administrators of the future. It is clear that young people are now more interested in the public service than they were in the 1950s. It is not clear what motivates them, whether they are going after a well-paid first job, or consider themselves as embarking on a life career in administration. If we knew how many of the FSEE or Management Interns had already left, or were thinking of leaving the service, the long-term prospect might be more acceptably gauged.

If we put the U.S. Civil Service back into its constitutional, political, economic and historical setting, it is, in my opinion, unrealistic to believe that America will ever become enamoured of, or show deep respect for, its Government servants in general. Any possibility of the swift emergence in government (the same is not perhaps true of business) of a self-confident, powerful, policy-determining group of career generalists should be coolly discounted. Americans still do not appreciate the virtues (if there are some) of the highly intelligent talented amateur. A man should have a clearly recognizable and saleable skill and it is for the exercise of this expertise that he is paid at preferential rates.

Nobody would claim that the Federal Service is highly efficient, or perhaps even efficient. Americans do not expect it to be so, and they have been fortunate so far in not needing to have a streamlined bureaucracy rapidly transforming political decisions into effective administration. And their present affluence puts them under no compulsion to take desperate measures to improve governmental efficiency. So much wealth is produced, and so much accomplished by ordinary economic activity—and the natural resources of the USA—that Federal Government activity is still—defence apart—marginal in the lives of most Americans. President Johnson's 'Great Society' vision and its anti-poverty programmes are in general supported as worthy ideals. But Congress and the people do not by their actions show the same concern for social amelioration as the President did in 1964. The great majority—probably four-fifths—of all Americans are prosperous. The minority, the poor, constitute a problem of conscience for a very small proportion of the affluent majority. Public opinion polls taken amongst whites in the USA (just before the Newark and Detroit riots of 1967) disclosed that only a tiny minority of respondents considered negroes to be treated unfairly in the USA.

Against this background it is unlikely that the future will show any great reversal of the tradition of recruitment for specialized skills in the Federal Service, and the use of specialists in general administration. The specialist is a qualified person with publicly accredited special training. To the extent that the American public does admire their public servants, they admire them for what they visibly do—as scientists, engineers, accountants, economists, social scientists, doctors, or lawyers. They admire too those who are intellectually able, who are persuasive writers or speakers, who make telling criticisms of the quality of American life, who advocate political or fiscal reforms, who analyse the course of American foreign policy: but these people are—or ought to be—writers of signed columns for the Press, or politicians.

AN AGENDA ITEM

Some years ago James Fesler, Professor of Public Administration at Yale University, noted the revival of an old agenda item: the specialist versus the generalist in administration.[1] The problem has been a serious one in Britain for a good time. According to Anthony Sampson 'the conflict between amateurs and professionals runs through many British institutions—more than on the Continent or in America—but it has its most troubled frontier in the Civil Service'.[2] Critical discussion of the Civil Service is part of the 'state of England' debate that has been under way for some years. There is a growing literature on our failure to meet the challenge of the mid-twentieth century and most pins some responsibility on the administrative system.[3] The present role of the 'generalist' administrator is a common thread. A recent Fabian pamphlet, indeed, said that the amateur versus professional issue was the central issue of Civil Service reform.[4] Much of the evidence to the Fulton Committee on the future structure of the Civil Service touches on this.

It is not our purpose to add to this often polemical debate by arguing the case for the specialist here.[5] Although this symposium was commissioned by the Institution of Professional Civil Servants, what they requested was an academic study, evidence to help the Fulton Committee and the interested public, not necessarily to support their own recommendations. Whether our evidence *does* support their case is for the reader to decide.

It seemed appropriate, however, to end this book with some consideration of general principles. The theory and practice of public administration have been examined in numerous textbooks, many large, most American. One might expect to find

[1] *Public Administration Review*, 1958.
[2] Anthony Sampson, *Anatomy of Britain Today*.
[3] E.g. Brian Chapman, *British Government Observed*; Andrew Shonfield, *Modern Capitalism*; Peter Shore, *Entitled to Know*.
[4] *The Administrators*.
[5] But see the author's 'Specialists as Administrators' in *State Service* (Journal of the Institution of Professional Civil Servants), February 1967.

guidance there, sections devoted to the sort of problems raised in this survey: the place of the professional in administration, the relationship between specialists and generalists, the case for and against the appointment of specialists to managerial posts, the relative merits of separate or combined administrative and advisory hierarchies. In fact, there has been surprisingly little discussion of these topics in organization theory, perhaps because much is written against an American background to which the issues of current British debate are only marginal. The two hierarchies problem, for example, is discussed in line and staff terms which do not coincide with ours; the specialist *v.* generalist issue is seen in terms of administrative professionalization rather than the appointment of members of other professions to administrative posts.

It may therefore be worth setting out some of the issues, posing problems and looking at alternative arguments, leaving the reader to draw his own conclusions as before. The purpose of this chapter is to raise questions rather than to answer them.

It is not merely that different answers can be given to the same questions. Their key terms are often used ambiguously. The answers to one will depend on how another has been interpreted. We may differ about the qualities of a good administrator even when we agree on what the functions of administration are. But we may also disagree about what is meant by administration and this will add a further element of disagreement to the preceding question. Our definition of administration will influence our views of organizational structure (single or dual hierarchy). But the relationship is reciprocal: our preference for one form of organization or another will determine the content we assign to administration.

THE ADMINISTRATIVE FUNCTION

What is the administrative function? The simplest starting point is to look at answers in terms of our present system, bearing in mind that these refer as much to what our Administrative Class does (or thinks it does) as to any attempt to isolate the essence of administration. In its evidence to the Fulton Committee, the representative association of the class described its work as 'bringing together the disparate issues involved in taking major decisions of policy, advising on what decisions should be and subsequently putting them into effect'. It is immediately obvious that two quite separate things are involved: policy-making (or, according to the letter of the British constitution, advice to Ministers on policy) and execution (i.e. decisions made within policy and the direction of subordinate staff). Traditionally, it is the former that has been emphasized.

It is thus possible to see administration very largely as a policy-making or policy-preparing activity. This is brought out in the following definition by an official committee: 'The analysis and co-ordination of ideas and proposals, the relation of these to political and economic conditions, and the expression of proposals and decisions in a form in which they can be assimilated and carried out by the Government machine.'[1]

The relationship between senior civil servants and Ministers is a key to understanding this approach. Members of the Administrative Class regard themselves first and foremost as Ministerial advisers. C. H. Sisson, himself a member of the class, says that they are 'near to being a part of the Minister's mind'.[2] Leaving aside the question of the actual relationship between the two (who influences whom?), it is clear that administrators form part of the policy-making side of Government.

What is striking is that such definitions emphasize a planning rather than an executory function: in business, that of a board of directors rather than managers; in the Army, of the General Staff rather than field commanders. This is reflected in an essay written by another member of the class: 'Administrative civil servants do not typically think of themselves as managers; by training and inclination they are fitted to regard themselves as advisers to Ministers and to the small group of very senior officials who help to fashion Ministerial policies.'[3] Seen in this way, administration has the characteristic of staff rather than line functions. There are some dangers of ambiguity here.

Another important aspect of these definitions is the emphasis placed on bringing together the many different elements in Governmental decisions: technical, financial, organizational and, perhaps above all, political. The administrator is the man whose function it is to weigh all these factors, to adjust the

[1] Report of the Working Party on the Role of Professional Engineers.
[2] C. H. Sisson, *The Spirit of British Administration*.
[3] Competition organized by the association of the Administrative Class and reported in *The Economist*, August 8, 1964.

technically desirable to the organizationally possible and the financially viable, taking account of what public opinion will stand and balancing the interests of affected groups. The IPCS, in its Fulton evidence, says that the Administrative Class consider themselves referees, reconciling interests, not managers making positive decisions of their own. This view has undoubtedly been shared in the past by many sections of that class. It has naturally affected their views of the qualities required of a good administrator (neutrality between proposals as well as between interests).

This raises the question of whether there is an administrative function (and an administrative skill, science or technique) common to all services and distinct from other, more specialized or technical functions (and from other recognized skills or branches of knowledge). The point has often been made that administration is both substantive and procedural. There is always a *what* of administration, the field for which the administrator is responsible (e.g. education, defence) and there is also a *how* of administration. The latter involves knowing how to plan and how to organize.[1] It is this approach to administration, rather than that associated with the British Administrative Class, that is usually discussed in American textbooks. It is significantly different in that it sees administration as a managerial technique rather than a quasi-political activity. It involves specialized knowledge of procedures *in addition to* knowledge of the substantive field of specialization.

There is also the more limited notion of the administrator whose work is virtually independent of the substantive field for which his Ministry happens to be responsible. The term *administration générale* is applied in France to divisions dealing with personnel, accounts and similar common service matters. The administrative function then becomes as specialized as any other, the man himself a professional with his own, rather narrow, substantive field of action (roughly: office management).

The relevance of these distinctions is obvious when we consider the old topic, 'administration: art or science?' The more specialized the function, the more likely that it can be reduced to taught principles. They are also relevant when we look at the specialist *v.* generalist debate. It may turn into an argument about the rival merits of various types of expert (as in some

[1] Cf. M. E. & G. O. Dimock, *Public Administration*.

sectors of industry where accountants—the financial experts—are moving into general management). In some countries the issue is not, as in Britain, an argument between general and specialist classes about who should fill top posts but simply a discussion whether the non-professional administrator should himself be trained as an administrative specialist with responsibilities in a fairly restricted field.

The Treasury proposals to Fulton recommend the amalgamation of the Administrative and Executive Classes in a new 'managerial' group. The Administrative Class also emphasizes its management functions. A word should therefore be said about the relationship between administration and management. Both terms are ambiguous and, however defined, tend to overlap. But Sir Frederic Hooper, a leading industrialist and recognized expert, does make a distinction.[1] It is the task of management to carry policy into effect: it is concerned with the organization of work and the direction of staff. The administrative side is the line organization in the British system and administrators are therefore responsible for execution as well as for policy but relatively little is made of this, perhaps because management *within* policy is largely the province of the Executive Class. More attention is likely to be paid where Ministries have extensive field services as in France. Clearly rather different abilities and different skills are required than those for the administrative functions discussed above (the ability to handle men in particular).

ADMINISTRATORS AND ADVISERS

All this really brings us to the organizational question: should there be one hierarchy or two? How strong is the case for dividing a Ministry into two sides, as in Britain: one hierarchy of officials responsible for the formulation of policy and the direction of services, another responsible for research and advice (and, in fact, for the management of the more technical aspects of the more technical branches of the service)?

Is this a form of line and staff organization? Generally speaking, according to Dimock, 'line connotes action, staff advice; line is hierarchical, staff collateral; line is authority, staff influence'. Let us leave aside the collateral aspect referred to (staff officers as

[1] *Management Survey.*

assistants to executives at their own level rather than as members of a specialist hierarchy with a Chief Adviser at the top). Line is seen as executive authority. What this division of functions misses out is policy-making. It is perhaps for this reason that 'what the correct relationship between the two types of activity should be has long been a matter of debate'. Planning does not fit easily into this theory of organization unless one assumes that it is a joint responsibility. In the British system, on the other hand, such decisions are formally a line rather than a staff matter.

We have already noted that the British model is slightly odd in that both line and staff appear to have advisory functions. If one takes the doctrine of Ministerial responsibility seriously, the British system operates with two lines of staff: the administrator advising the Minister through his own hierarchy, the specialist sometimes through his own, sometimes (and this used to be the official position) through the head of the administrative side.

It may be noticed that this is not the only way of dividing functions. Policy formulation could be linked with research under the wider heading of policy planning and this could be defined as a staff function, separated from the execution of policy directives. It associates staff rather than line as the senior partners with the Ministers. The champions of staff activity think it is they who should make policy while line officials merely carry it out. This is closer to military practice where the General Staff determines strategy; the field commanders head operations. It would also appear closer to the Swedish system of government with its separation of policy-making Ministries from executory agencies. Such a dual structure is possible regardless of whether the policy-making side is staffed by British-type generalists or by economists, engineers and other specialists. It could be argued that, on the face of it, it is at least as logical as the one we have. Members of the Administrative Class and senior specialists both advise Ministers, the two are merely brought closer together.

Let us return, however, to the present British model (perhaps one should say standard model as changes are already taking place in some sectors). A further point needs to be made. A dual organizational structure may, but need not, be linked to a dual class structure. It has until now, but the Treasury's Fulton proposals recommend that the highest administrative posts should be opened to the best men of all classes (in staffing terms,

N

this would come near to the unified higher Civil Service that the
IPCS recommend). They do not suggest that the structure itself
should be altered. It is apparent from previous chapters, however, that many countries do not operate such a dual-hierarchy
system. In France, for example, the heads of functional divisions
are their own and the Minister's senior advisers (though there
are advisory committees and civil servants in research and
planning posts).

The case for the British model can be argued in different ways.
There are claims of organizational expediency. It may be more
effective to separate out specialist research and specialist advice.
These functions are best carried out by officials who can devote
their full time to the study of their subject, undistracted by wider
considerations and unhampered by executive duties. Policy-
making, on the other hand, is best linked with the direction of
services through which the official acquires a sense of the ad-
ministratively practicable. There are dangers in divorcing policy
formulation from responsibility for execution, including problems of feedback.

A second line of argument concentrates less on the organizational than on the human case for a division of labour. This is
followed by the Working Party on the Role of Professional
Engineers: 'If one brain could provide the expertise of both
aspects (i.e. the administrative and the professional), it would
be the natural arrangement to make one man responsible for
both; but, failing that, two brains must do the work of one.'
Support of the Administrative Class often takes this form. The
specialist (sometimes qualified as *real* specialist) cannot make a
good administrator because one man has simply not the time
and energy to acquire the wide range of skills necessary to combine the two. Sometimes it is also suggested that it takes a
different sort of man to be an expert in different fields: the
problem is not only the limited capacity of one brain but that
temperament makes a man suitable for one sort of work but not
another. Whatever the reason, the Administrative Class has
stated that it does not believe the two roles can be combined.

All this does not deal with what some consider the real heart
of the problem: are there really two different jobs to be done or
need there be only one job, with perhaps a wider range of duties?
Is it necessary to have line *and* staff? There seems to be little
agreement even among organization experts. A former senior

official of General Motors apparently described staff activity as the chief element of progress in the science of management, while Peter Drucker, consultant of General Electric, maintained that it is undesirable to have separate staff functions at all.

Dimock sensibly points out (though in a rather different line-and-staff context from the British) that the whole idea of dividing functions is unrealistic and that the tendency in current organization theory is to play down the distinction. Two things have been recognized. First: both types of work are involved in most senior posts. The senior executive must himself do 'research', even if this is restricted to the study of reports by different specialists and the reconciliation of conflicting proposals. All senior officials are involved in planning. Second: the theoretical division of responsibilities in formal organization charts is often misleading. Authority is largely a matter of influence. It is hard to fix realistically the lines of command in a government department where many decisions emerge from committees composed of both sorts of official and where both may have the ear of the Minister.

The case for a single hierarchy follows from what has been said. It may not be a self-evident fact of life that one brain cannot do both sorts of work (the protagonists of the existing order do not refer to the results of any aptitude tests). The distinction between the two types of work may be too blurred for a rational division of labour. There may be a positive gain from the amalgamation of functions. Friction may be avoided. 'The experts in the Civil Service not surprisingly resent the apartheid between them and the administrators, and in the last twenty years a cold war has existed between the two sides.'[1] The morale of the specialist side may be undermined either by the frustration of their career prospects or because they feel that their advice meets with a barrier, rather than a filter, in the Administrative Class. A single hierarchy may simplify problems of communication, it may reduce the risk that specialist advice is not considered or transmitted incorrectly to the Minister. The specialist's advice is likely to be improved if he too works 'near to the Minister's mind' (i.e. if he too is concerned with the 'political' elements in a decision); it is likely to be improved if he has administrative experience and responsibility for the execution of the policies which he has helped to plan. Work may

[1] Anthony Sampson, op. cit.

be simplified and speeded up. Anthony Sampson quotes a senior civil servant as saying that a dual structure all the way up is terribly wasteful.

The case for a single hierarchy is clearest where the department has real managerial responsibilities. We have noted the Treasury's recognition of the dual task of the higher Civil Service: the traditional policy-making function and the newer function of managing the machinery of government. But it is not always clear what they are thinking of managing. Traditionally Ministries have been policy-making and supervisory offices, with responsibility for the operation of services in the hands of local authorities, nationalized industries, private enterprise, universities and other non-Civil Service organizations. Structure and staffing is somewhat different in Ministries with extensive field services (e.g. Post Office, Ministry of Transport). It is significant that the dual hierarchy does not exist in local government where the emphasis has always been more on the provision of services directed by professional chief officers who are also the council's immediate advisers. It may be much more difficult to rely on a general class of administrators if management comes to mean the direction of more or less specialized staff running more or less technical services. If the Government's involvement in industry, science and technology grows further, the argument for a change of structure at the centre may be reinforced.

Let us look finally at the recommendations of the IPCS. Professionals should have more responsibilities placed on them. Their relationship to the general classes should be changed to one in which there are completely *unified hierarchies*. There should also be a *unified higher Civil Service* with all classes below the highest leading to it. At the level of the higher Civil Service posts should be filled by the men best able to do the job. Some posts would be filled largely by men trained and practised in administrative skills, others will demand professional qualifications. The difference between the two types of officer will thus be reduced and many will be filled by one or the other, depending on the best man available. Note the two elements of these proposals. First: the abolition of the line/staff dichotomy at the higher levels and (a problem we have not touched on) an end to the division of responsibility between members of the professional and general classes for management where this applies (full responsibility for one man). Second: the reclassification of all senior civil servants as members of the managerial class (while retaining recruitment into professional classes at the start of a career) in recognition of the fact that work is likely to become less technical and more managerial as one moves up the scale.

THE ADMINISTRATOR AS GENERALIST

The simplest case for the generalist is that which says that the administrative function does not depend on any single form of technical expertise and that the specialist therefore has no particular qualifications for this sort of work. The question whether public health requires certain restrictions in regard to the right to sell foodstuffs should not be decided on medical grounds alone; such decisions are administrative, i.e. based on a series of technical, economic and social premises which may themselves have political implications. Poul Meyer, the Danish author of what was until recently one of the few European textbooks on public administration, makes this point and adds 'since administrative decisions are never of the same character as technical decisions, the technical expert does not in principle have *any* merits over other persons as a performer of administrative functions'.[1]

The little word *any* (italicized by the present writer) needs to be stressed. Given two men of equal administrative gifts, experience or knowledge, the specialist is not considered by Meyer to have any advantage over the generalist; he has nothing extra to add. Professional qualifications are dismissed as irrelevant. This is very much the line taken by the Treasury which would open higher administrative posts to members of the professional classes who show administrative ability but does not suggest that such qualifications need themselves be taken into account. There is no recognition that for many posts relevant specialist experience might be an *added* advantage. (Compare this with the IPCS recommendations above that some should be classified as requiring professional, as well as general-managerial, ability.)

This approach seems to imply that the technical element is a minor factor in the final decision or that there are so many different elements (involving different professions) that expertise

[1] Poul Meyer, *Administrative Organization*.

in one is no advantage in bringing together the lot. It also implies that the generalist administrator has available all the necessary specialist advice, can understand it and even judge between conflicting specialist advisers.

Meyer pushes his case further. He argues that specialist qualifications are a positive disadvantage. Where technical experts are employed in general administration, they do not confine themselves to purely technical decisions: consciously or unconsciously they allow social value judgments to influence their work. This argument is hard to follow. Presumably no administrator would confine himself to purely technical considerations. The expert may or may not be influenced by value judgments; but so may any administrator, however generalist. It would be necessary to take the argument further and claim that part of the general administrator's distinctive training lies in overcoming his own bias. The specialist could reply that exactly this is a basic element of any scientific education.

There are more serious anti-specialist arguments. The specialist may find it difficult to give sufficient weight to non-technical factors. He may underrate the political factors (public reactions). He may be insufficiently cost-conscious (it was sometimes said of French engineers that their railways hold many records but run at a loss, their power stations are magnificent but uneconomic). It has equally been said of the British generalist that he may come to identify himself with the clientele of his Ministry or the field of development for which he is responsible (thus we have the notion of 'spending' and 'saving' Ministries). The European general administrator, for his part, has often been been accused of an over-legalistic approach to problems because of his training in law.

There may be some element of truth in the theory that specialists are often one-sided. Sometimes this involves the sleight of hand: for specialist read *mere* specialist. But to an extent it could be the result of one-sided training or one-sided experience. The problem, then, is not inherent in membership of a profession and could be remedied by broader education and a wider range of postings in early years of service. If specialists are too narrow in their outlook, it could be argued that it is the system which has made them so and that the system could be altered. We have noted that the engineer in the French Civil Service is perhaps a different man from his professional counterpart in Britain. In any case, similar accusations of narrowness have been levelled against members of the Administrative Class. Except at the very highest level, they do not necessarily have a very wide range of experience either.

This brings us to an ambiguity in the use of the term 'generalist'. It may mean the man with a general background (i.e. not vocationally directed) as well as the man who performs general administrative functions. It is occasionally suggested that there is an inherent difference of temperament between those who chose an education in the humanities and, perhaps, some of the social sciences on the one hand, in science and technology on the other. The specialist has chosen his profession because of a particular bent, an overriding interest in a particular field. The generalist's outlook is more balanced (or less dedicated, depending on whether one is for or against). The engineer is an engineer because he wants to build bridges rather than do office work; he is more interested in the technical aspects of a problem than the social. Many factors influence a child's choice of studies but in Britain the decision to study a non-Arts subject may be more narrowly career-oriented than in some other countries. But even here the experience of industry is that many a young engineer's fancy lightly turns to thoughts of management.

A further version of the anti-specialist argument is that they tend to ride hobby-horses. They may not merely be committed to a subject but to a school of thought within it that is not even shared by all their professional colleagues. French engineers were at one time sharply split in their commitment to hydro-electric and coal-burning power stations. Economists are notoriously divided on most issues of economic policy. It needs the disinterested non-specialist to arbitrate between rival theories. There is no evidence, of course, that the generalist always escapes over-identification with a particular set of proposals, though it would be tempting to think that classics and history teach a certain scepticism. In any case the whole discussion unfortunately suffers from the lack of any real hard evidence.

The argument in favour of the generalist is perhaps carried furthest in the English literature by C. H. Sisson, himself a member of the Administrative Class. 'There is no need for the administrator to be a man of ideas. His distinguishing quality should rather be a certain freedom from ideas. The acts of administrators are, in effect, mere acts of recognition. It is the business of those who think they hold the truth on any subject to make themselves recognized.'[1] One must assume, of course, that the generalist can always recognize a scientific truth (or, with Mill, that given free discussion truth will out). More fundamental to this view is its underlying political implication. It sees the function of government as arbitration between interests, adjudication on proposals, regulation of the activities of others. This is a sophisticated version of the 'night-watchman' theory of the State and one's own view of the adequacy of generalists may then depend on how one sees the role of government today. 'The ethos of the generalist,' says Peter Shore, 'is that of the cultivated amateur, sceptical and detached —and quite unsuited to modern, complex and purposive government.'[2] The argument used against specialists can be turned in their favour: by their very calling, they are more likely to be *purposive*. It is to some extent a question of where the initiative for reform should come from, public administration or private enterprise, voluntary associations and research institutes.

Finally we must look at the argument for the generalist on which the present structure of the Civil Service is actually based. It is summed up by Lord Macaulay, foreshadowing the North-cote-Trevelyan Report. 'We believe that men who have been engaged, up to 21 or 22, in studies which have no immediate connection with the business of any profession, and of which the effect is merely to open, to invigorate, to enrich the mind, will generally be found in the business of every profession superior to men who have, at 18 or 19, devoted themselves to the special studies of their calling.'[3] This is the 'gifted amateur' theory on which the present entrance examinations to the Administrative Class are still based. It holds that a general education is more likely to fit a man to understand the complex problems of administration than narrow training (the open and the closed mind). Its truth depends on the system of higher education but is open to doubt. In any case, it is not clear that he remains a man of such wide culture after some years of service. A more restrained version is that natural intelligence is what counts in administration, not technical expertise (the

[1] C. H. Sisson, op. cit.
[2] Peter Shore, op. cit.
[3] *Report on the Selection and Examination of Candidates for the Indian Civil Service*, 1854.

trained mind can deal with any problem). While this argument may be used in defence of generalists, it is not one that benefits them to the exclusion of specialists who may have an equally intelligent mind.

THE ADMINISTRATOR AS SPECIALIST

The member of the Administrative Class is intended to be an all-rounder, a 'polyvalent administrator' as the French would say, capable of service in all branches of the administration. There is far less mobility in practice than this theory might lead one to expect: promotion tends to be vertical, not diagonal, except at the very highest levels. Chapman makes the point that the typical administrator is as circumscribed in experience as any specialist.[1] The idea is nevertheless fundamental. It is linked to a particular theory of organization. The British system of administration is conceived, on the whole, in horizontal rather than vertical terms. The nature of work changes as one moves upwards through the Clerical, Executive and Administrative levels, rather than sideways between different Ministries. The justification for centring the public service on three general (i.e. interdepartmental) classes is that what is common to work at any level in all departments outweighs that which is different between departments. The French Civil Service has both horizontal and vertical class divisions but the administrative system has a strongly vertical character, the emphasis is on features that distinguish one branch from another and therefore on specialist qualifications for administrators.

The term 'all-rounder' is used in another, closely related sense. A member of the Administrative Class is recruited for abilities which are a prerequisite of administration in all fields. A good honours degree in any subject should be reasonable evidence of intelligence: this enables him to grasp the essentials of any problem and spot the weaknesses in proposals put to him (the analytical mind). The emphasis on essay writing and précis in the entrance examinations should guarantee literacy, the ability to set out a problem in simple terms. Qualities of character are tested in interview: balanced judgment, a sense of responsibility, devotion to work, a co-operative spirit, initiative and leadership. Some would argue that such tests are

[1] Brian Chapman, op. cit.

not yet sufficiently reliable. It may also be that initiative and leadership are given less importance than they deserve, perhaps because they were less important in the traditional view of the service's function. Political sensitivity is acquired on the job.

The all-rounders have been increasingly criticized in recent years as amateurs, lacking any real comprehension of the field they administer. Thomas Balogh has called theirs the crossword-puzzle mind, out of touch with modern realities. If one bears in mind that virtually all serve in Whitehall (and have been recruited into Whitehall around the age of 22), it can be argued that they deal with paper problems of which they have no direct experience and which may, therefore, become mere intellectual exercises. This may be bound up with the basic tenet of the British system of government. The Administrative Class cling firmly to the doctrine that their primary function is to advise Ministers and their training in fact makes them execllent drafters of memoranda. There is now talk of a management class and management functions. If this is to mean the management of services as well as policy formulation, a different range of personal qualities may need to be stressed and their will be a greater need for training in management techniques.

In fact, members of the Administrative Class already see themselves as specialists in administration, having, in addition to the abilities listed above, acquired through experience a considerable store of knowledge and an 'expertise in working the Government machine' (the latter is something of a favourite phrase). There are also post-entry courses in managerial techniques. Nevertheless, both they and the Treasury are clearly anxious to acquire even greater expertise. They wish to extend courses which will turn them into a class of *professional* generalist administrators.

It is no doubt partly a reflection of the fashions of the time that this specialized body of knowledge is seen largely in terms of the quantitative techniques of economics, including statistics, accountancy and computer science. The magic words of the moment appear to be cost-benefit analysis.[1] As civil servants say, they are now becoming numerate as well as literate. These subjects are all relevant to policy planning. Organization and Methods also plays its part and this is directly related to management in the narrower sense (office management). At the

[1] See H.M. Treasury, *Glossary of Management Techniques*.

level at which these matters are studied, it would seem that they could be assimilated equally well by the professional classes. Little attention is paid to the social sciences, none to the physical sciences and technology, though it could be claimed that the latter do not have the same universal relevance. The fact remains that it is difficult to know exactly what this body of knowledge should be that all administrators ought to have. Nor is it entirely clear that it could not be additional to a specialized training directly related to the field administered.

Robert Presthus, Professor of Public Administration at Cornell University, wrote recently of the 'decline of the generalist myth'.[1] There is little doubt that the generalist theory is undergoing serious attack. There also seems little doubt that it was always something of a 'myth' in the sense that it was based on *a priori* assumptions about the nature of administration, the qualities required of an administrator and the sort of people likely to have these qualities. No data was collected, no tests run. The only real empirical evidence was that the system seemed to run fairly well. So long as this was not challenged, one could reasonably assume that the principles on which it was based were adequate. One could not assume that other systems would not work as well or even better. There has been no real attempt to try alternatives until the recent reorganization of some departments. Nor has there been much serious comparison with other countries, and this, as previous chapters have shown, tends to run into difficulties because of the very different contexts in which their administrations are set. This theoretical approach is strange in a country which prides itself on its pragmatism.

THE SPECIALIST AS ADMINISTRATOR

Let us accept again for a moment the dual hierarchy of administration/policy-making and specialization/advice, the horizontal division of work which separates the former from more routine office management and field operations, the notion of administration as an interdepartmental activity with its own common skills. It may still be argued, to put it at its lowest, that there is no reason to assume that the man with professional qualifications cannot do such work as well as any other.

[1] *Public Administration Review*, No. 4, 1964.

There is no evidence that an early choice of vocational training indicates the absence of some *natural* gift for administration. Common sense about human nature (and some observation of industry and local government) suggest that administrative ability as a personality trait is not related to educational options even where these are at the same time career options: the schoolboy is not the best judge of his own abilities nor can he assess realistically the satisfaction he will obtain from different sorts of career. No doubt the young man with a strong scientific bent may in early life be fascinated by the thought of research but the same can be said of some students in the humanities. Nor is there much evidence that vocational training (e.g. law, engineering, accountancy) necessarily kills such ability. It can be argued that British university courses in science and technology are rather narrow and that the atmosphere may encourage a vocational concentration. But it is equally true that the best Arts graduates are oriented towards the academic life, hence some of the present difficulties in Civil Service recruitment. Nor is their education necessarily more relevant. History may give the student a knowledge of what has been tried in the past, a certain understanding of the present and some sense of perspective, all useful attributes. But the social sciences should contribute even more to an understanding of the community and its needs, and yet they are not officially favoured. In Europe mathematics and law have long been favoured as general educational backgrounds. Engineering, a European might argue, has the advantage of combining a theoretical training with the testing of theory in practical application. The Arts graduate may be better able to express himself in plain, succinct language than the scientist. If this is true, it lies less in the nature of the disciplines than in the current syllabi. The remedy lies in educational reform.

There is little evidence either that the professional cannot pick up administrative skills as well as anyone else. The generalist comes to the job inexperienced (in Britain, indeed, at the relatively immature age of 21 or 22). The Administrative Class maintains in its Fulton evidence that its members have a 'unique experience' of operating the Government machine. In so far as this is true, it may be because they have had greater access to posts in which such experience can be acquired. In itself, it proves little. The uncharitable might say that if they really have such a near monopoly of administrative experience (and this is by no means true) it is simply because they have 'fixed' the system in that way. The experience of industry is that the scientist and other specialists are just as likely to develop managerial skills if entrusted with managerial functions early enough. The position would be different if administration was a profession, if administrators came to their work qualified by an extensive training in a recognized body of knowledge. This does not apply to relatively short post-entry courses, however, which the specialist could tackle as well as anyone.

The comments of the IPCS on this matter seem reasonable and are worth quoting. 'It is true that the scientist's interest in administration and management frequently develops as he gets older. But we are strongly opposed to the suggestion that scientists generally have no aptitude for administration. It ignores the extent to which they are already involved in the Civil Service, and the much greater extent to which they are involved in industry and in the public services of other countries. . . . It is important that career planning should stimulate and develop the interests of scientists in administration from an early stage and training must also be given.'

At this level we have an argument for the selection of senior administrators from either generalist or specialist classes, depending only on the administrative ability that a particular individual shows, i.e. the opening up of senior posts. This is what the Treasury recommends. How effective it would be would depend on the opportunities given to specialists in the formative stages of their careers to learn managerial skills and show their ability to use them. If the two-hierarchy system is maintained, this is not easy as members of the professional classes are likely to spend their early years in the specialized work for which they are directly qualified. This may of course be what the young professional, recently graduated, wants to do at the time (that is the Treasury's view); it may also be that early administrative responsibilities would whet his appetite for more. Career planning, to which the IPCS refers, is thus very important if he is to have a real chance of climbing to the top of the administrative ladder.

It is sometimes said that to use specialists in this way is a waste of scarce natural resources. A scientist is more usefully employed doing science than in doing jobs a non-scientist can do equally well. If one accepts the last premise, the first part of the statement may be true. But such arguments come preciously close to advocating a direction of labour, however indirect the method. Can one tell a man that he must remain a scientist, or 'rig' the system to this end, when he wants to become a manager, particularly if the manager enjoys a higher status, exercises more power and receives a higher salary.

This brings us to a different level of the argument in favour of specialists: that he should not merely be able to compete on equal terms for top posts but that for many such posts professional expertise should be a *sine qua non* of appointment.

Fesler summarized the specialist *v.* generalist debate in the following broad terms: 'One side says: a man must administer *something* and a knowledge of that something is a necessary qualification for high administrative rank. The other side says: at the higher reaches of administration, work is largely of a general character.' It is claimed for the good generalist that he soon masters the vocabulary of the specialist advisers and learns to understand their technical proposals. If this is not true, if the general administrator can no longer adequately perform his task by relying on specialists, a case for the specialist may be made simply by the generalist's default.

It is a truism that we live in an era of growing complexity, increased specialization of knowledge and professionalization of skill groups. Government is more and more involved in economic planning, in the development of science and technology, in 'social engineering'. It seems likely that the man of general culture will find it increasingly difficult to master the specialized vocabularies and may therefore no longer be able to 'use' the specialist. A central theme of Peter Shore's book is that our post-war history is one of wrong policy decisions resulting from misunderstanding advice or failure to obtain advice at all because problems were not identified in advance. And again we may quote the IPCS: 'It is clear that the public is uneasy about the contribution of the Civil Service to the national life. Most serious are the accusations that it is behind the time, that it fails to use modern methods, that it is out of touch with modern society, industry and commerce, science and technology, that its highest officers are drawn from too narrow a field, that its advice is based on amateur hunches rather than professional assessments and research.'

There are obvious dangers in the belief, traditional to much British thinking about government, that 'the expert should be on tap, not on top'. There is little point in turning on the tap if one cannot understand what comes out. The self-confident amateur who has misunderstood, without realizing it, is as dangerous as any over-enthusiastic specialist. How does the generalist judge whether technical advice is competent, how does he judge between conflicting technical opinions? If this is the function of the Chief Scientific Adviser, does this not free scientists from the taint of one-sidedness? In any case, it is not just a question of turning on the tap to get advice. One has first to know what sort of advice to ask for, what the problems are: those of the future as well as those of today. The administrator is more likely to be aware of the latter: they land on his desk and demand immediate solutions. Hard pressed for time, he cannot always think about the long term. He may not even be aware of such problems. The specialist, if he maintains a lively interest in his subject, is more likely to pursue these lines of thought. The failure to identify long-term problems well in advance is said to be one of the weaknesses of post-war government in Britain. It is no longer sufficient to put the specialist in a back room and occasionally look in to ask his advice. The questions, as well as the answers, must come from him. That means he must participate fully in the work of the department as an administrator himself. The barrier that two hierarchies and a separation of functions create must be removed.

The preceding argument is, naturally, an exaggeration. The British Civil Service in fact no longer works in this way. There is co-operation between administrators and specialists, a two-way flow of ideas. Lines of communication and influence are more fluid than the formal structure might indicate. But that itself may be a reason for re-examining the whole notion of separate hierarchies.

No one would suggest that a highly qualified engineer or a brilliant scientist should be appointed to high administrative position purely on the basis of his professional qualifications, regardless of his administrative abilities. Yet many of the anti-specialist arguments seem to assume this. They often rest on the definition of a specialist as a one-sided man, a man who specialized in a narrow field to the exclusion of all else. This mistake is more easily avoided if one uses the term 'professional' instead.

Membership of a profession can be defined by qualifications (i.e. training) and need not imply full-time pursuit of professional activities. A solicitor retains his qualifications when acting as a town clerk and can use his legal knowledge as an adjunct to his wider functions; an accountant does not lose his specialized skills on becoming a company director. In other words, one might expect *both* professional qualifications *and* general managerial ability to be important factors in the making of a good administrator. Thus we come back to the argument that says a man must administer *something* and that a knowledge of that something is a necessary background for success.

If one accepts this, one may come to the conclusion that a single hierarchy is best. If, for other reasons (e.g. rationalization of the administrative structure), one favours the single hierarchy, then specialist knowledge in the administrator becomes essential.

Of course, things are not so cut and dried. The distinction between line and staff may be blurred and the job description of many jobs might realistically include elements of both. There are, nevertheless, posts at different levels in which there is greater emphasis on one rather than another. There must always be posts mainly concerned with thought rather than action, with the gathering of information on which decisions can be based rather than with the actual taking of decisions. The French often describe these as *sections d'etudes*. But it is possible to integrate such posts into a single organizational hierarchy, certainly into a single class system. In France, for example, the normal career pattern is that a man will at some stages of his career undertake research (in the widest sense) and have planning or advisory functions; at other stages he will occupy managerial or policy-making posts.

It may be countered that such varied careers are a dissipation of energy and undermine the specialist's expertise in his own field, thus reducing his value. This is another version of the argument that a man can only be a specialist if he specializes full-time. It is true that the professional whose main work lies in administration will not be able to keep in touch with all the developments in his own subject, particularly as he moves up the ladder and has to deal with an ever wider range of issues. But this is not necessarily an argument for a separate hierarchy of advisers pursuing a separate specialized career. As it is, a Chief Scientific Adviser cannot hope to keep abreast of all the latest scientific theories. The very complexities referred to above will defeat him. He needs younger and more specialized men to work for him. The situation, however, is no different for the Permanent Secretary who has to rely on the briefs prepared by junior administrators. Senior men in all fields are in the same position. Little is lost, therefore, if specialization is not permanent, particularly if one remembers that pure research continues at the universities and other institutes.

One can put forward other, even more positive reasons for preferring specialists to generalists on top. The Labour Party's evidence to the Fulton Committee claims that administrative functions (i.e. the purely 'administrative' elements in management) are now less important than the technical. What is needed is positive government, identifying needs, long-term planning, purposive action in many social, economic and technological spheres. The *pure* administrator may by his training be inclined to concentrate on the speedy and frictionless despatch of business at the cost of creative policies. One can argue that the type of man the Administrative Class stands for is too politically conscious, too aware of conflicting interests, of the inevitably hostile reactions of certain groups and of short-term public opinion, too concerned with administrative (and even financial) difficulties.

The need nowadays is to push through long-term development programmes. The generalist with a classics background may have no natural interest in this sort of activity (equally, of course, he may: but his education alone is unlikely to stimulate it). One might expect a vocational education to reflect or stimulate a greater degree of commitment (though this too is something of an assumption). One might also expect the professional to be a little more impatient of administrative difficulties and, indeed, public opinion, more anxious to get things done, even at a cost. Perhaps too much emphasis is placed on avoiding friction: it may be less important to have a smooth-running machine than a machine which actually gets somewhere. But that obviously brings one back to one's own philosophy of politics.

THE STUDY OF ADMINISTRATION

Let us return to the question: what sort of a thing is administration? The generalist has long argued that it is an art. An art

O

is a combination of natural talents and skills learnt in practice. If the professional civil servant is to become a successful administrator, the able man must be picked out early enough to give him practical experience in his formative years. And, of course, the only way of finding out whether a man *is* a potential leader is to give him early responsibility. This is exactly what many large industrial concerns do. Young scientists are put into managerial positions for a trial period after which they may be promoted in the managerial hierarchy or return to their original scientific work.

The generalist has emphasized that political sensitivity is an important aspect of this art. If specialists are to acquire this, they too must be exposed to public opinion and conflicting pressures (as are Chief Officers in local government). This can be organized by career planning, giving the specialist work involving contact with politicians and interest groups at a time when his attitudes are still being formed.

But it is increasingly held that administration is a science which can be studied. We may avoid the perennial debate about the true nature of science, whether it means a systematic body of knowledge or merely all that is accurately known about a subject.[1] If one sees administration as an integrated discipline, one may incline to the American approach with its weighty textbooks and its full university courses. If one sees it merely as a bundle of knowledge, not necessarily forming a whole, one may favour the British approach: more limited courses in selected techniques, chosen because they appear useful tools of the trade at the time.

We have said that administration is always substantive and procedural. The *what* of administration involves knowledge of a field such as engineering, medicine or agronomy, the *how* of planning and organization. If, as in America, both are taught at universities, the intending administrator may well ask which he should study (the notion of a completely undirected education before entry does not appear to strike Dimock when he considers this problem). One may obtain a professional qualification in a substantive field at the university and acquire administrative skills within the Civil Service, through practice and post-entry courses in the more technical aspects of management. One may equally train first as an administrator and then familiarize

[1] Both in the *Pocket Oxford Dictionary*.

oneself with the substantive field of one's department on the job, aided again, perhaps, by short courses. The latter is only possible if mobility is restricted so that the civil servant deals with one subject long enough to get a real grasp of it. In Britain movement between departments is rare, except at the highest levels, but the young administrator is perhaps moved around too often within his department.

The question that arises is which of the two branches of knowledge is more easily acquired and might, therefore, be regarded as the secondary training. In its present state, administrative 'science' is perhaps more easily assimilated than most other sciences. Practical experience and short courses are perhaps more likely to turn the specialist into an administrator than the administrator into a specialist. But that too is open to challenge. In any case, it is obvious that both must acquire a greater understanding of the other's field. Peter Self, Professor of Public Administration in the University of London, makes this point in his Fulton evidence. In this way co-operation between them would improve, organization would become less formally hierarchic and some of the organizational problems we have discussed would disappear.

In the generalist v. specialist debate, the two sides start with different assumptions. As Anthony Sampson says, the specialist does not believe that administration is an art in itself, while the generalist insists that the trained mind can deal with any problem. Both may have overstated their case in the past. Both have emphasized their need for wider training in the evidence of Fulton. The association of the Administrative Class, indeed, recommends that there should be more formal training in administrative techniques (till now largely learnt on the job) and that they should also be given greater opportunity to increase their knowledge of the subjects with which they are concerned.[1] Perhaps the two will come together by their acceptance of a body of knowledge which is a *necessary* qualification and in which *all* can qualify.

There has been no real development of such a discipline at British universities. What goes under the title of Public Administration is often no more than a description of our governmental system, made more interesting, perhaps, by a discussion in

[1] See also H.M. Treasury, *Report of the Working Party on Management Training in the Civil Service*, 1967.

general terms of how the system might be reformed. It is not a study of administrative procedure. Nor have we produced many real textbooks dealing with administrative techniques.[1] We have long dismissed French and German studies of public administration for their over-legalistic approach. In both countries academics and civil servants have recently combined to produce substantial, and quite practical, works. This is a challenge that needs to be met.

C. H. Sisson may be right that no subject is more elusive than administrative studies. The slow development of the subject in this country undoubtedly has much to do with our uncertainty about its content. Civil servants themselves seem relatively uninterested in the study of public administration as an academic discipline, again perhaps because we have little to offer them yet. The present trend is to strengthen the Treasury's Centre for Administrative Studies and this appears to be concentrating on the quantitative techniques of planning. Peter Self criticizes the one-sidedness of courses, present and proposed. The study of social factors is not given sufficient weight, no doubt because such factors are less amenable to quantification. This may lead to a distorted view of problems and to a miscalculation of policies as the complexities of social causations are overlooked. The administrator, he suggest, needs a rounder background of economics and sociology. He could, at the same time, usefully study public administration itself.

This brings us, finally, to the study of comparative public administration and the contribution this symposium is intended to make. A quotation from Sir Ernest Barker may prove a fitting conclusion.[2]

'When we consider the history of the modern State, not only in education, but in all its services and activities, we cannot but recognize the debt which all States owe to one another. Each country has developed according to its own genius; and each has produced its own fruit. But each has produced some institution, or some method of public service, which has served as an example to others; and each, in turn, has borrowed from each. There has been a rivalry of methods, but it has not been unfriendly; one country has studied, adopted

[1] The works of E. N. Gladden, though too elementary, deserve mention as a pioneering exception.
[2] Sir Ernest Barker, *The Development of the Public Services in Western Europe*.

or tried to improve the methods of another, and all have combined, however unconsciously, to promote the growth of a common European standard of administration and public service.'

GEORGE ALLEN & UNWIN LTD
London: 40 Museum Street, WC1

Auckland: PO Box 36013, Northcote Central, N4
Bombay: 15 Graham Road, Ballard Estate, Bombay 1
Barbados: PO Box 222, Bridgetown
Beirut: Deeb Building, Jeanne d'Arc Street
Buenos Aires: Escritorio 454–459, Florida 165
Calcutta: 17 Chittaranjan Avenue, Calcutta 13
Cape Town: 68 Shortmarket Street
Hong Kong: 105 Wing On Mansion, 26 Hancow Road, Kowloon
Ibadan: PO Box 62
Karachi: Karachi Chambers, McLeod Road
Madras: Mohan Mansions, 38c Mount Road, Madras 6
Mexico: Villalongin 32, Mexico 5, DF
Nairobi: PO Box 30583
New Delhi: 13–14 Asaf Ali Road, New Delhi 1
Ontario: 81 Curlew Drive, Don Mills
Philippines: PO Box 4322, Manila
Rio de Janeiro: Caixa Postal 2537-Zc-00
Singapore: 36c Prinsep Street, Singapore 7
Sydney: NSW: Bradbury House, 55 York Street
Tokyo: PO Box 26, Kamata

THE ORGANIZATION OF BRITISH CENTRAL GOVERNMENT
A Survey by a Study Group of the Royal Institute of Public Administration

The role of government in Britain has changed radically since the First World War. In 1914 it had three main activities—the maintenance of law and order, the defence of the realm, and the conduct of external relations. Fifty years later, it has to take decisions affecting the economy, industry and commerce, the development of science and technology, and the social life of the nation. This book provides the first detailed account of how the machinery of central government has evolved to meet this changing role. It deals with each of the major areas of government action—finance, trade and industry; justice and public order; social services; external affairs; defence; and scientific research. Then follow chapters on the information services and other common service, on the evolution of the Cabinet and its committees, and other procedures for co-ordinating policy at the apex of government. One of the appendices lists with year, month and statutory source, every change of any importance in the central department, the Cabinet or the distribution of functions between departments, in the half-century of continuous change which the book covers. As a source of reference this is unique.

THE BRITISH APPROACH TO POLITICS
MICHAEL STEWART

Mr Stewart originally wrote this book for the Association for Education in Citizenship, which, after compiling a 'Bibliography of Social Studies', still sought the ideal book for its purpose. In writing his successful book Mr Stewart was aided by ample experience of teaching both in school and in the adult education movement.

Now, in its third large printing, the book is entirely revised and re-written. In the intervening years there has been something of a social revolution. The revised edition makes the book one of the few which can claim to be completely up-to-date and to take account of the changes brought about since the Second World War.

ADMINISTRATORS IN ACTION
Volume I
F. M. G. WILLSON

Many of the existing books on British Government deal predominantly with its structure and organization. Little light has been shed on the detailed processes of day-to-day administration. This is the first of a series sponsored by the Royal Institute of Public Administration which will make good this deficiency. It will provide the citizen, the official and the student with a closer insight into the problems and intricacies facing administrators and thereby contribute to a better understanding of the British system of government.

Each of the five cases in this volume spotlights an episode in recent British administration. From central government come the stories of how a personnel problem was handled by a central department, and a history of the negotiation of a financial agreement between the United Kingdom and Spain; from local government, studies of how Coventry moved its Wholesale Fruit and Vegetable Market from the old city centre to new quarters in the suburbs, and of the administrative difficulties created by a problem family; and from the nationalized industries, the description of how the South-Western Electricity Board centralized and mechanized its accounting procedures.

Volume II
GERALD RHODES

This second volume provides two further glimpses into how government departments carry out their responsibilities.

The two studies have features of special interest. The provision of a better network of roads and motorways is now a matter of great public importance. *The Wentworth By-Pass*, in dealing with the acquisition of land, gives an insight into the detailed negotiations which have to be carried out, and the conflicts between private and public interests which have to be settled satisfactorily before the work of construction can begin.

New Standards of Accommodation for the Crews of Merchant Ships is concerned with the application in the United Kingdom of the terms of an International Convention. It demonstrates the difficulty of drawing an International Convention in terms which are appropriate to the circumstances and customs of different parts of the world, and it provides an illuminating example of the process of consultation in which the British Government engages in the drafting of the Regulations.

ASPECTS OF ADMINISTRATION
A. AVASTHI and S. N. VARMI

This collection of essays is a welcome addition to the existing literature on the study of political science and public administration in India. The variety of subjects covered indicates not only the extensiveness of approach but also the results of investigations in new fields where adequate materials are not available. Some of the important subjects discussed are: district administration, community development, planning, corruption in public services, parliamentary democracy, patterns of authority in independent African states, and teaching and research in political science and public administration.

Contributors to this volume include Paul H. Appleby, Arthur W. MacMahon, William A. Robson, Jay B. Westcott, A. H. Hanson, Eddy Asirvatham, A. Avasthi, S. N. Varma, M. V. Pylee and P. J. Philip.

REPRESENTATIVE AND RESPONSIBLE GOVERNMENT
A. H. BIRCH

Here is a book which throws new light on the theory and practice of British politics. The concept of representative government is analysed and Professor Birch gives a brisk but comprehensive account of traditional British doctrines about the electoral system, the functions of MPs, and the role of Parliament in the political process. Among the twentieth-century ideas which he examines are the belief that politics is dominated by class conflict, the ideas of the Pluralists and Guild Socialists, the doctrine of the electoral mandate, and the view that political parties themselves should be democratically organized. In his analysis of responsibility in British politics Professor Birch disposes of a number of hoary myths about the British constitution, suggests that the conventions about ministerial responsibility to Parliament are important in ways rather different from those commonly claimed, and examines the limitations of the language in which constitutional matters are generally discussed. He considers the circumstances in which Parliament may still be the most effective channel of communication between the public and the government, and also discusses the role of other channels such as pressure groups, advisory committees, party organizations and the national press.

GREAT CITIES OF THE WORLD
Their Government, Politics and Planning
W. A. ROBSON

'Taken as a whole, however, this book is a most valuable addition to the literature of comparative local government, and the standard of the articles is high.... They vary inevitably in the amount of information they give, and in the insight which they show into the working of city government. They do however, provide an admirable and much needed source of information on a subject on which but little has been written in English before....' *Universities Quarterly*

'This is a book which can be recommended not only as a good book in itself, but as a *sine qua non* for the student of administration ... the book impressed the writer as being fresh, expert and informed. It is with every confidence that it is recommended for acquisition....'
Local Government Chronicle

GOVERNMENT AND POLITICS IN DENMARK
KENNETH E. MILLER

Why study Denmark? The author's preface gives several reasons:

'Denmark is one of the small countries of the world, in area and population, if not in spirit. But it has for a long time offered an example of political democracy, social progress, and governmental stability to a world where they have often been lacking. For the student of political science and for the general reader as well, Danish governmental institutions and political processes hold much of interest: the multi-party system, unicameralism, proportional representation, the problems of coalition and minority Governments, the welfare state, the ombudsman, the difficulties of a small state with powerful neighbours. This book seeks to describe and explain these and other aspects of the Danish political system, and to examine and analyse some of the problems of the system.'

A HISTORY OF LOCAL GOVERNMENT
K. B. SMELLIE

Modern English local government has developed from the industrial and scientific revolution and the growth of political democracy since 1832. The present system is the result of an interplay between political, economic, and scientific factors. The Poor Law Act of 1834 determined the main principles of central control of local authorities until 1929. The Municipal Corporations Act of 1835 inaugurated a system of local government by elected councils, and this was systematized by the Local Government Act of 1933. The Local Government Act of 1888 applied to the counties the principles of local self-government which had been developed by the boroughs after 1835. This structure of town and country government, was adapted without fundamental change, to the revolutions this century has seen in science and industry, in public finance and public administration. It is now on the eve of a radical reconstruction.

Professor Smellie has outlined the changes in structure in areas and in the relations between local and central authorities, from 1832 to 1967. His discussion of the causes of these changes explains the problems which local government now face. There is a separate chapter on London government, including details of the evolution of the Greater London Council, and an introductory chapter on the conditions of local government between 1689 and 1832.

GOVERNMENT AND POLITICS IN ISRAEL
OSCAR KRAINES

The author deals in turn with Knesset, the political parties and the electoral system, Cabinet, Presidents and Judiciary, the basis of citizenship and civil rights, the administrative structure, local government and foreign policy.

The book brings out the taut, precarious balance of the new State, at one point only nine miles wide, breaking the arc of hostile Arab states which stretches almost right across the Middle East. Secondly the author manages to reproduce the flavour of a State in which immigrants exceeded the original population and which supports four religious parties amongst the twenty-six which contested the elections in 1959. Finally the almost total lack of comparable serious studies lends a particular value to this volume.

THE PROFESSION OF GOVERNMENT
BRIAN CHAPMAN

This book may claim to be the first in any language to survey the civil services of the whole of western Europe, and is the product of ten years' travelling, research and discussion in thirteen countries. Material has been collected in eight languages, much of it previously unpublished and the work is to a considerable extent based on first-hand knowledge of the countries concerned. Dr Chapman has made a genuine comparative study; his book is not simply descriptive, but is an analysis of the most important questions facing modern public administration.

A lengthy historical introduction traces from Roman to modern times the concept and practice of public service, and brings out the underlying unity of European experience.

The rest of the book is divided into four Parts. The first chapter of Part One deals with the general composition and extent of the public service in different countries and the difficulties of definition. Other chapters examine in detail the questions of recruitment and training.

Part Two is concerned with the detailed conditions of service of public officials: their discipline, promotion, rights and duties, and their security of tenure.

Part Three considers the problem of controlling public administration. The whole complex of administrative jurisprudence and the various types of administrative courts in Europe are comprehensively examined for the first time in English. Individual chapters cover the history of administrative law, the composition and structure of administrative courts, and their methods of operation. There are further chapters on financial courts, and the extremely interesting case of the Scandinavian Ombudsman.

In Part Four, the author ventures into the no-man's-land between politics and administration. In a series of chapters he shows how intimately civil servants are connected with the political process, how far they are a pressure group in their own right, and the extent to which they have become a self-recruiting, self-administering, self-disciplining closed corporation, whose profession is the profession of government.

Dr Chapman's achievement is a formidable one which will be welcomed not only by students of politics and public administration, but also by lawyers, politicians and administrators, as well as by the informed general public. Many will agree that it is both provocative and stimulating and in places profound; it is most likely to become accepted by this generation as the standard work in its field.

THE GOVERNMENT OF REPUBLICAN ITALY
J. C. ADAMS and PAOLO BARILE

This is probably the first detailed treatment of Italy's post-war Constitution and government. It is a text-book and work of reference, authoritative, factual and clear, discussing both constitutional form and actual political practice against an adequate social and economic background.

The book starts with good chapters on historical and cultural background, a real discussion of basic underlying factors such as agriculture, industry, labour, education and Church, Church and State, civil liberties, relations of north and south. The authors then treat in turn the Constitution, Parliament, President and Executive, Central and Local Administration, Judiciary, Parties and elections, the Labour Movement, Italy as a Liberal Democracy.

This is not a book of the 'current events' class but a reliable survey of the enduring political factors.

HOUSING AND LOCAL GOVERNMENT
J. B. CULLINGWORTH

Housing policy in this country is currently undergoing major changes. The production of houses is being greatly increased, housing standards are being raised, housing subsidies have been recast and a 'complete overhaul' is underway. But perhaps most important of all, the aims of housing policy are being reviewed and for the first time a comprehensive approach is being made to the problems of house production, finance and the respective roles of the public and private sectors.

This is therefore an appropriate time for a review of the current situation, of the powers and policies of the State and local housing authorities, and of emerging problems. Mr Cullingworth provides such a review in this companion volume to his *Town and Country Planning in England and Wales*. A long historical introduction, which sketches the development of housing policy over the last hundred years, sets the scene. This is followed by chapters outlining the administrative framework, the powers of local housing authorities, the characteristics of council houses and the families who live in them. Other chapters deal with housing standards, finance, slum clearance, the improvement of older houses and a wide range of other important issues. A separate chapter discusses some of the social aspects of housing, and finally there is a general discussion of the role of the State and the objectives of State action. Each chapter has a full bibliography.

TOWN AND COUNTRY PLANNING
J. B. CULLINGWORTH

Mr Cullingworth has now revised his book and considerably extended it. He has brought all his tables up to date and has added a major new chapter which he significantly entitles 'The Throes of Change'. In this he deals with the many important developments since the book was written and analyses the direction which change is taking.

'. . . a unique contribution to its subject. . . . To members of Planning Authorities who have laboured throughout the post-war years to achieve something positive in planning development, often apparently in vain, as well as those immediately concerned this work will prove invaluable for reference and guidance.' *Municipal Review*

'. . . a most valuable contribution on how town planning works in England and Wales, together with an assembled critique of some of the ways of altering it . . . a comparative rarity—a textbook on the administrative and legal aspects of town planning which is readable. . . . This is a book which, while remaining authoritative, succeeds in raising some of the challenging issues which the long-overdue overhaul of town planning in Britain will have to face.' *Times Review of Industry*

MUNICIPAL HEALTH SERVICES
NORMAN WILSON

Municipal Health Services gives an account of the powers in regard to the personal health services which are possessed by local authorities; describes the manner in which these powers are exercised; and deals with principles and methods of administration and organisation. Since the range of the health services depends upon the type of local authority entrusted with them, it is with those provided by the county borough, which has the widest powers, that the book is more particularly concerned.

Norman Wilson was awarded the Diploma in Public Administration of Liverpool University with Distinction in 1933, and in 1936 the Degree of Master of Arts for a thesis on Public Health Administration. He incorporated part of this in *Public Health Services*, published in 1938 on behalf of the Institute of Public Administration.

He has contributed articles on public health and other social services to *Public Administration* and other journals.

DELEGATION IN LOCAL GOVERNMENT
PETER G. RICHARDS

Three modern Acts of Parliament, the Education Act, 1944, the Town and Country Planning Act, 1947, and the Civil Defence Act, 1948, have each made provision for the administration of these local government services to be shared between county and district councils. This is achieved through the technique of delegation which, although not new, has become much more important in recent years. Its growth has been due to two chief factors. Competing claims of county and district councils to control local government functions have been met with the compromise of delegation. The partnership that delegation implies has also enabled the joint use of the separate qualities of larger and smaller local authorities; backed by their financial resources, the counties undertake the over-all planning of delegated services, while detailed administration can be left to district councils which have a fuller knowledge of local conditions.

The many legal and administrative problems that have arisen from these arrangements are fully examined by Dr Richards, who is a Lecturer in Government in the University of Southampton. The book outlines the history of delegation since the establishment of the county councils in 1888 and it describes the use made of delegation over a wide range of local authority services.

THE ENGLISH LOCAL GOVERNMENT SYSTEM
J. H. WARREN

Generations of students have used this book, now in its eleventh printing. But this is only because it has been kept up-to-date, at first by Mr Warren himself, subsequently by Dr Richards, who has also taken over the editorship of the series.

Dr Richards knows intimately the examinations for which this book is used by students at universities, those in the Local Government Service or in technical colleges, or working on their own. He also knows intimately the whole field of local government and the changes which are now taking place in the structure as we inherited it.

The extent of his considerable revisions he has itemized in his new preface. What further changes lie ahead he has considered so far as possible. The book is again revised, reset and up-to-date, an essential textbook for the student, still one of the best surveys for the general reader.

GEORGE ALLEN & UNWIN LTD